"The easy path may be more convenient, but it's never as fulfilling. Instead of looking backward at what could have been, start looking forward at what could be! Mark Batterson's *Win the Day* will help you step away from the familiar and onto the path of accomplishing your God-sized dreams."

—CRAIG GROESCHEL, pastor of Life.Church and
New York Times bestselling author

"At a time when life seems more overwhelming than ever, Mark Batterson offers seven practical habits that can help you overcome your regrets and accomplish what you're called to do every day. Mark's characteristic research, insight, and optimism make *Win the Day* a powerful combination of inspiration and application. The best way to change your life is to start by changing today. This book will help you do just that."

—CAREY NIEUWHOF, bestselling author,
podcast host, and speaker

"*Win the Day* is a timely guide to stressing less in a world that gives us more than enough to stress about. Mark Batterson gives you seven practical steps for living boldly, accomplishing more, and seizing hold of God-sized dreams."

—RYAN SAUNDERS, professional basketball coach

"Sometimes we worry about the future so much that we fail to make the most of right now. It's a trap we can all fall into (and it's so common that we don't even realize we're stuck). In *Win the Day*, Mark gives practical handles to help you accomplish God-sized dreams—one day at a time."

—STEVEN FURTICK, pastor of Elevation Church and
New York Times bestselling author

Do It for a Day

Do It for a Day

How to Make or Break
Any Habit in 30 Days

MARK BATTERSON

MULTNOMAH

DO IT FOR A DAY

LIBRARY OF CONGRESS CATALOGING-IN-PUBLICATION DATA

Names: Batterson, Mark, author.
Title: Do it for a day: how to make or break any habit in 30 days / Mark Batterson.
Description: First edition. | Colorado Springs: Multnomah, [2021] | Includes bibliographical references.
Identifiers: LCCN 2021018807 | ISBN 9780593192849 (hardcover: (acid free paper) | ISBN 9780593192856 (ebook)
Subjects: LCSH: Habit-breaking—Religious aspects—Christianity. | Habit. | Sermon on the mount—Criticism, interpretation, etc.
Classification: LCC BV4598.7 .B46 1989 | DDC 248.4—dc23
LC record available at https://lccn.loc.gov/2021018807

Printed in Canada on acid-free paper

waterbrookmultnomah.com

2 4 6 8 9 7 5 3 1

First Edition

Interior book design by Virginia Norey

Contents

Do It for a Day Manifesto

Almost anyone can accomplish almost anything
if they work at it long enough, hard enough,
and smart enough.

Destiny is not a mystery. Destiny is daily habits.
It's mind over matter. It's nurture over nature.
It's a daily grind in the same direction.

If you want every day to count, count the days.
If you want to change your life, change your story.
If you want God to do the super, you've got to do the natural.

Time is measured in minutes. Life is measured in moments.
Bury dead yesterdays. Imagine unborn tomorrows.
Make every day a masterpiece!

If you do little things like they're big things,
God will do big things like they're little things.
If you stay humble and stay hungry,
there's nothing God can't do in you or through you.

Show me the size of your dream,
and I'll show you the size of your God.
Show me your habits, and I'll show you your future.

The obstacle is not the enemy. The obstacle is the way.
Do the best you can with what you have where you are.
Dream big. Start small. Think long.

Can you do it for a day?
That's the question. You know the answer.
Habits happen one day, one step, one rep at a time.

If you want to walk on water, you have to get out of the boat.
Faith is taking the first step before God reveals the second step.
Wade into the water!

Yesterday is history.
Tomorrow is mystery.
Do it for a day!

Introduction

Domino Habits

S how me your habits, and I'll show you your future.
It's that simple.
It's that complicated.

For better or worse, our lives are the sum of our physical, mental, and spiritual habits. Bad habits always come back to bite us. Good habits always come back to bless us. Either way, you cannot break the law of measures. The law of measures will make or break you. "With the measure you use," Jesus said, "it will be measured to you."[1] There are no shortcuts, loopholes, or cheat codes. Simply put, *you'll get out of it whatever you put into it.* And by *it*, I mean everything. Destiny is not a mystery; destiny is daily habits.

You are one habit away from getting into shape.

You are one habit away from financial freedom.

You are one habit away from mental health.

You are one habit away from a happy, healthy marriage.

You are one habit away from any goal you set.

The only catch? It has to be a *daily* habit!

Over the next thirty days, I want to help you hack your habits. I'll cite dozens of stories and studies, as well as best practices. We'll look at the art and science of habit formation from multiple angles—psychological, neurological, and theological. The goal? To tap your full potential. Why? Potential is God's gift to you. What you do with it is your gift back to God. How? By making or breaking the habits that will make or break you.

There is nothing simple about habit formation. It's as complicated as the cerebral cortex. It'll take longer than you like and be harder than you hope. The good news? Every habit is learned, which means every habit can be unlearned and relearned. Of course, you'll have to overcome task avoidance. It's our natural tendency to avoid things we're not particularly good at. Making and breaking habits takes us back to kindergarten. We have to be willing to fail, willing to fall, and willing to look foolish.

We'll break bad habits using a tried-and-true technique called *habit switching*. We'll build good habits using a bait-and-switch technique called *habit stacking*. We'll identify high-leverage habits—*domino habits*—that yield the highest return on investment. We'll engage in some goal setting, and we'll reverse engineer those life goals into daily habits.

You've probably noticed that this book doesn't have chapters—it has days. Why? The pacing is important. Don't try to do too much too fast. When it comes to habit formation, that's a recipe for failure. If you want to make or break a habit, put the title of this book into practice—*Do It for a Day*!

The average reading speed is approximately 250 words per minute, so each day's reading should take about ten minutes. That said, I would encourage you to slow the pace by taking time to reflect on the question at the end of each day's reading: *How do I make it a habit?* You'll get out of this book precisely what you put into it.

During the first eight days, we'll create the framework for making and breaking habits. Then we'll spend three days on each of the seven habits that were introduced in the prequel to this book, *Win the Day*. Those habits are sequenced in the same order—*flip the script, kiss the wave, eat the frog, fly the kite, cut the rope, wind the clock,* and *seed the clouds*. Don't worry if you haven't read *Win the Day*. The power of those daily habits will become clear soon enough.

Finally, this book works best with the buddy system. Take the 30 Day Habit Challenge with your friends or family, your staff or team, or even your entire organization. One, it's far more fun. Two, a rising tide floats all boats. Over time, you'll become the average of the twelve people you spend the most time with.[2] If you don't elevate their game, you're holding yourself back.

HABITUALIZATION

According to a Duke University study, 45 percent of daily behavior is automatic.[3] Without the ability to automate, we'd have to relearn everything we do every single day. Habitualization saves us tremendous time and energy, but that savings comes at a cost. When a thought pattern or behavior pattern becomes second nature, we rarely give it a second thought. That's where *Do It for a Day* enters the equation. It's designed to help you deconstruct and reconstruct your daily habits.

"All our life," said the father of American psychology, William James, "is but a mass of habits—practical, emotional, and intellectual—systematically organized for our weal or woe, and bearing us irresistibly toward our destiny."[4]

All of us are creatures of habit. Some of those habits are subconscious. I'm not sure why, but I always set my alarm to an even number. Other habits are consciously chosen, often to correct past mistakes. After I fill up with gas, I always check the side-view mirror before pulling away. Why? Because one time I failed to do so, and I pulled the gas hose that was still in my tank right off the pump! That reminds me . . . I always check my zipper before getting onstage to speak. You can guess why! On a more serious note, I always take my shoes off before writing as a ritual reminder that I'm on holy ground.

A habit is any behavior that you put on repeat, consciously or subconsciously. There are *micro habits,* such as the way you brush your teeth or hold your fork. There are *macro habits,* such as your coping mechanisms during crisis or your defense mechanisms when criticized. Big or small, good or bad, habits are recurrent ways of thinking, feeling, and acting. Some habits are as old as the adaptive strategies we employed as kids to gain attention. On that note, the hardest habits to break are the ones that are almost as old as we are.

There is some debate as to how long it takes to make or break a habit. Estimates range from 21 days to 254 days. The reality? It depends on the habit, and it depends on the person. Habit formation is not one-size-fits-all. Habits are as unique as you are. However, I'm confident that thirty days will generate the momentum you need to establish a winning streak.

THE HOLY GRAIL

Almost a century ago, a behavioral psychologist named B. F. Skinner theorized that behavior follows a predictable pattern—stimulus, response, reward.[5] Stimuli fall into two categories: aversive and reinforcing. Skinner believed that, by reverse engineering the stimuli, any behavior could be reconditioned.

The black box is a cluster of brain cells deep within the cerebral cortex called the basal ganglia.

When it comes to habit formation, the basal ganglia is the holy grail. It's the place where habits are stored. It's the switch that flips our behaviors. It's the engine that powers *action selection,* helping us recognize patterns from the past while determining the best course of action when alternative options are presented. The basal ganglia is our chief executive officer when it comes to everyday decisions.

Fast-forward to the end of the twentieth century, and researchers at the Massachusetts Institute of Technology got a good look at the holy grail via neuroimaging technology. Building off B. F. Skinner, their research yielded a three-step process whereby habits are formed. They called it the *habit loop,* and it consists of cue, routine, and reward. The *cue* activates an automatic response. The *routine* puts the behavior on repeat. The *reward* perpetuates the pattern by dangling the proverbial carrot.[6]

To make or break a habit cycle, you have to (1) *identify the prompt,* (2) *interrupt the pattern,* and (3) *imagine the prize.* That sounds simple enough, but it takes a ton of trial and error. It also requires raw honesty and holy curiosity. You have to approach habit formation from a third-person perspective. Your life is the lab, and *everything is an experiment.*

I have a friend who has commanded ships as a rear admiral and has managed highly sensitive intelligence as the homeland security and counterterrorism adviser to the president. He operates with a simple MO: "I reserve the right to get smarter later." I love that approach to crisis management, and the same goes for habit formation.

THE HABIT CYCLE

The science of habit formation is evolving in amazing ways, but the idea is as old as the Sermon on the Mount. If you reverse engineer the longest discourse of Jesus in the Gospels, it's a master class on the habit cycle.

Jesus didn't offer an orientation to His disciples; He provided a disorientation. The sermon includes six antitheses aimed at unlearning bad habits. "You have heard that it was said," Jesus said six times, "but I tell you."[7] Jesus was uninstalling old default settings like "An eye for an eye." He was updating and upgrading with a new mindset—Turn the other cheek.[8] When someone slaps us, our natural reaction is to slap back. Or is that just me? Jesus issued a counterintuitive command that requires reconditioning of our reflexes.

Is it possible that Jesus knew a little something about conditioned reflexes before Ivan Pavlov came along? That Jesus knew about operant conditioning before B. F. Skinner and behavior modification?

That Jesus knew a little something about the basal ganglia before the advent of neuroimaging?

Instead of fighting fire with fire, the Sermon on the Mount offers a counternarrative that is counterintuitive. As a Christ follower, I am called to love my enemies and pray for those who persecute me. Those aren't natural reactions! Neither is going the extra mile or sacrificing the shirt off my own back.[9] But that is the Jesus Way, and it's not just "out with the old and in with the new." It's a third way, a better way, when it comes to habit formation.

Jesus identified common cues that tempt us and test us and tick us off. Then He interrupted the pattern in ingenious ways. In a dog-eat-dog world, the Sermon on the Mount calls us to live counter-culturally. Jesus stopped the vicious cycle and replaced it with a virtuous cycle. How? Jesus called His followers to a routine of *radical love*. Simply put, love everybody always! Jesus called His followers to *radical forgiveness*. Instead of baiting, trolling, shaming, or canceling, we forgive seventy times seven. Jesus called His followers to *radical generosity*—the ethic of the extra mile.

After *identifying the prompt* and *interrupting the pattern*, Jesus helped us *imagine the prize*. What is it? The grand prize is hearing the heavenly Father say, "Well done, good and faithful servant."[10] The grand prize is storing up treasures in heaven by doing to others as you would have them do to you. Why? "Your Father, who sees everything, will reward you."[11]

DOMINO HABITS

In 1974, Bob Speca was a sophomore at Marple Newton High School in Broomall, Pennsylvania. That's when he was introduced to mathematical induction. His teacher, Mr. Dobransky, likened the theory to the domino effect. Bob Speca bought two boxes of dominoes that afternoon, and the rest is history.

From that day forward, Speca would devote his life to domino stacking and toppling. He appeared on *The Tonight Show Starring Johnny Carson,* showing off his skills. *The Guinness Book of Records* even created a category to recognize his accomplishments. Speca set the first world record in domino toppling with a chain reaction numbering 11,111. He would break his own world record five times, topping out at 97,500 dominoes.[12]

Around the time Bob Speca was setting world records, a physicist named Lorne Whitehead took a scientific interest in the domino chain reaction. Whitehead discovered that a domino is capable of knocking over a domino that is one and a half times its size. A two-inch domino can topple a three-inch domino. A three-inch domino can tumble a four-and-a-half-inch domino, ad infinitum.[13]

By the time you get to the eighteenth domino, you could knock over the Leaning Tower of Pisa. Of course, it's leaning so that isn't entirely fair! The twenty-first domino could take down the Washington Monument. The twenty-third domino could waffle the Eiffel Tower. *And* the twenty-seventh domino could cartwheel the one-hundred-sixty-story Burj Khalifa.

Remember the math induction theory? Instead of a fancy formula, dominoes offer a real-world example. Knock one over and the sky is the limit. The math induction theory states that we can climb as high as we like on a ladder. How? By starting with the bottom rung of the ladder and climbing one rung at a time. The theory is relatively new, but the idea is as old as the Tower of Babel.

"Nothing they set out to do will be impossible for them."[14]

Translation? *Almost anyone can accomplish almost anything if they work at it long enough, hard enough, and smart enough.* That is our working theory over the next thirty days, and the key is domino habits—little habits that have an exponential effect over time.

You are capable of more than you can imagine. Yes, you! The goal of this book is to help you prove it to yourself. How? One habit at a time, one rung at a time, one day at a time!

PICK A HABIT

This book makes a bold promise: *How to Make or Break Any Habit in 30 Days*. I don't want to overpromise and underdeliver, so let me shoot straight. You won't accomplish 100 percent of the goals you don't set. Goals give us targets to aim at, but life goals are lag measures. Goals are the desired outcomes, but you have to identify the inputs that will produce those results. How? You have to reverse engineer your life goals and turn them into daily habits.

Before we embark on this thirty-day challenge, *pick a habit, any habit*.

It can be a *physical* habit like doing your age in sit-ups every day, a *mental* habit like five minutes of meditation every morning, a *spiritual* habit like kneeling next to your bed every night, an *emotional* habit like keeping a daily gratitude journal, or a *relational* habit like smiling at everyone you encounter.

Pick a habit, any habit. Do you have it? Once you pick a habit, you put it into practice by making it as easy as 1, 2, 3. You have to "3M" the habit. How? By making it *measurable, meaningful,* and *maintainable.*

1. Make It *Measurable*

In 2017, I ran my first marathon. I didn't go out and run 26.2 miles the day after deciding to do it. That's a good way to pull a hamstring! The first thing I did was download a training plan, and then I worked the plan—seventy-two training runs totaling 475 miles over six months. The training plan made my goal measurable by reverse engineering it into daily distances.

Getting into shape and losing weight are hopes, not habits. You have to make it measurable by counting calories or mapping miles. Once it's measurable, it's manageable. Give yourself a daily gratitude quota. Download a Bible reading plan. Limit screen time to a set time.

Once you set the goal, you need to add timelines and deadlines.

A dream without a deadline is DOA—dead on arrival. When it comes to goal setting and habit building, deadlines are lifelines. The bottom line? Measure what you want to see more of. If you want to *break records*, you have to *keep records*!

2. Make It *Meaningful*

Running a marathon ranks as one of the greatest accomplishments of my life. Why? I suffered from severe asthma for forty years. There weren't forty days in forty years that I didn't have to use my rescue inhaler. I slept with it under my pillow and played sports with it in my sock. Then I prayed a bold prayer on July 2, 2016, and God healed my lungs. I haven't touched or used an inhaler from that day to this day.

I ran the Chicago Marathon to celebrate that miracle. Why Chicago? Yes, it's one of the flattest marathon courses in the country! But that isn't the reason. I grew up in Naperville, a suburb of Chicago. That's where I spent many weeks in the intensive care unit at Edward Hospital. That's where I was code blue, taking what I thought was my last breath.

The Chicago Marathon was my way of proving to myself what's possible. My training plan made it measurable, but the miracle is what made it meaningful. When my hamstrings started cramping at mile sixteen, the memory of that miracle is what kept me going. Having accomplished that life goal, I'm dreaming bigger, praying harder, and thinking longer. That's how you steward a miracle. You believe God for even bigger and better miracles. Ironman, here I come!

3. Make It *Maintainable*

Along with being measurable and meaningful, habits have to be maintainable. It's okay to dream big, but you have to start small. "The best way to motivate people, day in and day out," said Harvard professor Teresa Amabile, "is by facilitating *progress*—even small wins."[15] Don't despise the day of small beginnings! While you're at it, don't worry about next week, next month, or next year!

Can you do it for a day?

That's the question, and you already know the answer. Anybody can do anything for a day! Do it two days in a row, and there is a domino chain reaction. If you focus on inputs, God will take care of outcomes. With each small win, the next win gets a little easier. Why? Because you get a little stronger. Those 1 percent improvements add up like the math induction theory! Of course, you still have to rinse and repeat. You've got to get up every day and do it all over again. There is no other way to win the day!

THE EIGHTH WONDER OF THE WORLD

It takes very little effort to push over a single domino—.024 microjoules of input energy. That's the flick of your pinkie finger! By the time you topple the thirteenth domino, the kinetic energy is two billion times greater than the energy it took to knock over the first domino.[16] My point? You've got this! Even better, God's got this! If you do little things like they're big things, God will do big things like they're little things.

There are two types of progression in mathematics—linear and exponential. Linear progression is simple addition: 1 + 1 = 2. Exponential progression is compound doubling: 10 x 10 = 100. If you take thirty linear steps, you're ninety feet from where you started. If you take thirty exponential steps, you've circled the earth twenty-six times![17]

A two-inch domino may seem insignificant, but extrapolated across time and space, it has an exponential effect. The same is true of domino habits. Do your age in sit-ups, and sooner or later, it will add up to a six-pack. Write one hundred words a day, and sooner or later, it will add up to a book. Start a training plan, and sooner or later, it will add up to a marathon. Every decision you make, every action you take, starts a domino chain reaction!

This may seem like a self-help book. I promise you, it is so much more than that. At the end of the day, your habits aren't just about you. They're all about loving God and loving others. Bad habits can have a negative impact, an epigenetic effect, to the third and fourth generations. You don't break bad habits just for you. You do it for your kids and grandkids. You do it for your friends and family, neighbors and employers. Ultimately, you do it with the help and for the glory of Father, Son, and Holy Spirit.

What God does for us is never just for us. It's also for the third and fourth generations. We think right here, right now. God is thinking nations and generations. Good habits don't just add up; they multiply like compound interest. Speaking of, Albert Einstein reportedly called compound interest the eighth wonder of the world.[18]

We overestimate what we can accomplish in a day, but we underestimate what God can do in a year or two or ten. Consistency beats intensity seven days a week and twice on Sunday! Why? Daily habits pay dividends the rest of your life! Give it enough time, and you can transform your body, mind, marriage, finances, and attitude.

A six-pack may be one hundred pounds from here.

A marathon may be 475 miles of training down the road.

A published book may be fifty thousand words away.

Debt-free may be $100,000 beyond your budget.

Restoring your marriage may be seventeen counseling sessions from now.

Pick a habit, any habit. Make it measurable, meaningful, and maintainable. Then, with a flick of your finger, knock over that first domino. Good habits are good, but God habits have an exponential effect. They establish the baseline and trend line of your life. The only ceiling on your intimacy with God and impact on the world is daily habits, and the compound interest is incalculable. God habits don't just pay dividends here and now; they are the legacy we leave for all eternity!

Yesterday is history.

Tomorrow is mystery.

Do it for a day!

Day 1

Wade into the Water

The Sea saw him and fled.
—Psalm 114:3

There is a legend in Judaism about a man named Nahshon. He gets only one *begat* in the Bible. Of course, that's one more than you and me! Nahshon disappears almost as soon as he makes his genealogical debut, but the Talmud credits him with saving the nation of Israel by one act of courage.[1]

When the Israelites were trapped between the Egyptian army and the Red Sea, no one knew what to do. It seemed like a no-win situation. That's when God issued a command: "Tell the people of Israel to go forward."[2] The problem with that was this—the Red Sea was staring them in the face! None of the tribes wanted to go first, and who can blame them? It felt like a death wish. While the Israelites argued, the leader of the tribe of Judah stepped up and stepped into the Red Sea.

According to rabbinic tradition, Nahshon wades into the water like Aquaman. All right, I may be taking a little liberty by adding Aquaman to the equation, but that's how I envision this epic moment. Nahshon wades into the Red Sea until he's neck-deep, right up to his nostrils. That's when and where and how the Red Sea split in half. It was God who made a sidewalk through the sea, but it was Nahshon who made the miracle possible. How? By wading into the water! In the words of the psalmist, "The Sea saw him and fled."[3]

There's an old axiom: *If you want to walk on water, you have to get out of the boat.* That is absolutely true, but here's one more for good measure: *if you want God to make a sidewalk through the sea, you've got to get your feet wet.* Most of us spend the majority of our lives waiting for God to split the Red Sea. Maybe, just maybe, God is waiting for you to wade into the water. What I know for sure is this: if you want God to do the super, you've got to do the natural.

You have to make a defining decision.

You have to take a calculated risk.

You have to make a selfless sacrifice.

You have to take a flying leap of faith.

That's all it takes for God to make a sidewalk through the sea, but you've got to get your feet wet. And the first step is always the hardest step. Why? You have to overcome the law of inertia by exercising initiative. You have to overcome fear by exercising faith. If you aren't ready to take that step of faith on day 1, keep reading. God will give you the wisdom, the courage, and the faith you need by day 30!

"There are decades where nothing happens," Vladimir Lenin is purported to have said, "and there are weeks when decades happen." Let me up the ante: *there are days when decades happen!* This is one of those days, if you want it to be. You are one habit away from a totally different life! The next thirty days can set the table for the next thirty years. This is the first day of the rest of your life. If you believe that, mark the moment by jotting down the date in the margin.

This book is your rite of passage to a new chapter, a new normal, a new you. But you have to wade into the water, right up to your nostrils. Faith is being sure of what you hope for—a clearly defined goal. But faith is more than imagining unborn tomorrows. It's taking initiative today. Faith is taking the first step before God reveals the second step.

What is your next step?

What are you waiting for?

Let me eliminate a few excuses up front.

One, *I'm not qualified.*

Welcome to the club! God doesn't call the qualified; He qualifies the called. God wants to use your strong hand. He's the one who gave you those gifts! But God also wants to use your weak hand. Why? That's where His power is made perfect.[4] Your weakness is God's opportunity to put His glory on display. How? By doing things you can't take credit for.

Two, *I'm not ready.*

Guess what? You never will be. I wasn't ready to get married. Lora and I weren't ready to have kids. I wasn't ready to start a church. We weren't ready to open a coffeehouse on Capitol Hill or the DC Dream Center. And we weren't ready to buy and build out a city block called the Capital Turnaround. If you wait until you're ready, you'll be waiting until the day you die! Quit living as if the purpose of life is to arrive safely at death. If God gives you a green light, it's not *ready, set, go.* Faith flips the script—*go, set, ready!*

Three, *I'm waiting for the right opportunity.*

Aren't we all? I know people who say they'll give more if they make more, but I'm not buying what they're selling. If you aren't generous with a little, you won't be generous with a lot. Generosity starts right here, right now! I know people who say they'll serve more when they have more time. You don't *find time;* you have to *make time*! I know people who say they'll step up when the big opportunity presents itself. Not if you aren't seizing the little opportunities that are all around you all the time! Quit trying to win the lottery, and start winning the day.

Forty years after wading into the waters of the Red Sea, the Israelites find themselves obstructed by a similar obstacle. It's a divine déjà vu. All that separates them from the promised land is the Jordan River. It's almost like God tips the cap to Nahshon by giving the priests who carry the ark of the covenant a curious command:

When you reach the banks of the Jordan River, take a few steps into the river.[5]

This is where so many of us get stuck. We stand on the shoreline, waiting for God to part the water. Then we wonder why nothing is happening. All the while, God is waiting for us to wade into the water. There is a sacred sequence encoded in this ancient algorithm. If you want God to make a sidewalk through the sea, you've got to get your feet wet.

We all want a miracle. Of course, none of us wants to be in a situation that necessitates one. Guess what? You can't have one without the other. What we perceive to be an impossibility presents a unique opportunity. That is when we exercise our faith. How? By taking the first step!

How do I make it a habit?

Baby steps.

Those are the words of Dr. Leo Marvin. Yes, he's the fictional psychiatrist in a very funny film, *What About Bob?* That doesn't make it any less true. Just a little more fun! When it comes to making and breaking habits, it helps to have a few laughs along the way. Why? Because you'll take a few falls and experience a few fails. You have to laugh it off, get back up, and try again. Or in some instances, try different.

We often get stuck trying to figure out steps two, three, and four. Yes, failing to plan is planning to fail. But habit formation always begins with one small step. You can't steal second base if you keep your foot on first.

I believe in setting God-sized goals—go big or go home! But when it comes to forming habits, small wins is the name of the game. Trying to jump-start your goals by getting a jump on the day? Set a goal of seeing the sunrise seven days in a row. Want to write a book? Take a page out of Tim Ferriss's book, and write "two crappy pages a day."[6]

What river are you trying to cross?

What is the first step you need to take?

If it's running a marathon, you wade into the water by paying the registration fee. Now you've got skin in the game. If the goal is reading the Bible cover to cover, download a reading plan and ask a friend to join you. If it's getting your graduate degree, fill out the application. The same goes for your dream job or summer internship. If it's resolving a personal issue or restoring a relationship, make the counseling appointment.

I admire plotters, with two *t*'s. Plotters are people who see further into the future than the rest of us. Can I tell you who I admire even more? Plodders, with two *d*'s. Plodders are the people who get up and grind it out every day. Plodders put one foot in front of the other like everybody else, but they don't stop when they run into the Red Sea. They wade into the water like Nahshon, the patron saint of plodders.

What if Nahshon had stepped into the water and stopped? *Well, that didn't work.* What if he had called it quits when he was waist-deep? *This isn't happening.* What if he had backed up when the water reached his chinny chin chin? *That was a waste of time.* The answer is simple: Nahshon would have forfeited the miracle right before it happened.

The challenge on day 1? Pick a habit, any habit. Then get your feet wet by taking a baby step! This is the day when decades happen.

Wade into the water!

Day 2

Take the Stairs

God did not lead them along the main road that runs
through Philistine territory, even though that was the
shortest route to the Promised Land.
—EXODUS 13:17, NLT

In 1987, a group of engineers, entrepreneurs, and earth scientists set out to build an artificial ecosystem in Oracle, Arizona. Biosphere 2 encompassed 3.14 acres, making it the largest closed system ever created. Designed as the ideal ecosystem for plant life to thrive, the climate-controlled environment included purified air, clean water, nutrient-rich soil, and natural light. Despite what seemed like perfect conditions, something curious kept happening. The trees that were planted would grow to a certain height, and then they would fall over. After some head-scratching, the scientists finally figured out what was missing. The biosphere lacked a critical component for growth. Care to venture a guess?

In their natural habitat, trees are buffeted by winds that blow every which way. Trees respond to that wind resistance by growing stronger bark and deeper roots. Without adversity, trees atrophy. Newsflash: humans do too!

One of the mistakes we make as parents and as leaders is this: we do everything within our power to create emotional and relational and spiritual biospheres. We avoid conflict. We mitigate risk. We minimize discomfort. We sidestep sacrifice. Then we wonder why people grow to a certain stature and stop. We wonder why leaders fall. We wonder why friendships experience a falling out. Like seeds planted in rocky soil, they lack the root systems to sustain growth.

You don't have to go out and look for resistance. It will find you soon enough! My advice? Don't look for a work-around; work through it. Just as Nahshon waded into the water, you have to kiss the wave. The obstacle is not the enemy; the obstacle is the way. In fact, *harder is better*! Without that mindset, you won't make it to day 30.

When God delivered the Israelites out of Egypt, He didn't take the shortcut to the promised land. He took the scenic route! Why? They weren't ready. The goal of going after a God-sized dream isn't simply accomplishing it. It's who you become in the process—big dreams make big people! Don't be so anxious to get out of difficult situations that you fail to get anything out of difficult situations. You've got to learn the lesson, cultivate the character, and curate the change.

Habit formation is not linear. It's two steps forward, one step back. Did you know that there were forty-two stations of the Exodus? They zigged and zagged all over tarnation! You will experience setbacks during this thirty-day challenge, but that is when you need to press in and pray through. Those are the days when you need to double down. It can't just be *rise and shine;* it's got to be *rain or shine*!

When you encounter an obstacle, any obstacle, think of it as resistance training. On days when you experience decision fatigue, God is building emotional fortitude. On days when you feel like throwing in the towel, God is preparing you for something bigger, something better. And, I might add, it's those bad days that help us appreciate the good days!

As a leader, I get frustrated when I cast a vision and people don't get it. Or worse, they oppose it. That said, I've learned to appreciate the resistance because it has a refining effect on vision. It forces me to anticipate objections and answer questions, thereby clarifying the vision.

I don't care if your name is Moses and you come down from Mount Sinai with stone tablets inscribed by the finger of God— you'll still experience resistance. It's called the diffusion of innovation bell curve—16 percent of people are resistors.[1]

As leaders, we love early adopters who are on the other side of the bell curve. They're the people who will walk off the cliff with us! Can I let you in on a little leadership secret? I've come to appreciate laggards just as much, if not more, because they force us to become better vision casters. Don't hate the haters! Listen to them. Learn from them. You may not win them over to your way of thinking, but it'll cultivate mutual respect.

Can I take issue with a cultural trend? Giving every kid a trophy regardless of performance has unintended consequences like Biosphere 2. If everyone gets a trophy, emotional-fortitude muscles atrophy. You never learn how to cope with disappointment. You never learn how to get up after being knocked down. You never learn how to dig a little deeper.

In her brilliant book *Mindset,* Carol Dweck made a distinction between two very different mindsets.[2] A *fixed* mindset is the belief that our capabilities are set in stone. It's nature over nurture—*I was born this way.* With that frame of mind, you try to avoid failure. Why? If you fail, you're a failure. Failure is seen as an indictment rather than an opportunity to learn. People with fixed mindsets are always on trial, always trying to prove themselves. They are only as good as their last game, last election, last case, or last performance.

A *growth* mindset is the belief that capabilities can be cultivated, regardless of circumstances. It's nurture over nature. It's mind over matter. It's the belief that *almost anyone can accomplish almost anything if they work at it long enough, hard enough, and smart enough!* Your failure doesn't own you if you own it. How? You leverage it by learning from it. Nine times out of ten, failure is the result of poorly managed success. But let me flip that script—*success is the result of well-managed failure.*

I'm not ignoring genetic or epigenetic factors when it comes to habit formation. There are heritable traits that give us advantages and disadvantages. If you're five foot seven and you want to play in the NBA, may the Force be with you, because the odds are against you. You'll have to work longer, work harder, and work smarter. But don't tell me it can't be done! Why? At five foot seven, Spud Webb didn't just play in the NBA—he won the 1986 dunk contest.

Psychologist Benjamin Bloom once conducted a study of 120 outstanding achievers in a wide variety of occupations from concert pianists to Olympic swimmers to research scientists. Most of them were *not* remarkable as children. There was little evidence of future accomplishment. What set them apart? "After forty years of intensive research . . . my major conclusion is: What any person in the world can learn, *almost* all persons can learn."[3]

Is that not empowering? Talk about leveling the playing field. I don't want to turn habit formation into a competition, but the prize generally goes to those who work longer, harder, and smarter! Simply put, *the only limit is your dedication to learning.* If you stay humble and stay hungry, there's nothing God can't do in you or through you.

Habit formation is as unique as your history, personality, and chronotype. If you're a lark, you've got to get up early to go after your goals. If you're an owl, you burn the midnight oil. Either way, you've got to figure out what works for you. And give the same grace to others! In the words of Oswald Chambers, "Let God be as original with other people as He is with you."[4]

Habit formation is as different as thinkers and feelers, introverts and extroverts, goal setters and problem solvers. One way or the other, habit formation starts with a growth mindset. It welcomes resistance as a means of growing stronger. Whatever habit you're trying to cultivate, it will get harder before it gets easier. That's par for the course!

How do I make it a habit?

Take the stairs!

I mean that literally and figuratively. Yes, the elevator is easier. But the path of least resistance won't get you where you want to go. When given the choice, don't take the easy way out. It's a mindset and a metaphor. When presented with the option of an elevator or the stairs, you make a predecision to take the stairs. Why? Harder is better! The stairs and the elevator will get you to the same place, but you'll be in better shape having taken the stairs.

Taking the stairs is all about adding more resistance, but that doesn't mean it has to be less fun. A few years ago, Volkswagen Sweden staged a public intervention aimed at better health. They employed something called the fun theory: "Fun is the easiest way to change people's behavior for the better."[5] The masterminds behind this intervention installed a piano staircase next to an escalator at a subway station in Stockholm. The stairs looked like and functioned like keys on a piano. That interactive staircase resulted in a 66 percent rise in use![6]

The moral of the study? Along with adding resistance, add an element of fun. "A major criterion for judging the anxiety level of any society," said Edwin Friedman, "is the loss of its capacity to be playful."[7] All work and no play makes Jack a dull boy!

Habit formation is serious business, but you have to have fun along the way. Self-deprecating humor allows you to learn from your mistakes by laughing at them. My advice? Take God seriously, but take yourself less seriously. Habit formation is hard enough as it is!

"If anyone forces you to go one mile," Jesus said, "go with them two miles."[8] In other words, *go the extra mile.* Make it your mantra, your mission, your MO. A Roman soldier was allowed to commandeer a Jewish citizen for a thousand paces. The first mile was required, but Jesus upped the ante. He challenged His followers to exceed expectations by going above and beyond. It's the road less traveled, but there aren't any traffic jams.

When I exercise, I listen to podcasts and playlists. It's one way I habit stack. I exercise my mind while I exercise my body. A few of my favorite podcasts are *Radiolab, 99% Invisible, Freakonomics Radio,* and *Revisionist History.* Why do I do it? Podcasts are one way I cross-pollinate my mind by learning from a wide variety of disciplines. Plus, they distract me from the pain I'm putting myself through!

I also love worshipping while I'm running. How can I not after God healed my lungs? I often listen to one of my worship playlists. That said, when I need to push my limits, I go old school. I put the *Rocky IV* soundtrack on repeat. Welcome to my world! When I listen to the training montage, I picture Rocky doing inverted sit-ups in an old barn, shoulder pressing an oxcart, and doing lunges in the Siberian snow. I also hear his trainer yelling, "No pain, no pain, no pain!"

That is a growth mindset. It's the old axiom *No pain, no gain.* That's how you make and break habits. And harder is better.

Take the stairs!

Day 3

Get Off the Grid

With the Lord a day is like a thousand years,
and a thousand years are like a day.
—2 PETER 3:8

When the Russian comedian Yakov Smirnoff immigrated to the United States, he was asked what he loved most about America. His answer? American grocery stores. "I walked down an aisle and saw powdered milk; just add water and you get milk. Right next to it was powdered orange juice; just add water and you get orange juice. Then I saw baby powder, and I thought to myself, *What a country!*"[1]

Instant everything. We wish, right? We live in a culture that aims at fifteen minutes of fame rather than fifty years of faithfulness. We want the quick fix. Even better, get rich quick. We are an instant-gratification culture, and it's evidenced by how frustrated we become with the smallest delays.

Case in point? You're about to board an airplane that will fly five hundred miles per hour at thirty thousand feet, getting you all the way across the country in five hours flat, and you're unbelievably frustrated by a fifteen-minute delay! I get it, and I'm guilty as charged. But it beats a covered wagon, doesn't it? It took a covered wagon, traveling at the speed of oxen, six months to cross the country! And there was no economy plus—I promise you that.

If you're going to dream big, you need to start small and think long. This goes back to the growth mindset from day 2. *Harder is better,* and *slower is faster.* That's as counterintuitive as it is countercultural, but that doesn't make it any less true. Whatever habit you're trying to make or break, it'll take more than a minute. You have to hitch the wagon and commit yourself to the long haul called the habit cycle.

In the sixteenth century, an English playwright named John Heywood died about a decade after William Shakespeare was born. He was a lot less famous than Shakespeare, but I bet you've quoted him without even knowing it. A few of his idioms include "many hands make light work," "better late than never," and "a rolling stone gathers no moss." His most famous axiom? *Rome wasn't built in a day.*[2]

Can I be brutally honest? Habit formation feels like it takes forever. That's when you have to remind yourself that Rome wasn't built in a day! Making habits and breaking habits will take longer than you like, no doubt. But the more time you invest, the more meaningful it is.

Fun fact? In 1947, General Mills introduced its first instant cake mix. They expected instant success, but the cake mix didn't sell well. The company was confused because it had simplified a difficult task. All you had to do was add water. It was easy-peasy. And that was precisely the problem; it was *too easy*!

General Mills commissioned a marketing expert, Ernest Dichter, to figure out why the instant mix wasn't resonating with consumers. His conclusion? We bake a cake for special occasions. In other words, it's an expression of love. *Less effort* made it *less meaningful*.

Remember 3M? Our habits have to be *measurable, meaningful, and maintainable*. The cake mix was so simple that it felt self-indulgent. What did General Mills do? They made it more meaningful by making it less easy! They made it take more time! When consumers had to add eggs and measure milk, sales soared.[3]

The lesson? *Harder is better,* and *slower is faster.* And it's not just true of cake mix. If you were looking for easy answers and quick fixes, you bought the wrong book. This thirty-day challenge won't be easy, and I make no apologies for that. By definition, a challenge involves a degree of difficulty. The technical term is *desirable difficulty*, and it's a critical piece of the habit-formation puzzle. I shared an equation in *Win the Day* that I want to solve in *Do It for a Day*:

Deliberate Practice + Desirable Difficulty = Durable Learning[4]

We'll reverse engineer the entire equation over the next thirty days, but let me start with *desirable difficulty*. It sounds like an oxymoron, as oxymoronic as James 1:2: "Consider it pure joy . . . whenever you face trials of many kinds." Really? Why? Because those trials are opportunities to prove yourself. You can't spell *testimony* without the word *test*. When you pass the test, you graduate to the next level. Plus, you'll be stronger on the other side.

Coined by Robert A. Bjork, *desirable difficulty* refers to a task that requires considerable effort.[5] Difficult tasks slow down the learning process at first, but they yield a long-term benefit called durable learning. If something is too easy, we get bored. If something is too difficult, we quit. *Desirable difficulty* is the middle ground where growth happens.

The sweet spot is called JMD—*just manageable difficulty*. It's a little outside your comfort zone. It's a little beyond your resources. It's a little past your pay grade. That's why we need coaches, therapists, and trainers. We need someone who pushes us past our perceived limits.

Have you ever heard of the 40 percent rule? When your mind tells you to quit—you feel like you've given it everything you've got—you've tapped only 40 percent of your potential. That idea originates with ultramarathon runner and former Navy SEAL David Goggins.[6] When you feel like you've reached the end of your rope, you have 60 percent more potential than you are even aware of. If you're going to tap your full potential, you have to push past those mental blocks.

As a writer and a pastor, I feel like my job is to *comfort the afflicted* and *afflict the comfortable*. My goal is to coax you out of your comfort zone and into your growth zone. You have to get comfortable with discomfort. How? By adding time and resistance. When you push past previous limits and achieve a PR—personal record—the ceiling becomes the floor!

How do I make it a habit?

Retreat.

The word *retreat* means "to move back." The irony? That's how you make forward progress. It's as counterintuitive as the law of diminishing returns—less is more.

If you want to make or break a habit, it's a lot like learning a new dance. My repertoire is pretty limited, but I can *floss* and *churn the butter,* and I do a pretty mean *running man.* How did I learn those dance moves? I had to break it down and slow it down. Then, and only then, was I able to go faster. Simply put, you cannot hurry habits. You have to retreat in order to advance.

Remember Alice in Wonderland? She ran as fast as she could to keep up with the Red Queen, but she didn't gain any ground. Ever feel like that? "*Here,* you see, it takes all the running *you* can do, to keep in the same place," said the queen. "If you want to get somewhere else, you must run at least twice as fast as that!"[7] How do we get off the merry-go-round that goes faster and faster? You've got to get off the grid. How? Here's a simple idea: *day off, phone off.*

Next time you read the Gospels, notice how often Jesus withdrew. Jesus was retreating all the time—climbing mountains, walking beaches, sailing across the Sea of Galilee. He even spent forty days in the wilderness. Evidently, the best way to make progress is by retreating with great frequency and intentionality! Jesus operated with a sense of urgency, yet He was unhurried. In the words of Japanese theologian Kōsuke Koyama, He is the "three mile an hour God."[8]

I live by a little formula: *change of pace + change of place = change of perspective.* There are moments when we need to pick up the pace because of laziness, but more often than not, we need to slow the pace because of busyness. "If the devil cannot make us bad," said Corrie ten Boom, "he will make us busy."[9] Why is it that the Sabbath is the longest of the Ten Commandments? Perhaps because it's the hardest one to keep! You have to slow down, which is tough to do in a rat race.

At the end of every year, Lora and I take a two-day planning retreat. Along with budgeting and calendaring, we review our gratitude journals and set goals for the coming year. We employ a wide variety of techniques to keep us centered, including a word of the year and a verse of the year. You don't have to go somewhere exotic. It can be a staycation. But you do need to set aside time for a set purpose. In addition to that planning retreat, we try to schedule a silent retreat once a year. With all the white noise these days, we need to do some ear cleansing! Finally, I'd recommend one weekend a year to set goals, review goals, and reverse engineer your goals into daily habits.

Get off the grid!

Day 4

Lick the Honey

Write the vision, and make it plain upon tables.
—Habakkuk 2:2, kjv

In 1965, a social psychologist named Howard Leventhal designed four pamphlets for the purpose of promoting the tetanus vaccine among Yale University seniors.[1] Tetanus is a bacterial infection that bonds to nerve endings, causing muscle spasms so severe that they can break bones. Those pamphlets were divided into two categories—low fear and high fear. The difference? The low-fear pamphlet had no pictures. The high-fear pamphlet included rather shocking photographs of those suffering the side effects of tetanus.

Not surprisingly, twice as many students who received the high-fear pamphlet indicated that they *intended* to get vaccinated. Fear is a powerful motivator, but evidently, it's not powerful enough to guarantee follow-through. There was only a 1 percent difference in the rate of vaccination among low-fear and high-fear students!

But Leventhal had added a second variable that proved to be far more powerful than good old-fashioned fear. Along with low-fear and high-fear designations, the pamphlets were divided into low-specificity and high-specificity categories. The nonspecific pamphlet advocated for the vaccine, but it didn't specify *when* or *where* or *how*. The high-specificity pamphlet included a campus map, as well as the hours and location of the health center where students could get the vaccination.

The results? Only 3 percent of the low-specificity students got the vaccination. The success rate among high-specificity students was ten times higher—30 percent of them got the tetanus vaccine.[2] Specificity was the silver bullet, and it still is! The technical term is *implementation intention,* and it's critical when it comes to making and breaking habits. If you don't specify *when* and *where* and *how,* good luck with that. Luck is what you'll need.

Imagine setting up an appointment with someone and asking them *when* and *where* they want to meet. They reply, "Whenever, wherever." The flexibility is much appreciated, but that meeting ain't never going to happen, is it? Good intentions are good, but they aren't good enough. Remember 3M? Your habits have to be *measurable, meaningful,* and *maintainable.*

One key to making your habits maintainable is the slogan at the end of every episode of the original *Batman* TV series: *Same bat time, same bat channel.* Make an appointment with yourself. For what? For everything! Schedule date nights, gym time, and personal retreats. No, you don't have to schedule bathroom time. That's taking it too far. But generally speaking, if it's not in your calendar, it's not going to happen!

In the field of behavioral economics, nudge theory analyzes the way small prompts can have a major impact on behavior. Remember the piano stairs from day 2? They're a classic example of what D. J. Stewart called the art of the nudge. It's identifying the prompts that interrupt the pattern, which is more than half the battle when it comes to habit formation.

If you visit the men's restrooms at Schiphol Airport in Amsterdam, you'll see that an image of a black housefly is sketched in the urinals. According to Aad Kieboom, the man responsible for the addition of the flies, "If a man sees a fly, he aims at it." Duly noted, and for the record, it has reduced spillage by 80 percent.[3]

Aad Kieboom is a *choice architect.* Truth be told, all of us are! As parents, we cue our kids via choice architecture all the time. How? We turn vegetables into airplanes and fly them into their mouths! Our tactics get more sophisticated as they age, and we resort to things like reverse psychology. But the principle of choice architecture remains the same. We engineer ways of incentivizing or disincentivizing different behaviors. Of course, we do the same thing with ourselves. It's the third phase of the habit cycle—*imagine the prize*. And it's the key to self-motivation.

Richard Thaler and Cass Sunstein shared a fascinating example of choice architecture in their brilliant book, *Nudge*.[4] In Chicago, there is a dangerous stretch of highway where Lake Shore Drive takes a tight turn at Oak Street. When I was a student at the University of Chicago, I made that drive many times. The Department of Transportation tried to curb accidents by installing a sign that said Dangerous Curve Ahead. It had very little effect on the accident rate. In 2006, they took a different tack. A series of lines were painted on Lake Shore Drive that had a subconscious effect on drivers. As cars approach the curve, the gaps between the lines get smaller, giving the impression that cars are going faster. The lines are a subconscious cue that causes drivers to slow down. The result? A 36 percent reduction in accidents.[5]

How do we implement these kinds of prompts when it comes to habit formation? How do we nudge ourselves and others? How do we architect cues for the students we teach, the athletes we coach, and the children we parent? How do we reverse engineer our environments to maximize good habits and minimize bad habits?

Nudge theory may be new, but the idea is as old as the Torah. If you lived in Judea in the first century, your formal education would begin at the age of six in the local synagogue school called Bet Sefer. The first lesson? The rabbi would cover the students' slates with honey[6] and instruct them to lick the honey while reciting Psalm 119:103: "How sweet are your words to my taste, sweeter than honey to my mouth!"

The teacher was creating a positive association, a positive addiction. The goal was to catalyze a craving for the Word of God—helping students "taste and see that the LORD is good."[7] What do you think those students thought of every time they tasted honey?

It was their first lesson, and it left a lasting taste in their mouths. Fun fact? Honey is the only food that lasts forever. It will crystallize over time, but the nectar from flowers combined with the enzymes inside bees creates a chemistry that is nonperishable.[8]

There is an old adage: *You can lead a horse to water, but you can't make it drink.* That's true, but you can salt the oats! Are you picking up what I'm throwing down? Habit formation doesn't just reroute neuronal connections; it creates new cravings. The key is feeding good cravings while starving bad ones.

When Randy Pausch worked at Carnegie Mellon University, he served as an academic reviewer. Getting professors to read and review densely written research papers was as hard as herding cats. Pausch got tired of nagging professors who were past due, so he came up with a unique way of nudging them. He sent a note and a box of Girl Scout Thin Mint cookies with every paper that needed to be reviewed: "Thank you for agreeing to do this. The enclosed Thin Mints are your reward. But no fair eating them until you review the paper." Brilliant, right? Not only did that put a smile on their faces, but it also created a craving. Instead of pestering those professors, all Pausch had to do was ask them a question: "Did you eat the Thin Mints yet?"[9]

Remember B. F. Skinner? He believed that behavioral cues fall into two basic categories: aversive and reinforcing. When it comes to making good habits, you have to reinforce them with the right prompts. You have to dangle a carrot or, even better, Thin Mint cookies. When it comes to breaking bad habits, aversive stimuli are an effective stopgap.

When I was in junior high, I was a compulsive nail biter. How did I break that habit? I started wearing a clear nail polish that makes you sick to your stomach if you ingest it. That aversive stimulus was an effective short-term strategy, but there is a better way to recycle your bad habits. It's called *habit switching.* It's breaking a bad habit by replacing it with a good habit.

"Addiction is not all bad," argued Dr. William Glasser in his book

Positive Addiction.[10] Negative addictions destroy our lives one drink, one click, one hit at a time. Positive addictions have the opposite effect. In a sense, all of us are addicts. The question is this: Are those addictions positive or negative, healthy or unhealthy, holy or unholy?

You can break a bad habit by *not* doing it, and it might work for a week or two. But it's not a long-term solution. Spiritually speaking, you don't stop sinning by *not* sinning. That's like someone saying, "Don't think about the Jolly Green Giant." What image just popped into your head? In psychology, it's called a double bind. If I say to you "Be spontaneous," you can't be. It creates a no-win situation, and the same goes for every temptation we face. I wish it were as easy as *just say no*. It's not. You need a *yes* that is bigger and better than the *no*! You need a vision that is bigger and better than the obstacle you're trying to overcome. That's where habit switching enters the equation.

Habit switching is replacing a bad habit with a good habit, and it takes time and effort. According to Dr. Glasser, cultivating a positive addiction requires a minimum of forty to sixty minutes a day. And it might take six months or longer.[11] Of course, thirty days will give you a running start. Don't get overwhelmed by how long it might take. *Do it for a day!*

Habit formation is choice architecture, and choice architecture is all about creating the right cues, the right cravings. You have to change your default settings by making predecisions—the decisions you make before you have to make a decision. Not only do predecisions reduce decision fatigue, but they also have a domino effect.

Is there a predecision you need to make?

Is there a default setting you need to change?

Is there a prompt you need to put in place?

When Lora and I got married, we decided that we would never not tithe. We don't make that decision every time we get a paycheck. That would be exhausting! We made that predecision on day 1, and it's had a domino effect. Budgeting is a great example of choice architecture. It creates default settings by establishing boundaries and priorities. It's also an example of implementation intention. The same goes for calendaring. If you don't predecide how you're going to use your time, someone else will. Your bank statement and your calendar don't lie. They reveal what your core values really are!

How do I make it a habit?

Put it in writing!

That principle has a hundred applications, but putting things in writing has two primary benefits. The first is clarity. The process of putting things on paper forces us to be precise. It's the way we take our thoughts captive with the twenty-six letters of the English alphabet and make them obedient to Christ.[12] That goes for goals as well as gratitude!

The second effect is memory. Writing things down has a generation effect—we demonstrate better memory for the things we've written down than things we simply read. The shortest pencil is longer than the longest memory. Writing encodes things into long-term memory.

Are your life goals in writing? How about your core values? What about your personal definition of success? Do you keep a gratitude journal? A prayer journal?

In the Deuteronomic code, a curious command is given to ancient Jewish kings: "When he takes the throne of his kingdom, he is to write for himself on a scroll a copy of this law." The king had places to go and things to do! Why take the time to write out the entire Torah in longhand? Was that really necessary? The answer is embedded in the amendment: "So that he may learn to revere the LORD his God and follow carefully all the words of this law."[13]

I call this the king habit, and it involved three provisions. First, the king had to write out the Torah. Second, the king had to keep that copy on his person at all times. Third, the king had to read from it daily. I'll give you a pass on the first provision. If you have a smartphone, the second provision is as simple as downloading a digital Bible. The key is the third provision, and the best way to put it into practice is a daily Bible reading plan. It's one of the best pre-decisions you'll ever make. Not only does it serve as preventive medicine; it also creates a craving for God's Word.

Lick the honey!

Day 5

Circle the Mountain

Say to this mountain, "May you be lifted up
and thrown into the sea."
—MARK 11:23, NLT

Outside the ancient city of Kyoto in Japan, there is a monastery that dates back to the ninth century. Its founder, Sōō Oshō, was the first monk to complete an ancient challenge called the *kaihōgyō*.[1] In English, it means "circling the mountain." As part of their quest for enlightenment, monks-in-training must complete a marathon-length circuit around Mount Hiei. They do this one hundred days in a row! And that's entry level. Upon completing the hundred-day challenge, they qualify for the thousand-day challenge!

See, this thirty-day challenge isn't so bad!

Only forty-six marathon monks have completed the thousand-day challenge since 1885. Those who complete the challenge—one thousand marathons in one thousand days—cover a distance that is greater than the circumference of the earth!

To embark on that challenge, a marathon monk must petition his superiors for that privilege. If he is granted permission, there is no turning back. A marathon monk is allowed to quit during the first one hundred days, but day 101 is the point of no return. Not unlike an Old Testament vow, there is no opting out. The monk commits himself to complete the challenge or die trying. The trail around Mount Hiei is marked by the graves of monks who did just that.

When I first heard about the marathon monks, I had a hard time believing that one thousand marathons in one thousand days is even possible. One marathon is hard enough! How do they do it? They eliminate all other options. It's do or die!

There is a genius to this sacred ritual on day 101. Technically speaking, it's called a *commitment device,* and it comes in quite a few flavors. If you're trying to break a bad habit, impose a fine on yourself every time you fail to fulfill your commitment. Of course, you'll need someone to keep you honest. If you're looking to leverage positive reinforcement, why not try a box of Thin Mint cookies like Randy Pausch? The only limit on commitment devices is your creativity!

It took me thirteen years, and quite a few false starts, to write my first book. How did I finally pull it off? I leveraged my thirty-fifth birthday as a deadline. I had to make a commitment to myself: *I'm not going to turn thirty-five without a book to show for it.*

All of us are incredibly creative when it comes to finding excuses! If you're looking for an excuse, you'll always find one. If you give yourself an escape clause, you'll eventually take it. Habit formation requires implementation intention upfront, but a commitment device is the insurance policy. The good news? "At the moment of commitment," said the German poet Johann Wolfgang von Goethe, "the entire universe conspires to assist you."[2]

Can I let you in on a little secret? As a pastor, I often include things in my messages as a way of "going public," thereby holding myself accountable. Sometimes it's casting corporate vision, like launching a new campus or building our DC Dream Center. Sometimes it's more personal. Before I started training for the Chicago Marathon, I announced that I was going to run it. Why? I knew it would keep me accountable! One facet of a commitment device is going public somehow. That's precisely what the apostle Paul modeled: "He publicly announced the date when their vows would end."[3]

One key to creating a habit loop is not giving yourself any loopholes. You have to pick a habit, any habit. You have to make it measurable, meaningful, and maintainable. Then you have to wade into the water thirty days in a row. Or in the case of the marathon monks, you have to circle the mountain every day for a thousand days!

As a true freshman, Herschel Walker broke almost every NCAA record on the books for running backs—most yards, most yards per carry, most touchdowns. He won the Heisman Trophy his junior year. In 2002, he was selected as the second-greatest player in college football history behind Red Grange.[4]

How did Herschel Walker do it? You guessed it—a commitment device. Until the age of twelve, Walker's passion was poetry and reading. One day he read a book "about a Marine who did all these push-ups and sit-ups."[5] That paragraph proved to be a prompt. Walker began an exercise regimen that involved thousands of sit-ups and push-ups, and he never stopped. Even after retiring from professional football, he kept doing two thousand sit-ups and push-ups every day. I think that qualifies as a positive addiction!

Remember our working theory? *Almost anyone can accomplish almost anything if they work at it long enough, hard enough, and smarter enough.* The marathon monks are exhibit A. You don't run a thousand marathons in a row without a growth mindset. If you focus on the size of the mountain, you'll quit before you start. The marathon monks can't see all the way around the mountain. So what do they do? They focus one hundred feet in front of themselves, and they keep putting one foot in front of the other. They are plodders, par excellence!

I've already introduced two dimensions of habit formation— *harder is better* and *slower is faster.* Let me add one more to the mix: *smaller is bigger.*

If you have faith as small as a mustard seed, you can say to this mountain, "Move from here to there," and it will move.[6]

A mustard seed measures only two millimeters in diameter, yet it grows into a nine-foot tree. If that isn't exponential, I'm not sure what is. If my math is correct, that seed grows into something that is 1,371 times its original size! Contained within that seed is a remarkable nutritional profile that includes vitamins A, B6, B12, C, E, and K. It's a source of calcium, iron, magnesium, phosphorus, potassium, sodium, and zinc. It has anti-inflammatory properties. Plus, it tastes fantastic on pretzels!

If you didn't know what it was—a mustard seed—you would never imagine what it could become. That is the essence of faith. We plant and water, but God gives the increase. God is great not just because nothing is too big. God is great because nothing is too small.

National Community Church has given more than $25 million to kingdom causes, but it started with our first fifty-dollar check. We've taken 273 mission trips, but it started with the first team of seven people. Don't despise the day of small beginnings! Just as God's power is made perfect in weakness, His sovereignty is revealed in our smallness.

When it comes to habit formation, it's easy to get overwhelmed. That's how I felt when I started training for a marathon. That's how I feel at the beginning of every book project. Some days I feel that way just getting out of bed. My advice? Quit worrying about outcomes, and keep planting mustard seeds of faith.

You have the authority to move mountains. Yes, you! You are capable of more than you can imagine, and I don't just mean 60 percent more. How do I know this? Because God is "able to do immeasurably more than all we ask or imagine, according to his power that is at work within us"![7] Again, potential is God's gift to us. What we do with it is our gift back to God. You tap that potential by using the equation I introduced on day 3:

Deliberate Practice + Desirable Difficulty = Durable Learning

According to Anders Ericsson, the Swedish psychologist who first described the ten-thousand-hours rule, *deliberate practice* demands near maximal effort.[8] Anything less than 70 percent effort doesn't disrupt homeostasis. It maintains the status quo, which makes it counterproductive.

When it comes to physical habits, 70 percent effort is relatively easy to measure. Especially if you wear a smart watch. You figure out your maximum heart rate by subtracting your age from 220. Your target heart rate is the minimum number of heartbeats per minute to reach a level of exertion necessary for cardiovascular fitness. According to the CDC, that's somewhere between 64 percent and 76 percent.[9] A happy medium is the 70 percent effort that Anders Ericsson advocated.

How is it going with the habit you're trying to make or break? Don't get discouraged by a perceived lack of progress. Seeds have to take root before they can bear fruit. Keep giving it 70 percent effort, and it won't just add up. The effort will multiply like the marathon monks.

How do I make it a habit?

Take inventory!

Benjamin Franklin is famous for his consistent pursuit of self-improvement. He identified thirteen virtues that he wanted to cultivate, and then he developed a tool to make them measurable and maintainable. He started with concise definitions. Temperance? "Eat not to dullness; drink not to elevation." Silence? "Speak not but what may benefit others or yourself." Tranquility? "Be not disturbed at trifles."[10]

Benjamin Franklin created what we would call a habit journal. He allotted a page for each virtue, and then he divided it into days. At the end of every day, Franklin would grade himself on one of the virtues. That habit journal served as a commitment device and a daily inventory. By his own admission, Franklin never perfected any of the thirteen virtues. In fact, he fell far short. "Yet I was, by the endeavor, a better and a happier man than I otherwise should have been if I had not attempted it."[11]

In the largest and longest weight-loss study ever conducted, those who kept a food diary lost twice as much weight. "It seems that the simple act of writing down what you eat encourages people to consume fewer calories," said the lead researcher.[12] You have to identify the prompt before you can change it.

If you want to break records, you have to keep records. You have to track calories, map miles, and count blessings. The magic of measuring habits is that it heightens our self-awareness by creating a feedback loop. It connects the dots between cause and effect.

Habit formation requires honest self-evaluation. It also requires friends who care enough to confront. The best feedback loops have two ears! When it comes to breaking bad habits, few organizations have found more success than Alcoholics Anonymous. The founder, Bill Wilson, implemented a twelve-step program to help participants overcome their addictions. Step four says, "[We] made a searching and fearless moral inventory of ourselves."[13] In other words, identify the prompt that causes you to drink uncontrollably.

The twelves steps are highly acclaimed and widely used, but if AA has a secret sauce, it's ninety meetings in ninety days. Why? These meetings interrupt the pattern of participants. Instead of hitting happy hour after office hours, participants attend AA meetings!

Ask someone who has gone through AA how long they've been sober, and they can tell you the exact number of days. Why? It's all about that winning streak. They can even show you their ninety-day chip. They count the days they've been sober the same way the marathon monks circle Mount Hiei. Whatever habit you're trying to make or break, you have to take inventory by creating a feedback loop. Then you have to keep at it, one day at a time.

Circle the mountain!

Day 6

Stack the Habit

Burn fragrant incense on the altar every morning.
—Exodus 30:7

A hundred years ago, only 7 percent of Americans brushed their teeth. I know—gross! When the United States started drafting recruits for World War I, so many soldiers had rotting teeth that poor dental hygiene posed a national security risk. That raises the question, How did toothbrushing become a national habit?

Before answering that question, let me double back to the basal ganglia. It's the part of the brain that stores recurrent patterns and recalls repeated actions. It's the way we get from the bedroom to the bathroom in the middle of the night. For that matter, it's the way we drive two-ton vehicles in ten-foot lanes traveling seventy miles per hour. Of course, it was very different the first time you tried navigating a new space in the dark, wasn't it? Instead of finding the bathroom, you probably found the door with your forehead or the coffee table with your shin!

That said, you eventually get so good at repeated routines that you could do them with your eyes closed. My favorite example? Michael Jordan shooting a free throw with his eyes closed against the Denver Nuggets during the 1991 NBA season. Yes, he made it.

What does any of that have to do with brushing your teeth?

In 1929, a toothpaste company called Pepsodent launched a marketing campaign that would transform the habits of a nation. Within a few years, more than half the American population were brushing their teeth daily. I know—still gross that almost half were not. But that represents one of the most significant statistical shifts in daily habits ever!

The genius behind that campaign was an advertiser named Claude Hopkins, and the key was creating a cue. While researching dental textbooks, Hopkins took note of the mucin plaque that covers our teeth. Hopkins called it film, and he turned it into a prompt. "Just run your tongue across your teeth," read one Pepsodent ad. "*You'll feel a film*—that's what makes your teeth look 'off color' and invites decay."[1]

Along with creating a cue, Hopkins also created a craving. The secret ingredients in Pepsodent were citric acid and a dash of mint oil. That combination of chemicals created a tingling sensation on the tongue that people equated with clean teeth. The tingling sensation was the prize.

Remember the habit cycle—the three-step process whereby habits are formed? One, a *prompt* activates an automatic response. Two, a *pattern* is put on repeat. Three, a *prize* functions as a dangling carrot. In order to make or break a habit, you have to identify the prompt, interrupt the pattern, and imagine the prize. Intentionally or not, Claude Hopkins managed to do all three with Pepsodent.

The prompt was getting people to run their tongues over their teeth. The prize was the tingling sensation after brushing. The pattern was taking a few minutes to brush before bed, then rinse and repeat the next morning!

The tingling sensation caused by toothbrushing is only a century old, but leveraging the five senses in habit formation is as old as frankincense. Did you know that ten chapters in the book of Exodus are devoted to the aesthetics of the tabernacle, right down to the color of the curtains, the feng shui of the furniture, and a precise prescription for incense? The devil isn't in the details; God is. The question, of course, is, Why?

Before I answer that question, let me share one of my favorite studies. Freshly popped popcorn contains a complex mixture of twenty-three odor compounds.[2] When the smell of popcorn floods a movie theater, it does more than make you hungry. It enhances your ability to recall memories. Simply put, the smell of popcorn is a memory stimulant. Why do I love that study so much? Because National Community Church (NCC) has met in movie theaters for twenty-five years!

Praise the Lord and Pass the Popcorn!

That was the headline of an article that was written about us during our early days as a church, and it has become one of our mantras. The smell of popcorn is our incense at NCC. For moviegoers, the smell of popcorn triggers the opening trailers. When I smell popcorn, it cues worship! If these memory studies are accurate, our congregants might have the best sermon recall in the country!

Why did God give the priests a precise prescription for incense in the tabernacle? For the same reason companies spend millions of dollars creating a unique scent to prompt your olfactory nerves. Can you say Cinnabon? That scent triggers salivation, even in the most sanctified among us! God was habit stacking—using a unique scent to trigger worship recall. And it was as regular a routine as toothbrushing is for us.

Aaron must burn fragrant incense on the altar every morning when he tends the lamps. He must burn incense again when he lights the lamps at twilight so incense will burn regularly before the Lord for the generations to come.[3]

Every time the people approached the place of worship, the smell of incense evoked memories of worship. Incense was their cue, their call to worship. And that's the tip of the iceberg. It's why they wore tassels called tzitzit. Those tassels weren't fashion statements. They were physical prompts to help them remember the commandments.[4] It's why they hung mezuzahs, ritual reminders, on their doorposts.

Those aren't just ancient rituals or silly superstitions. They're straight genius! God was helping His people form habits. How? By creating prompts out of daily routines. One of the best ways to create new prompts is by leveraging bedtime. What is the last thing you do every day? Instead of consuming social media, close your eyes and confess your sin. Instead of counting sheep, count your blessings.

What is the first thing you do when you get up in the morning? Here's an idea: kneel next to your bed for a few minutes during this thirty-day challenge! Physical posture is a powerful prompt. Your physical posture affects your heart posture and vice versa. When you kneel and pray, it sets the tone for the rest of the day.

All this is easier said than done, so let me double back to the idea of craving. You can discipline yourself for a season, but lasting change needs to happen from the inside out. How? By changing your cravings. By rewriting the rewards. By renewing your mind. "Until you make the unconscious conscious," said Carl Jung, "it will direct your life and you will call it fate."[5]

According to molecular physiologist Stephen Smith, there are more than 125 trillion synapses in the cerebral cortex. That's roughly equal to the number of stars in 1,250 Milky Way galaxies![6] Each synaptic gap measures less than a thousandth of a millimeter. When it comes to habit formation, that microscopic gap is where the magic happens. It's so small, by the way, that a mustard seed of faith looms large!

Why are habits so hard to make and break? The short answer is dopamine. It's one of seven small-molecule neurotransmitters that deliver chemical messages between nerve cells. Dopamine is often referred to as the feel-good neurotransmitter, and it trains our brains to seek out pleasurable experiences while avoiding unpleasant ones. It also plays a key role in planning by helping us predict the impact of everyday activities.

"You're probably 99.9 percent unaware of dopamine release," said neuroscientist Read Montague, "but you're probably 99.9 percent driven by the information and emotions it conveys to other parts of the brain."[7] I know that sounds complicated, and it is. But that little fact gives me an extra measure of grace when I don't understand why people act the way they do. Of course, the same goes for me! "I do not understand what I do," said the apostle Paul. "For what I want to do I do not do, but what I hate I do."[8]

There are many mysteries in the universe, but the greatest mystery may be the four pounds of gray matter housed within the human cranium. That's where memories are stored, dreams are conceived, and habits are formed. That's also where the Holy Spirit does His best work. Just as He hovers over all of creation, He resides within the trillions of synapses that crisscross the cerebral cortex. He sanctifies our amygdala with stirrings. He consecrates our basal ganglia with promptings.

"Delight yourself in the LORD," said the psalmist, "and He will give you the desires of your heart."[9] At the risk of oversimplifying something that is mystical, we could say that God alters our neurochemistry by conceiving new desires within us. Let's try to incarnate this idea.

How do I make it a habit?

Stack the habit.

Many years ago, we did a little experiment at National Community Church. We called it an experilent because we did it during the liturgical season called Lent. At 7:14 every morning, we hit our knees no matter where we were. The most memorable moment for me was kneeling at gate D8 in the Cleveland airport. Did it feel a little awkward? Absolutely! But I didn't want to break my streak. A little pride died as I knelt in that waiting area, and that's not just a good thing. That's a God thing.

If you're going to interrupt the pattern, you have to experiment with different prompts. How? You leverage your regular routines by habit stacking. Habit stacking is coupling habits that are hard to form with things we do normally and naturally. My office is right above the coffeehouse we own and operate, so I start my day with a small latte, two shots of espresso. Why? The Holy Spirit + caffeine = awesome! That latte is my prompt to do my daily Bible reading plan. The prize is caffeine, which, in my experience, makes the Bible read even better!

One key to stacking your habits is reverse engineering your daily routines and finding ways to steward them. Turn your commute into a classroom by listening to audiobooks. Instead of couch surfing, exercise while you watch television. You can even leverage your bathroom time. How? Put a book in there! Anyone can read a book a month that way, and some of you have more potential than that.

Did you know that your body is two-thirds water? You are Venice with all its waterways. Your brain is 73 percent water. Your lungs are 83 percent water. Your muscles are 79 percent water. Even your bones are 31 percent water.[10] Make no bones about it—water is critical to your overall health. It flushes out impurities, enhances your immune system, and is the conduit that carries electrical currents across your synapses.

Did you know that four-fifths of us are dehydrated every day? And that's people who have access to clean water via pipes that deliver it directly to our homes. The average adult produces a quart and a half of urine daily, and we lose another quart and a half through our skin. My point? Fill up your water bottle when you go to the bathroom! And don't go to the bathroom again until you drink that water bottle. And when you sit down in the bathroom, instead of mindlessly scrolling your smartphone, pick up that book and start reading! It's a simple way of leveraging something we do every day.

Stack the habit!

Day 7

Take the Shot

Do not be conformed to this world,
but be transformed by the renewing of your mind.
—Romans 12:2, nasb

In 1932, two brothers were playing basketball on their family farm in Hillsdale, Wyoming. The older brother was six foot five. The younger brother was five foot seven. It was a classic case of David versus Goliath, and you might be tempted to think that the shorter brother was at a distinct disadvantage. On one level, you would be right. The younger brother couldn't even get a shot off because the game of basketball at this point was played with both feet firmly planted on the ground. Why? Well, the jump shot didn't exist—yet.

"This is not the game for you," said the older brother to the younger brother. "It's for big men. It's for tall men." The younger brother could have quit, but he dared to do something that had never been done before. Kenny Sailors jumped into the air, put the ball over his head, and shot the basketball with one hand.

In his documentary film *Jump Shot*,[1] Steph Curry shared the remarkable story of Kenny Sailors. He may be the best basketball player that hardly anyone has heard of. In 1943, he led the University of Wyoming Cowboys all the way to Madison Square Garden. Not only did his team win the NCAA championship, but Kenny Sailors was also named the tournament MVP.

In January 1946, *Life* magazine published a photograph that would change the game of basketball forever. It was a snapshot of

Kenny Sailors elevating above his defender and shooting his patented jump shot while everyone else was on the ground. It was the shot heard round the world. That picture in *Life* piqued the imagination of the next generation of athletes and gave them permission to play a different way.

If you want to repeat history, do it the way it's always been done. If you want to write history, do it the way it's never been done!

We have the natural tendency to do it the way we've always done it. And by *it,* I mean almost everything. It's called heuristics, and it's one of the biases Jesus was trying to break with the Sermon on the Mount. It begins with eight blessings that we call the beatitudes, and they are as counterintuitive as a backwards bike. Yes, I bought a backwards bike, but I have yet to successfully ride it. Why? I can't seem to train my brain to turn left in order to turn right. The beatitudes are a lot like that backwards bike. Those who *mourn* will be comforted. The *meek* shall inherit the earth. Those who *hunger* and *thirst* for righteousness will be filled.[2]

The Sermon on the Mount is a coup d'état against conformity. If you're going to make or break habits, you have to go against the grain. You have to identify the prompt, then interrupt the pattern by reconditioning your reflexes. That takes moral courage and tons of patience.

On August 10, 1948, a television producer named Allen Funt debuted a reality TV show called *Candid Camera.* The genius of the hidden-camera show is that it caught people in the act of being themselves. Along with producing lots of laughs, it offered a fascinating look into the human psyche.

In one very funny and rather infamous episode, "Face the Rear," an unsuspecting person boarded an elevator and did what normal people do—face the front. That's when three actors entered the elevator and faced the rear. Hidden cameras captured the angst of the person who was now staring those actors in the face. *To turn or not to turn—that is the question.* When a fourth actor entered the elevator and faced the rear, the peer pressure was too much. Without exception, every person facing the front turned around and faced the rear![3]

Do not be conformed to this world, but be transformed by the renewing of your mind.[4]

Conformed or transformed? It's one or the other. We are bombarded by news and fake news all day, every day. Online advertisers use clickbait to compete for our attention. Social media algorithms are designed to keep us in our echo chambers. It's not easy facing the front. Why? Our tendency is conformity!

What percentage of your thoughts, words, and actions are a regurgitation of the news feeds you subscribe to and the social media accounts you follow? What percentage of your thoughts, words, and actions are a revelation you're getting from God's Word? An honest answer to those questions will reveal whether you are mindlessly conforming to or courageously transforming the world around you.

In 1951, a social psychologist named Solomon Asch did a series of groundbreaking studies in the psychology of conformity.[5] He gave students a "vision test," in which they had to determine which lines were the same length. If you've seen the test, you know how easy it was! But Asch had planted "confederates" who gave the wrong answer. About 75 percent of the participants second-guessed their better judgment and went along with the consensus at least once. His conclusion? *People are willing to ignore reality for the sake of conformity!*

Morality is not rooted in an opinion poll. It's not decided by the Supreme Court either! My advice? *Let your conscience be your guide.* Scripture is our final authority. If you're going to live a countercultural life, you've got to give the Holy Spirit veto power. The same goes for making and breaking habits.

The internal presence of the Holy Spirit has to be greater than the external pressure of the world around us. By *external pressure,* I

mean everything from implicit bias to cancel culture to moral rela-
tivism. R. A. Torrey framed the Spirit-filled life this way:

> If we think of the Holy Spirit, as so many do, as merely a power
> or influence, our constant thought will be, How can I get more
> of the Holy Spirit, but if we think of Him in the biblical way as a
> divine person, our thought will rather be, How can the Holy
> Spirit have more of me?[6]

How much of you does the Holy Spirit have? Does He have all
the pieces of your complex personality? If you don't consecrate your
personality, it becomes a crutch. Quit blaming disobedience on an
Enneagram number or Myers-Briggs letter!

For more than thirty years, Gordon MacKenzie held the title of
Creative Paradox at Hallmark Cards. His job was challenging corporate normalcy! His side hustle was creativity workshops at elemen-
tary schools, and those workshops led to a fascinating observation.

MacKenzie would ask the kids an opening question: "How many
artists are there in the room?" The pattern of responses was always
the same. In the first grade, the entire class waved their arms. Every
child saw themselves as an artist. In the second grade, half the kids
raised their hands. In the third grade, the number dropped to one-
third. By the time he got to the sixth grade, only one or two kids
would self-consciously raise their hands.

> Every school I visited was participating in the suppression of
> creative genius.
> Why? . . .
> Well, it is not intentional. It is not a plot. Genius is an inno-
> cent casualty in society's efforts to train children away from
> natural-born foolishness.

MacKenzie continued, "From cradle to grave, the pressure is on:
Be Normal." For the record, normality is overrated. It's just confor-

mity by another name. MacKenzie came to this conclusion: "My guess is that there was a time—perhaps when you were very young—when you had at least a fleeting notion of your own genius and were just waiting for some authority figure to come along and validate it for you. But none ever came."[7]

Enter Jesus!

Jesus is the epitome of nonconformity! Just look at all the reactions He got from the "normal" people of His day. He sets us free from self-consciousness by helping us rediscover our inner child. "Unless you change and become like little children," Jesus said, "you will never enter the kingdom of heaven."[8] The key to nonconformity is becoming like Christ. The result is becoming like little children.

Juxtapose that with this.

According to a study by Stanford professor and psychiatrist Dr. William Fry, the average kindergarten student laughs 300 times a day. The average adult laughs just 17 times per day![9] Somewhere between childhood and adulthood, we lose 283 laughs per day. It's time to reclaim that birthright, along with everything else our bad habits have robbed us of. Like smiling, laughing releases a cocktail of chemicals that reduce stress and operate as natural painkillers.[10]

According to Rolf Smith, children ask 125 questions per day. The average adult asks 6.[11] Somewhere between childhood and adulthood, we lose 119 questions per day. Part of becoming like little children is recapturing holy curiosity. Did you know that Jesus asked more questions than He answered? He was asked 183 questions in the Gospels, but He asked no less than 307 questions! The more you know, the more you know how much you don't know. Questions are a good measure of your curiosity quotient.

In one study on divergent thinking, 98 percent of children between the ages of three and five scored in the genius category! Between the ages of eight and ten, that number dropped to 32 percent. By the time those kids became teenagers, the number dropped to 10 percent. And only 2 percent of those over the age of twenty-five scored in the genius category for divergent thinking![12]

Where did it go? It's the casualty of conformity. If you're going to break habits, you have to break with the status quo. You have to swim upstream by living a countercultural life.

If you reverse engineer the Jesus Way, it sure seems like Jesus went out of His way to offend the chief conformists of His day. He could have healed any day of the week, but He chose the Sabbath. Why? Why not heal two birds with one stone! By healing on the Sabbath, Jesus confronted the religiosity of the rule makers. They codified no less than 613 rules, an impossible burden to bear! Jesus changed the game with one Great Commandment.

My advice? *Thou shalt offend Pharisees!* Quit living according to the expectations of people who don't know you, love you, or care about you. Walk to the beat of a different drummer. Rewrite the rules, just like Jesus. Take your prompts from the Holy Spirit, and dare to be different.

How do I make it a habit?

Change the game!

Half a century ago, a psychologist named Albert Bandura did a series of studies designed to cure children who were deathly afraid of dogs.[13] He showed the kids short videos of other children encountering dogs. The children in the videos didn't display any fear as they moved closer and closer, finally petting the dogs. The technical term is *systematic desensitization,* and it can be effective in curing our fears.

After a month of visual conditioning, the kids were placed in a similar situation to the one they had watched. An unfamiliar dog would have terrified them a month earlier, but that exposure therapy had given them newfound confidence. Most of them were able to approach the dogs and pet them. According to Bandura, we are conditioned by what we see more than we know. For better or for worse, we mirror the behavior of others. Bandura branded it "modeling," and fashion is a great example. Ever look back at an old outfit and wonder what you were thinking? In high school, I wore almost all my sweatshirts inside out. Why? Everyone else was wearing them inside out. Consciously or subconsciously, we take our fashion cues from others. We also take political cues, relational cues, and emotional cues from others.

How have you been subconsciously conditioned by culture?

Are there any ways you need to be reconditioned?

If you want to make or break a habit, you have to interrupt the pattern. How? You have to change the game. That's what Kenny Sailors did when he had the courage to take his unorthodox jump shot. It goes without saying, but I'll say it anyway: *you won't make any of the shots you don't take.* If you want to make a difference, you have to dare to be different. Does that mean every attempt will succeed? Far from it.

According to Steve Harvey, Michael Jordan made 146 attempted game-winning shots during his college and professional career. Any guess how many he took? A lot more than he made! Jordan took 946 shots, which means he missed 800. But that isn't what you remember, is it? You remember the bank shot that won the NCAA championship for his North Carolina Tar Heels on March 29, 1982. You remember the jumper against the Utah Jazz in Game 7 to win his sixth NBA championship.

We're one week into our thirty-day challenge. How are you doing on the habit you're trying to make or break? If you're struggling, find a way to change the game. How? Turn it into a game! Rewrite the rules in a way that makes the habit more measurable, meaningful, and maintainable. And remember, even if you feel like you're falling short, I bet you've gotten further than you would have if you hadn't set the goal in the first place.

Take the shot!

Day 8

Remember the Future

Faith is being sure of what we hope for.
—Hebrews 11:1, NIRV

On September 9, 1965, James Stockdale was flying a mission over North Vietnam when the plane he piloted was shot down. He parachuted into a village where he was captured by the Vietcong. Stockdale would spend almost eight years as a prisoner of war at the infamous Hanoi Hilton. His concrete cell measured three feet by nine feet, with no windows. As a senior naval officer, he was routinely tortured and denied medical treatment.

How do you survive eight years in those kinds of circumstances? How do you overcome that kind of physical and psychological trauma? In the words of James Stockdale, "I never lost faith in the end of the story."[1]

If you forget how the story ends, it's awfully easy to lose faith, lose hope, lose courage. I know life is unfair. I know pain and suffering are far too prevalent. I know there are an awful lot of wrongs that need to be made right. Can I tell you what else I know? I know how the story ends! The kingdom of this world is becoming the kingdom of our Lord and of His Christ, and He will reign forever and ever.[2] "God's aim looks like missing the mark," said Oswald Chambers, "because we are too short-sighted to see what He is aiming at."[3] We don't believe in happily ever after. We believe in something so much bigger and better and longer and stronger—happily *forever* after!

When it comes to making and breaking habits, remembering the past is incredibly important. It's one way we pop the periscope on our present circumstances and gain perspective. "The farther backward you can look," said Winston Churchill, "the farther forward you can see."[4] Hindsight is incredibly important, but it has to be coupled with foresight.

History is the way we remember the past.

Prophecy is the way we remember the future.

The Bible gives us a sneak peek at where history is headed. The day is coming when every nation, tribe, people, and language will worship around the throne.[5] The way you remember the future is by going to the back of the Book. While we're on the subject, prayer is the way we write history before it happens!

When I was a student, I loved open-book tests. They weren't any easier than closed-book tests, but I knew I could find the answer if I looked long enough, hard enough, and smart enough. Life is an open-book test, and the way you pass the test is by going to the back of *the* Book. Don't lose faith in the end of the story!

In his classic book *Good to Great,* Jim Collins asked James Stockdale about the prisoners who didn't survive their captivity. According to Stockdale, it was the optimists who didn't make it. Why? They were perpetually disappointed by false expectations. *We'll be released by Christmas,* they would say to themselves. But Christmas would come and go, along with Easter and Thanksgiving. "They died of a broken heart," said Stockdale. How did Stockdale survive? "I never doubted not only that I would get out, but also that I would prevail in the end." But Stockdale didn't stop there: "[I would] turn the experience into the defining event of my life, which, in retrospect, I would not trade."[6]

A few years ago, I was part of a panel with my friend Bob Goff. Bob has a way of dropping the mic by dropping one-liners. I can't even remember the original question, but I love Bob's answer: "The best chapter titles come later." It's true, isn't it? You can't have a chapter titled "Comeback" without a chapter titled "Setback." The same goes for "Failure" and "Success." Maybe you're in a chapter titled "Pain and Suffering." Don't lose faith in the end of the story. "Hope and Healing" are coming!

Fun fact? During that same panel discussion, Bob Goff shared a story that predates his daughter. Before she was born, Bob wrote a note forgiving her for getting into an accident and crashing their car. He put that note in a jar, then buried it in the ground. And sure enough, seventeen years later his daughter crashed their car! Bob gave her a shovel, along with the latitude and longitude of where that jar was buried. She dug it up and discovered that her father had forgiven her before she was even born. That's awesome, isn't it? If that isn't remembering the future, I'm not sure what is!

Let me double back to James Stockdale for a moment. Reflecting on eight years as a POW, Stockdale said, "You must never confuse faith that you will prevail in the end—which you can never afford to lose—with the discipline to confront the most brutal facts of your current reality, whatever they might be."[7] Jim Collins dubbed it the Stockdale Paradox, and it's one key to making and breaking habits. You have to confront the brutal facts, but you do so with unwavering faith.

Jesus said it this way: "In this world you will have trouble." Pain and suffering shouldn't come as a surprise. Why? We live in a broken world, a fallen world. But Jesus added a critical conjunction: "But take heart! I have overcome the world."[8]

When injustice slaps you in the face, it stings. When sorrow overwhelms your soul, it's hard to stay afloat. When you crash into cancer or go through a divorce, it's hard to know which way is up. I'll say it once again for good measure: *don't lose faith in the end of the story!* You have to imagine the prize. You have to be sure of what you hope for and certain of what you do not see.[9] That's easier said than done, but when you can't see past today, *do it for a day*! Let me bring this idea down to earth and apply it to habit formation.

On August 13, 2008, Michael Phelps won the gold medal in the two-hundred-meter butterfly, setting a new world record. It was one of six gold medals that Phelps won in the Beijing games, but it may be his most impressive. Why? His goggles were dislodged when he dove into the pool, and he lost his vision. When Phelps made the last turn, all he could do was count his strokes. He had to swim blind, sort of. The reality? He had already made the swim that morning in his mind. And the night before. And the day before, and the day before that. Michael Phelps had been visualizing his races since he was a teenager.

As a teenager, Phelps had a hard time calming down before races. His coach, Bob Bowman, bought him a book of relaxation exercises that Phelps's mom read to him every night. The book contained a script—"Tighten your right hand into a fist and release it. Imagine the tension melting away." That exercise helped Phelps relax and eventually fall asleep. It also exercised his imagination!

After every practice, Coach Bowman told him to go home and "watch the videotape." Michael Phelps would visualize the perfect race twice a day, every day. During practices and meets, his coach would shout, "Put in the videotape!" Every time Phelps dove into the pool, he was remembering the future. It was mind over matter. That's how he won the gold medal, even when his goggles filled with water. A lesser swimmer might have panicked, but not Michael Phelps. When a reporter asked him what it felt like to swim blind, Phelps said, "It felt like I imagined it would."[10]

We have a tendency to remember what we should forget and forget what we should remember. That's how we get stuck in the past or fixated on the future. How do we manage memory and steward imagination? We remember the past by building altars. We remember the future by setting goals. Then we visualize them in vivid detail, like Michael Phelps did.

Keep going to the back of the Book.

Keep putting in the videotape.

Starting tomorrow, we will unpack seven daily habits—*flip the script, kiss the wave, eat the frog, fly the kite, cut the rope, wind the clock,* and *seed the clouds.* Try to be fully present each day. That's a constant battle, so let me share a centering prayer. It's not unlike the visualization exercise Michael Phelps practiced, but it adds God to the equation. It will help you remember the future while staying focused on each day's challenge.

The Quakers often employed body posture in their prayers. They would start with their hands out, palms down, symbolizing the things they needed to let go of. Give it a try! Is there anything you've been obsessing over? Anything you're anxious about? Is there anyone you need to forgive, including yourself? Let go and let God. God's got this. God's got you.

Once you feel like you've placed all your hurts and habits and hang-ups in the hands of God, turn your hands over. In a posture of receptivity, welcome His presence, His power, His peace. Let it guard your heart and your mind.[11] While you're at it, ask for a fresh infilling of His Spirit. "To be filled with the Holy Spirit," said Simon Ponsonby, "leaves no room to be filled with anything else."[12]

There is an old adage: *Look both ways.* It's timeless advice, isn't it? It's awfully important when it comes to crossing the street. It's equally important when it comes to making and breaking habits. At this juncture in our journey, take a deep breath. If you're anything like me, you have a long way to go when it comes to making and breaking habits. It feels like two steps forward and one step back. That can be discouraging, but keep reminding yourself of how far you've come.

How do I make it a habit?

Is this where you stop?

Dan Sullivan is the cofounder of Strategic Coach and an expert in entrepreneurship. He attributes his success to a no-quit mindset. After high school, he went on an Outward Bound expedition in Scotland. During an excruciating hike through treacherous terrain, Sullivan took off his backpack and sat down. He was ready to quit.

That's when one of the Outward Bound guides asked him a question that would change the trajectory of his life: "Is this where you stop?" The confused look on Sullivan's face prompted an explanation: "Everybody stops somewhere. Is this where you stop?"[13]

Sullivan was spent, well past 40 percent! We've all been there and done that, right? You feel like you have nothing left in the tank. That's when you have to make a choice. Is this where you stop? Or is this when you dig a little deeper, try a little longer? At some point, almost everything you've accomplished seemed impossible. When you were six months old, that was true of walking. When you were in kindergarten, you weren't solving algebraic equations. Your goal may seem like it's a thousand miles away, but if you keep putting one foot in front of the other, you'll get there sooner or later!

The hill in front of Dan Sullivan looked like Everest, but that's when he made a declaration: "This is not where I stop." Sullivan is a plodder, with two *d*'s! He picked up his pack and put one foot in front of the other. When he reached his destination several days later, the same guide who asked him that game-changing question said this: "If you had stopped on the hill that day, your life would have been difficult. You would have been tempted to quit anytime you faced a struggle in the future." Whenever Dan Sullivan faces what seems to be an insurmountable challenge, he asks himself that question: *Is this where I stop?* "I've always answered that question," he said, "with a resounding no."[14]

I've been tempted to quit a time or two or ten. The thing that has kept me going? Remembering the future. In my first year pastoring, I was tempted to throw in the towel. If I had quit, it would have affected only twenty people at the time. And all of them could have found a more mature church to attend. But I also would have been quitting on the tens of thousands of people we would affect in the future. I would have been quitting on the 273 mission trips we've taken. I would have been quitting on Ebenezers Coffeehouse and the DC Dream Center.

Are you picking up what I'm throwing down? When you get

overwhelmed by your present circumstances, remember the future. Go back to your life-goal list. Go back to your core values. Go back to the back of the Book.

I have no idea what habit you're trying to make or break, but let me pop the question at this juncture: *Is this where you stop?* If you're still breathing, God hasn't given up on you. Don't give up on God. And don't give up on yourself.

Remember the future!

Habit 1—Flip the Script

*If you want to change your life,
start by changing your story.*

In the science of cybernetics, there are two kinds of change. First-order change is *behavioral*—it's doing something *more* or *less*. If you're trying to lose weight, eating less and exercising more are steps in the right direction.

First-order change may facilitate a quick fix, but second-order change passes the test of time. Second-order change is *conceptual*—it's mind over matter, and that's where the magic happens. Everything is created twice. The first creation is *internal*. The second creation is *physical*. Everything was once a thought. That includes you. You are a unique expression of God's imagination. You don't just bear His image; you are His idea!

We tend to think of habits as *external* exercises that increase proficiency or productivity. Playing scales. Drawing sketches. Shooting free throws. External habits will pay dividends, no doubt. But the biggest returns on investment come from *internal* habits that no one sees. Your internal monologue. Your explanatory style. The stories you tell yourself day in and day out.

I've had the joy and privilege of leading National Community Church in Washington, DC, for a quarter century. During that time, I've led every kind of person under the sun. I've led every combination of letters on the Myers-Briggs and every number on the Enneagram. I've led people you would clone if you could. I've led my fair share of EGR people—extra grace required. Can I tell you the hardest person I've ever had to lead? You know exactly who it is, don't you? The hardest person to lead, hands down, is the person I see in the mirror every morning! No one is harder to lead than me, myself, and I.

Leadership starts with self-leadership, and self-leadership starts with daily habits. It's cultivating private habits that aren't affected by publicity, positive or negative. It's doing the right thing, regardless of who's watching or not watching. If you want to win the day, you have to win in the dark! In my book, success is when those who know you best respect you most. It's being a better person in private than you are in public. Or at the very least, the same person!

On average, sixty thousand thoughts fire across our synapses every day. If your thoughts about yourself were transcribed, what would they say? According to a study done by the Cleveland Clinic, 80 percent of our thoughts are negative.[1] That's a scary thought, pun intended. That's why sanctifying your self-talk is so important. Self-talk is the source code. That's where the battle is won or lost.

As he thinketh in his heart, so is he.[2]

It's no secret that our thoughts have psychological and physiological effects. Your thoughts have the power to lower your blood pressure, slow your pulse, and boost your immunity. Of course, they have the power to do the opposite too. Either way, your explanations are more important than your experiences! If you don't like your life, you may be telling yourself the wrong story. You have to flip the script. If you want to change your life, you have to change your story!

John Quincy Adams was right: "Whoever tells the best story wins."[3] Any guess who tells the best stories? The answer is the Author and Finisher of our faith! Of course, you have to give Him complete editorial control. The still, small voice of the Holy Spirit has to be the loudest voice in your life. You have to take your cues from Scripture. When you do, Scripture becomes your script-cure. Then, and only then, does God begin writing His-story—*history* with a hyphen—in and through your life.

Do you know the greatest predictor of children's emotional well-being? It's not getting them into a great school, giving them lots of hugs, or taking them on a pilgrimage to Disney World. According to researchers at Emory University, the number one indicator of emotional well-being is knowing their family history.[4]

Each of us is born into someone else's story. For better or for worse, you need to know your backstory. Fun thought? I bet Jesus heard a few bedtime stories about Nahshon. Why? Jesus was one of his begats, which means Nahshon was part of His backstory. Your backstory is the script you were handed the day you were born. That said, we're handed another script the day we're born again. We aren't just adopted into the family of God; we get grafted into God's story! If you're in Christ, you're of the lineage of Nahshon. It's in your blood, your bloodline! And God wants to write a sequel through your life.

It's time to flip the script!

Day 9

Change Your Story

I can do all things through Christ who strengthens me.
—Philippians 4:13, NKJV

B*eamonesque.*

It ranks as one of my favorite words. Yes, it's actually in the dictionary! It's a superlative that means unexpected excellence, and its etymology traces back to an iconic moment during the 1968 Olympics. The genesis of that word is an achievement so astonishing that it became known as "the jump." *Sports Illustrated* dubbed it one of the five greatest sporting moments of the twentieth century.

The long jump competition included gold medalists from the previous two Olympics, America's Ralph Boston and Britain's Lynn Davies. The favorite to win gold was Russia's Igor Ter-Ovanesyan, the world record holder. But it was a long-shot long jumper named Bob Beamon who would come out of nowhere and jump into the history books.

Bob Beamon took nineteen strides, planted his right foot, flew more than six feet into the air, threw his arms behind his back, and landed in the sand. The whole thing took less than six seconds, but it took more than twenty minutes to measure that jump. Olympic officials had installed an electronic measuring device that ran the length of the long-jump pit, but Beamon outjumped the electronics! Officials had to find an old-fashioned tape measure. Even then, they had a hard time believing the tale of the tape.

The world record going into the Olympic Games was twenty-seven feet, four and three-quarters inches. In the prior one hundred years, that record had been broken thirteen times by an average of two and a half inches. Bob Beamon obliterated the world record by almost two feet. None of the other competitors even eclipsed twenty-seven feet. Bob Beamon landed twenty-nine feet, two and a half inches from where he took off.[1] Not only did he set a new world record, but a new word was conceived in the unabridged dictionary—*Beamonesque*. It describes a result that is so far superior to anything previously accomplished that it's almost inconceivable.

Most of us aren't going to break world records or become world famous, and that's okay. *Beamonesque* has nothing to do with fame or fortune. It's reserved for long shots, like you and me. *Beamonesque* is blue collar. It refers to ordinary people who accomplish extraordinary things with a little extra faith, a little extra hope, a little extra love. And, I might add, a little extra effort.

Once again for good measure: *almost anyone can accomplish almost anything if they work at it long enough, hard enough, and smart enough.* The way you tap that God-given potential is by telling yourself a better story. On that note, here's the rest of the story.

Bob Beamon won the gold, won the day. But there's more to his story than individual effort. There always is, isn't there? Beamon almost failed to reach the finals, fouling on his first two jumps. It was his teammate Ralph Boston who calmed him down and coached him up. Right before Beamon's third and final attempt, Boston whispered these words into his ear:

Take off early. You have room to spare. Give 'em two inches on the front. You'll take two feet when you land. Your legs have never been as strong as they are right now. At this moment your body weighs nothing. Your mind has wings. Use them. Fly up. Fly out.[2]

How did Bob Beamon set a new world record? With a new story—"Your mind has wings." With a better story—"Your body weighs nothing." Bob Beamon made "the jump," but Ralph Boston handed him the script—"Give 'em two inches on the front. You'll take two feet when you land."

All of us need someone who believes in us more than we believe in ourselves. We need people who push us past our limits by reminding us of who we are and what we're capable of. For six unforgettable seconds, Bob Beamon borrowed Ralph Boston's faith.

Who is the loudest voice in your life?

The answer to that question will determine your destiny, and there are lots of voices to choose from. For some, it's the voice of *conformity*. If you allow it, culture will try to name you and tame you. There are social media algorithms designed to keep us in our echo chambers, not to mention the white noise of news and fake news. You may even have a few people trolling, shaming, and baiting you.

For others, it's the voice of *condemnation*. The accuser of the brethren is like a broken record reminding us of everything we've done wrong over and over again. He is also identified as the father of lies, which is where many of our false assumptions, false narratives, and false identities originate.

Finally, there is the voice of *criticism*. If you give your inner critic the mic, good luck. You won't get a word in edgewise! In the infamous words of comic-strip character Pogo, "We have met the enemy and he is us!"[3] And that's no joke!

There is another voice—a still, small voice. Like Ralph Boston, the Holy Spirit is whispering words of encouragement. What words? The same words He inspired thousands of years ago! We don't just read them; they read us. Why? They are living and active!

If God is for us, who can be against us?[4]

He who is in you is greater than he who is in the world.[5]

All things work together for good to those who love God.[6]

I can do all things through Christ who strengthens me.[7]

Remember the habit cycle? If you want to make or break a habit, you have to *identify the prompt*. If you want to change your life, you have to change your story. How? The key is the cue. You rewrite your story by letting Scripture overwrite your false narratives. Nothing prompts faith more than the promises of God. Of course, you have to rehearse them over and over again! Overwriting doesn't happen overnight.

"If you want a new idea," said Ivan Pavlov, "read an old book."[8] I love reading history and biography. Those genres help me see my life and my circumstances through a wide-angle lens. That said, no book is older and no book is better than the Bible.

"Since the day the Temple was destroyed," says the Talmud, "[God] has only one place in His world, only the four cubits of *halakha*."[9] *Halakha* is Hebrew for the law, both oral and written. It means "the way of walking." The curve ball is four cubits. What's that about?[10] Four cubits is roughly six feet, which is both a clue and a cue. It's a code word for an individual's personal space. You are a walking, talking translation of the halakha. In other words, your life is a unique translation of Scripture. The question is this: Is your life a good translation?

The first habit is flip the script, and the key is flipping open the Bible. The Bible is your backstory, and you are the rest of the story. If you want to get a word *from* God, you've got to get into the Word *of* God. When you open the Bible, God opens His mouth. The more you read it, the louder God's voice gets. Holy Scripture becomes the source code that rewrites your life story.

How do I make it a habit?

Be still.

For the past thirty-plus years, an acoustic ecologist named Gordon Hempton has been compiling what he calls "The List of the Last Great Quiet Places." It consists of places with at least fifteen minutes of uninterrupted quiet during daylight hours. At last count there were only twelve quiet places in the entire United States![11] And we wonder why the soul suffers.

By definition, white noise is a sound that contains every frequency a human can hear. Because it contains every frequency, it's very difficult to distinguish any frequency, especially the still, small voice of God. Chronic noise may be the greatest impediment to our spiritual growth, and it's not just spirituality that suffers. Noise affects everything from creativity to productivity!

In a study of students at a grade school in Manhattan, psychologist Arline Bronzaft found that children assigned to classrooms on the side of the school facing the elevated train tracks were eleven months behind their counterparts on the quieter side of the building.[12] After New York City Transit installed noise-abatement equipment on the tracks, a follow-up study found no difference between the groups.

Can I go out on a limb? Your life is too loud, and your schedule is too busy. That's why it's so easy to forget that God is God. "Be still," He said, "and know that I am God."[13]

The author, professor, and priest Henri Nouwen believed that silence was an act of war against the competing voices within us. That war is fought on many fronts, and it's a daily battle. "Every time you listen with great attentiveness to the voice that calls you the Beloved," said Nouwen, "you will discover within yourself a desire to hear that voice longer and more deeply."[14]

A simple next step? Download a daily Bible reading plan. While you're at it, check out the five-day reading plan based on my book *Whisper*.[15] If you're an auditory learner, download an audio version. If you start taking your prompts from Scripture, those cues will become convictions that function as a moral compass. Over time, the still, small voice of the Holy Spirit will become the loudest voice in your life. His promptings will rewrite and reroute your life in supernatural ways. Before you know it, God will be writing His story in you and through you.

Change your story!

Day 10

Fix Your Focus

You intended to harm me, but God intended it for good.
—Genesis 50:20

In December 1944, American forces were surrounded by enemy troops at Bastogne, Belgium. The German general demanded immediate and unconditional surrender. The situation seemed hopeless—supplies were low and morale was even lower.

General Anthony McAuliffe assembled the 101st Airborne Division and surveyed the situation: "Men, we are surrounded by the enemy." You know what comes next, right? The white flag! But General McAuliffe wasn't wired that way. He changed the course of history by flipping the script. Instead of waving the white flag, he shifted their perspective with a little reframing: "We have the greatest opportunity ever presented an army. We can attack in any direction."[1]

In psychology, cognitive reappraisal is a fancy phrase for telling yourself a different story about what's happening. It's flipping the script by looking at your circumstances from a different vantage point. Here's a fictitious example I came across many years ago:

Dear Mom and Dad,
I have so much to tell you. Because of the fire in my dorm set off by student riots, I experienced temporary lung damage and had to go to the hospital. While I was there, I fell in love with an orderly, and we have moved in together. I dropped out

of school when I found out I was pregnant, and he got fired because of his drinking. So we're going to move to Alaska, where we might get married after the birth of our baby.

Your loving daughter.

PS: None of this really happened, but I did flunk my chemistry class and wanted to keep it in perspective.[2]

One way to keep your sense of perspective is by keeping your sense of humor. Remember day 7? A little humor goes a long way when it comes to habit formation. If you can't laugh at yourself, it's awfully hard to change yourself. The happiest, healthiest, and holiest people on the planet are those who laugh at themselves the most.

When it comes to cognitive reappraisal, Joseph is exhibit A. He was betrayed by his brothers, sold into slavery, and found guilty of a crime he didn't commit. After thirteen years of pain and suffering, Joseph could have played the victim card. Right? Then, when he was promoted, he could have played God. It was within Joseph's power to even the score by exacting revenge on his brothers. He didn't do any of those things. Joseph looked back on all the ups and downs, all the twists and turns, and said,

You intended to harm me, but God intended it for good . . . the saving of many lives.[3]

According to Dr. Martin Seligman, former president of the American Psychological Association, all of us have an explanatory style: "Explanatory style is the manner in which you habitually explain to yourself why events happen."[4] It's those explanations—not the experiences themselves—that make or break us.

What was Joseph's explanatory style? Long before the Stockdale Paradox was put into print, Joseph confronted the brutal facts— "You intended to harm me." But he didn't lose faith in the end of the story! Joseph had a God's-eye view. He flipped the script by identifying the metanarrative—"But God intended it for good . . . the saving of many lives."

Hold that thought and consider these two questions.

One, *How happy are you?*

Two, *How many dates did you have last month?*

Those are the questions posed to college students who participated in a study on cognitive bias. Researchers found no correlation between level of happiness and number of dates. Then the researchers flipped the questions and, I might suggest, flipped the script.

One, *How many dates did you have last month?*

Two, *How happy are you?*

All of a sudden, there was a strong correlation between the number of dates the students had been on and their level of happiness. What happened? By getting those students to focus on their dating status first and foremost, the researchers were able to alter their outlook on life.[5]

It's called the focusing illusion, and it's a cognitive bias whereby humans tend to rely too much on the first piece of information presented to them. It's why we judge a book by its cover. It's why first impressions leave a lasting impression.

In a similar study conducted at the University at Buffalo, subjects were asked to complete this sentence: *I'm glad I'm not a _____.* After subjects filled in the blank five times, researchers noted a measurable increase in levels of satisfaction. Why? It's called a downward counterfactual. It may sound masochistic, but it's reminding yourself of how things could be worse.

A second group of subjects were asked to complete this sentence: *I wish I were a _____.* After they completed it five times, there was a measurable decrease in levels of satisfaction. Why? It's called an upward counterfactual. No matter how good you've got it, it could always be better, couldn't it?[6]

Happiness is reality minus expectations, right?

Here's the bottom line: Your feelings aren't determined by your circumstances. Your feelings are a function of your focus. Simply put, *your focus determines your reality.* How do we fix our thoughts? By fixing our focus! That idea is as old as these words written by the apostle Paul from a prison cell right around AD 62:

Fix your thoughts on what is true, and honorable, and right, and pure, and lovely, and admirable.[7]

I once heard marriage guru Gary Smalley say that every marriage is about 80 percent good and 20 percent bad. In other words, we all have marital issues we need to fix. According to Smalley, the difference between happy and unhappy marriages is focus. Yes, you need to fix the 20 percent that is bad. But you need to fix your focus on the 80 percent that is good. In the world of organizational leadership, it's called appreciative inquiry. It identifies what's working, and then it does more of that.

If you're frustrated with your spouse, refocus on the things that made you fall in love in the first place. The same is true of the job you used to love. We don't see the world as it is. We see the world as we are! Much of what we see is a projection of our personality, our pain, our past, and our prejudice. This is why hurt people hurt people. This is also why forgiven people forgive people. Yes, seeing is believing. But believing is also seeing. "What the eye sees," said author Richard Restak, "is determined by what the brain has learned."[8]

Restak shared a motto that has become a personal mantra: "Learn more, see more."[9] When astronomers look into the night sky, they connect the dots called constellations. They see more because they know more. When musicians listen to a song, they hear the harmonies. They hear more because they know more. The more you know, the more you see!

Remember the twelve spies who spent forty days in the promised land? They went to the same places, encountered the same people, and surveyed the same cities. Ten of them were focused on the size of the giants in the land, which functioned as an upward counterfactual. "They are stronger than we are."[10] That statement might have been true, but were they stronger than almighty God? When you measure your problems against your ability, your resources, or your education, you always come up short.

Positivity and negativity are projections of our personality, our psychology, and our theology. And don't tell me it's not a big deal. It was the negativity of the ten spies that kept Israel out of the promised land for forty years!

If you are full of fear, you'll find something to be afraid of.

If you are full of doubt, you'll find something to second-guess.

If you are full of hurt, you'll find something to hate.

If you are full of pride, you'll find something to criticize.

"We seemed like grasshoppers in our own eyes," they self-assessed, "and we looked the same to them."[11] How did they know how they looked to them? They were playing the comparison game, and they literally came up short. Their negativity resulted in a bad report, and that bad report was the by-product of the focusing illusion. The only way to fix your focus is by measuring your problems against the character of God—His goodness, His faithfulness, and His sovereignty.

"I am not what I think I am," said Charles Horton Cooley, co-founder of the American Sociological Association, "and I am not what you think I am. I am what I think you think I am."[12] That's a bit of a tongue twister. How much wood could a woodchuck chuck if a woodchuck could chuck wood?

Cooley called it the looking-glass self,[13] and it's our sense of self that we base on how we believe others see us. That's why we need to fix our eyes on Jesus, the Author and Finisher of our faith. We take our cues from Scripture, and it becomes our script-cure. Then we interrupt the pattern by fixing our focus.

James, the half brother of Jesus, likened Scripture to a looking glass.[14] That's how we discover our identity, our destiny, and our authority in Christ. You can't let other people narrate your life. If you do, you'll spend your entire life living up or living down to their expectations! You have to let go and let God narrate.

There is no place for pride when you follow Christ. That said, false humility is just as dangerous. It's thinking of yourself as anything less than who God says you are. You are the apple of God's eye. You are God's workmanship. You are more than a conqueror![15]

How big is your God? Is He bigger than your biggest problem? Your biggest challenge? Your biggest mistake? "A low view of God is the cause of a hundred lesser evils," said A. W. Tozer. A high view of God is the solution to "ten thousand temporal problems."[16] Show me the size of your dream, and I'll show you the size of your God.

How do I make it a habit?

Count your blessings.

In a classic study on counterfactuals, psychologist Vicki Medvec revealed the relative importance of attitudes over and against circumstances. Medvec studied Olympic medalists and discovered that bronze medalists were quantifiably happier than silver medalists. That makes no sense, right? The silver medalists beat the bronze medalists! The difference? Silver medalists tended to focus on how close they came to winning gold, so they weren't satisfied with silver. Bronze medalists tended to focus on how close they came to not winning a medal, so they were happy to be on the medal stand at all.[17]

You get to choose your focus, and that choice will determine your reality. My advice? Choose joy. Yes, it's a choice. Joy isn't getting what you want. It's appreciating what you have. How? By taking inventory at the end of the day. Don't just count sheep; count your blessings.

If you are looking for something to complain about, you'll always find it.

If you are looking for something to praise God about, you'll always find it.

I can take someone who can complain about *anything* and turn them into someone who is grateful for *everything*. How? You have to interrupt the pattern via habit switching. If you commit yourself to finding one thing you are genuinely grateful for every day and writing it down in a good old-fashioned gratitude journal, I can cure you of complaining. Over time, gratitude will flip the script from negativity to positivity. How? By sanctifying a cluster of cells at the base of your brain stem called the reticular activating system. It's the part of the brain that determines what you notice. It's why goal setting is so important. When you set a goal, it creates a category in your reticular activating system and you now notice everything that will help you accomplish that goal. The same goes for gratitude!

We try to start every meeting at National Community Church by sharing wins. Why? It's appreciative inquiry. You need to celebrate what you want to see more of. Ministry is hard enough as it is. Sharing wins reminds us of why we do what we do! It reminds us of what God is doing in us and through us. It's a domino habit that creates positive energy. By the time we're done sharing wins, we have enough energy to deal with the problems.

Fix your focus!

Day 11

Know Your Name

I will give to each one a white stone,
and on the stone will be engraved a new name
that no one understands except the one who receives it.
—Revelation 2:17, NLT

When Diana Nyad was nine years old, she stood on a beach in Fort Lauderdale, Florida. Looking out over the ocean, she asked her mother an innocent question: "Where is Cuba?" Nyad's mom pointed toward the horizon. "It's right over there," she said. "You can't see it, but it's so close, you could almost swim there."

In narratology, what happened on the beach that day is an *inciting incident*. It's a turning point in a plotline. It's the first stage of the hero's journey—the call to adventure. That sentence was destined to become Nyad's signature story. It was more than a prompt. It was the prize that Nyad would spend much of her life pursuing.

Twenty years later, Diana Nyad would attempt to swim from Cuba to Florida. She swam seventy-eight miles in forty-two hours, but strong winds stopped her short of her goal. The dream of becoming the first person to swim across the Straits of Florida would then lie dormant for three decades. When Diana turned sixty, she figured it was now or never. Her second attempt was cut short by an asthma attack. Her third attempt failed because she was stung by a Portuguese man-of-war, not once but twice. Her fourth attempt ended with nine jellyfish stings. End of story, right? Not so fast.

On the morning of August 31, 2013, sixty-four-year-old Diana

Nyad would start one last attempt. Fifty-three hours later, Nyad swam ashore in Key West. Her tongue was swollen because of salt water, but her message was loud and clear: "We should never, ever give up," she said. "You are never too old to chase your dream."[1]

How did Diana Nyad endure the physical pain and mental agony of swimming 110 miles? Especially when so-called experts said it was humanly impossible! Why did she refuse to give up, even after four failed attempts? Motivation is as complicated as the 125 trillion synapses that crisscross the cerebral cortex, but the genesis of Nyad's dream traces all the way back to her fifth birthday. It was a day when decades happen.

Her father called her into the den and made a proclamation in his thick Greek accent: "I have been waiting so very long for this day. Now you are five. Today is the day you are ready to understand the most significant thing I will ever tell you." He opened an unabridged dictionary and pointed to her name.

> Your name: Nyad. First definition, from Greek mythology. . . .
> The nymphs that swam in the lakes, oceans, rivers, and fountains to protect the waters for the gods. Listen to me, darling, because now is coming the most important part. Next . . . a girl or woman champion swimmer. . . . Darling, this is your destiny![2]

How did Nyad do what no one had done before?[3] She knew her name! She owned her name, and then her name owned her. Her name was both the prompt and the prize, and she never lost sight of it.

If I asked, "Who are you?" how would you answer that question? We have lots of identities—race and religion, gender and geography, political party and marital status. I'm a husband to Lora and a father to Parker, Summer, and Josiah. I'm a pastor and an author. I'm an ENFP on the Myers-Briggs and a type 3 achiever on the Enneagram.

All those identities are pieces of my puzzle, but none of them represents my primary identity. My primary identity is who I am in Christ. The phrase *in Christ* is found 164 times in the Pauline epistles. It's the key that unlocks our identity, our destiny, and our authority.

You are not defined by the things you've done wrong. You are defined by what Christ did right—His righteousness. I may not know you from Adam, but I know who you are. You are the image of God. You are the apple of God's eye. You are God's workmanship, created in Christ Jesus to do good works prepared for you in advance.[4]

In Paul's letter to the Ephesians, much of the first chapter is a poem. It's twelve verses in English, but it's one sentence in the original language. It's the longest sentence in the Bible. If you read it right, you'll never see yourself the same way again. It flips the script by revealing who you are and whose you are:

You are *blessed* with every spiritual blessing in Christ.

You were *chosen* before the beginning of time.

You are *blameless* in the eyes of God.

You are *adopted* by the heavenly Father.

You are *redeemed* by the blood of Christ.

You are *sealed* by the Holy Spirit.

You are *stamped* with the image of God.[5]

In the beginning, God created us in His image.[6] We've been creating God in our image ever since. That's how we end up with false identities, false narratives, and false securities. Identity issues are idolatry issues. "The human heart," said John Calvin, "is a perpetual idol factory."[7] An idol is anything you love more, trust more, or worship more than God. For some, it's fame and fortune. For others, it's their profile on LinkedIn, the size of their bank account, or the number of followers they have on social media.

Identity issues can be caused by low self-esteem, no doubt. The hardest person to forgive is yourself. You are not your failures. Of course, you aren't your successes either! I have a theory when it

comes to identity, and it'll sound counterintuitive at first. The more
you have going for you, the more potential you have for identity
problems. Why? It's easier to base your identity on the wrong
thing—what's right with you, rather than the righteousness of
Christ.

There is a phrase that is put on repeat in the Torah—"put his
Name." God is always looking for naming opportunities. He puts
His name on places, but He also puts His name on people. That said,
let me flip the script. One of the greatest privileges God gave Adam
was the right to name the animals. Imagine all the animals lining up
and Adam pulling names out of the hat. A few names, like *pink fairy
armadillo*, probably raised some eyebrows. I'm sure there were
plenty of laughs too! Try saying *hippopotamus* five times fast.

In Judaism, naming rights is a sacred responsibility and a prophetic privilege. It's not just calling something what it is. It's calling
out what it can be. Naming has the power to alter identity, alter
destiny. Jacob took on a new name that became a nation, *Israel*. A
rather impetuous disciple named Simon was renamed the Rock,
Peter. When God wants to rewrite our stories, He often gives us a
new name. It's a new cue, and it can change our trajectory.

Remember the priestly blessing that was pronounced on the
people of Israel?

> The LORD bless you
>   and keep you;
> the LORD make his face shine on you
>   and be gracious to you;
> the LORD turn his face toward you
>   and give you peace.[8]

I love this blessing. I even wrote a book about it, *Double Blessing*.
There are few privileges I treasure more than pronouncing this
blessing on people. It's as powerful now as it was then, but the best
part is the postscript:

So they shall put my name on the children of Israel, and I will bless them.[9]

Whose name did the priest put on the people? God's name! There are more than four hundred names for God in Scripture. Which one was the priest supposed to put on them? The answer is all of them!

The phraseology—*put my name on them*—is synonymous with putting clothes on. We clothe ourselves with Christ, and Christ also clothes Himself with us. Gideon is exhibit A: "The Spirit of the Lord clothed Gideon with Himself and took possession of him."[10] It's almost like God took Gideon into the fitting room and tried him on for size. Guess what? It's a custom fit.

What name of God do you need to clothe yourself with? He is Jehovah Jireh, God our provider. He is Jehovah Nissi, God our banner. He is Jehovah Shammah, our ever-present help in time of need. His name is Wonderful, Counselor, Mighty God, Prince of Peace.[11] Don't let culture name you or tame you. Peel off those false labels, and let God put His everlasting name on you!

For more than forty years, I self-identified as asthmatic. That changed on July 2, 2016. It was a day when decades happen, and I mean that literally. I had asked God to heal my lungs hundreds of times over four decades. Why did it happen when it happened? I have no earthly idea. God's timing is above my pay grade, but I know how it happened. Jehovah Rapha, God my healer, put His name on me!

When the sharks circle and the jellyfish sting, when dehydration and hallucinations set in, you need to know your name! Your name may not be in the dictionary, like Diana Nyad's. But it is in the Bible. No, not your birth name—the names of God placed on you through Jesus.

If you want a habit to stick, it has to become your identity. You don't just run; you're a *runner*. You don't just write; you're a *writer*. You don't just dance; you're a *dancer*. When a habit becomes part of your identity, it's no longer an extrinsic motivation. It's intrinsic!

If a habit is incongruent with your identity, it won't pass the test of time. That goes for good habits and bad habits. If you're trying to break a bad habit, you have to differentiate yourself from that identity. That's not who you are anymore! Remember Jeremiah? God told him not to say, "I am too young."[12] Fill in the blank with any false identity you have assumed. Whatever you verbalize, you give power to. For better or for worse, words are self-fulfilling prophecies.

Was it hard not thinking of myself as asthmatic? An asthma attack was my earliest memory, so that's the only identity I'd ever known. I had to habit switch and identity switch! I'm *not* asthmatic anymore. I'm a *runner*. More specifically, I'm a *marathoner*. I didn't just do it; I am it.

"Treat a man as he is and he will remain as he is," said Johann Wolfgang von Goethe. "Treat a man as he can be and should be and he will become as he can be or should be."[13] No one was better at that than Jesus. Maybe it's because He knew His name!

How do I make it a habit?

Fake it until you make it!

In Judaism, there are four dimensions of discipleship. When someone follows a rabbi, the first responsibility is *memorizing his words.* The second responsibility is *adopting his unique interpretation of Scripture,* called a yoke. The third responsibility is *imitating his way of life.* The fourth responsibility is *discipling others the same way you were discipled.* You flip the script by flipping the blessing! Discipleship is growing fruit on someone else's tree.

Juxtapose that with this.

In Hollywood, there is a unique form of acting called method acting. Actors take extreme measures to get into character. Dustin

Hoffman went three days without sleep to prep for a scene in *Marathon Man*. Meryl Streep learned Polish and German for *Sophie's Choice*. Christian Bale lost sixty pounds to play an emaciated insomniac in *The Machinist*. Jamie Foxx glued his eyes shut to play Ray Charles. And Leonardo DiCaprio slept in an animal carcass while filming *The Revenant*.[14]

Discipleship is method acting. It's getting into the character of Christ. It's taking your cues from the script of Scripture, and it advocates extreme measures. Remember the Sermon on the Mount? Jesus told His followers to cut off their hands and gouge out their eyes if that's what it takes to break a habit cycle.[15] Yes, Jesus was speaking in hyperbole! Please don't take it literally, but we'd better take it seriously. When it comes to making and breaking habits, desperate times call for desperate measures.

My advice? *Fake it until you make it.* No, I'm not advocating hypocrisy. But you have to reverse engineer the habit cycle. How? If you wait to interrupt the pattern until you feel like it, you're going to be in the waiting room a long time! Actions don't follow feelings as much as feelings follow actions. Remember what Jesus said? "Where your treasure is, there your heart will be also."[16] When you're trying to make a habit, it will feel awkward at first. You may even feel like an impostor. Keep on keeping on! At some point, the script will flip.

If you keep running, you'll become a *runner*.

If you keep leading, you'll become a *leader*.

If you keep writing, you'll become a *writer*.

Fill in the blank with whatever it is you want to become. Eventually you will own that identity and that identity will own you.

Know your name!

Habit 2—Kiss the Wave

The obstacle is not the enemy;
the obstacle is the way.

During his forty-five-year career as a composer, Ludwig van Beethoven wrote 722 symphonies, sonatas, and concertos. Even more amazing? Many of those compositions were written after Beethoven had lost his hearing.

When Beethoven first noticed his hearing loss, he was devastated. Without the ability to hear the music he made, his life felt meaningless. Beethoven got stuck in the first stage of grief—denial. He played the piano so loudly that he injured his hands, not to mention other people's ears! "In forte passages," said his friend and fellow composer Ludwig Spohr, "the poor deaf man pounded on the keys until the strings jangled."

Eventually Beethoven learned to kiss the wave. How? With softer sound waves! By putting a pencil in his mouth, he was able to feel the timbre of the notes. Was it ideal? Far from it. But kissing the wave is doing the best you can with what you have where you are. It confronts the brutal facts, but those brutal facts force us to innovate.

An analysis of Beethoven's music by the *British Medical Journal* reveals that high notes accounted for 80 percent of his music in his twenties but only 20 percent in his forties. Not only did Beethoven adapt to his hearing loss, but he also amended his melodies with lower frequencies. Because he couldn't hear his own music, he had to listen to his intuition and employ his imagination even more.[1]

Beethoven's Ninth Symphony ranks as one of his greatest musical achievements. "The symphonic game-changer," notes *BBC Music Magazine,* "has both terrified and inspired composers ever since."[2] Beethoven was deaf when he wrote what is considered by many the greatest orchestral piece ever written. He insisted on conducting that symphony himself. Unaware of the thunderous applause afterward, Beethoven had to be turned by one of the musicians to discover a standing ovation.

How could Beethoven make even better music after losing his hearing? "As his hearing deteriorated," said Arthur Brooks, "he was less influenced by the prevailing compositional fashions, and more by the musical structures forming inside his own head."[3] His music was inside out rather than outside in. He was driven by creative conviction instead of conforming to musical trends! His loss of hearing changed the prompt, the pattern, and the prize.

Born a few years after Beethoven died, Charles Spurgeon struggled with depression much of his life. How did he manage it? "I have learned to kiss the wave," said Spurgeon, "that throws me against the Rock of Ages."[4] Kissing the wave is not a death wish, but it's not afraid of death either. It's coming to terms with your own mortality, then living life to the fullest.

In 2017, my wife, Lora, was diagnosed with stage 1 breast cancer. Soon after she was diagnosed, she read a piece of poetry that posed a question: "What have you come to teach me?" It's a difficult question to ask, but there is no other way to kiss the wave. In 2020, Lora had a second bout with breast cancer. It felt like a sucker punch, but we kissed the wave all over again. Why? It's the only way to win the fight against cancer.

Kissing the wave takes a learning posture coupled with a growth mindset. God can certainly deliver us *from* trials and tribulations, and He sometimes does. More often than not, however, God delivers us *through* them. Either way, you've got to learn the lesson, cultivate the character, and curate the change. The obstacle is *not* the enemy; the obstacle is the way!

Kissing the wave is taking full responsibility for every situation you find yourself in. No, it's not taking the blame for things that aren't your fault. That's called a false confession, and it makes us prisoners of the past. Add a hyphen to the word *responsibility,* and it turns into *response-ability.* It's the ability to choose your response in any set of circumstances. It allows you to embrace adversity as opportunity. Why? God is using your present-tense challenges to prepare you for future-tense opportunities.

According to the CDC, nearly one-third of Americans are struggling with anxiety or depression. And I'm guessing the other two-thirds have bouts here and there. And a Gallup poll indicated that 60 percent of Americans experience daily stress.[5] I've seen two counselors in the last two years as I try to manage stress more effectively. Can I share a conviction? *Everyone needs counseling at some point!* Why? All of us have issues!

Live long enough, and the waves of grief, the waves of injustice, and the waves of pain and suffering will crash into your life. If you feel like you're drowning, you aren't alone. The good news? There is a God who sympathizes with our weaknesses. And He doesn't just have compassion on us. He's the God who rebukes the wind and says to the waves, "Peace, be still."[6]

In his autobiography, *God in My Corner,* the two-time heavyweight champion of the world George Foreman has a section titled "Storms Don't Last." He shared a story about an elderly woman who was asked her favorite verse of Scripture. She cited these words that appear 463 times in the KJV: "And it came to pass." Why? "Whenever a trial comes, it doesn't come to stay," she said. "It comes—to pass."[7] The season you find yourself in may be incredibly difficult, but it didn't come to stay. This too shall pass!

Remember what Bob Goff said? "The best chapter titles come

later." If you're in a chapter titled "Failure," don't forget that success is well-managed failure. If you're in a chapter titled "Setback," God is already preparing your comeback. Don't lose faith in the end of the story.

It's time to kiss the wave!

Day 12

Do It Scared

Fear not, stand firm, and see the salvation of the Lord.
—Exodus 14:13, esv

On March 26, 1913, something quite curious happened in Columbus, Ohio. Around noon, a man started running through town. It was discovered, after the fact, that he was running because he was late for an appointment. Regardless of the reason, a little boy started running after him. That's when someone is alleged to have yelled, "The dam has broke!"[1]

It was a classic case of crying wolf. The next thing you knew, thousands of citizens were running who knows where, who knows why! "Never before in the history of Columbus was there such a scene of panic," said the *Columbus Citizen* the next day. "Through alleys, down streets, down stairways, out of windows, people hurried, tumbled ran, shouted and fairly fought each other in their almost mad rush."

The story was buried on page 8 of another local newspaper, the *Columbus Dispatch*, probably out of embarrassment.[2] In all fairness, the Midwest had experienced torrential downpours and flash floods in the days prior to this noncatastrophe. Nonetheless, it was a false alarm based on fake news. The irony is that even if the storage dam had burst, it was several miles outside town. Those who ran for their lives might have gotten their feet wet, but that's about it. There was no reason to panic, but reasonable thinking is out the window when we give in to groupthink.

Remember Nahshon? He waded into the water, and God made a sidewalk through the sea, but let me back up that bus. A few moments before the Red Sea split, the Israelites were trapped between the water and the Egyptian army. It was fight or flight, right? In situations like that, many people let fear dictate their decisions. What did Nahshon do? He kissed the wave, quite literally!

Kissing the wave is facing your fear and doing it scared. By *it,* I mean anything that scares you. "Find out what a person fears most," said Carl Jung, "and that is where he will develop next."[3] If your dream doesn't scare you, it's too small. Kissing the wave is living according to your convictions, even if that puts you on the other side of the majority. It's staying in your lane and staying the course, even when the odds are against you. It's being a nonanxious presence in the face of adversity.

When Israel was trapped by the Egyptian army, the people panicked. That's the natural reaction, right? Before casting judgment, put yourself in their sandals. You see a giant dust cloud, and you hear the sound of horses and chariots. It's awfully hard not to hit the panic button with that kind of prompt.

It's your reaction in that kind of situation that will make or break you. In the words of a friend who trained marines for many years, "You don't rise to the occasion; you revert to the level of your training." Oorah!

There is a scene in *Ford v Ferrari* where Carroll Shelby, the race car driver played by Matt Damon, says, "There's a point— 7,000 rpm—where everything fades. The machine becomes weightless. Just disappears. And all that's left is a body moving through space and time. 7,000 rpm. That's where you meet it. . . . [It] asks you a question. The only question that matters: *Who are you?*"[4]

Who are you at 7,000 rpm? That takes us back to day 11, doesn't it? When all else fails, you need to know your name. When all hell breaks loose, you need to know His name! Then, and only then, are you ready to kiss the wave.

Fear not, stand firm, and see the salvation of the LORD.[5]

According to psychologists, we're born with only two fears—the fear of falling and the fear of loud noises.[6] Every other fear is learned, which means every other fear can be unlearned. Faith is the process of unlearning fear. How? "Perfect love casts out fear."[7] If you fear God—if you revere God above all else—you don't have to fear anything. Not only is it the beginning of wisdom, but it's also the end of every other fear!

The cure for the fear of failure is not success. The cure for the fear of failure is failure, in small enough doses that you build up an immunity to it. It works the same way as a vaccination. You need to identify the strain of the fear virus that infects you—fear of failure, fear of rejection, fear of intimacy, fear of people's opinions, fear of certain social situations. You have to identify it but not so you can avoid it. Remember the idea of systematic desensitization from day 7? You have to expose yourself to the thing you fear. How? By doing it scared. That's how you interrupt the pattern. Do it enough times, and you will build up an immunity to it.

Kissing the wave is not running away from what you're afraid of. It's wading into those waters, like Nahshon. It takes courage to kiss the wave, but that's how you surf the wave of suffering. You don't have to like it, but you do have to learn from it.

In October 2009, Lora and I were on a coffee date on my day off when I made the mistake of answering my phone. It was the manager of the movie theaters at Union Station, which is where National Community had gathered for thirteen years. Fun fact? We had toyed with the idea of changing our name to the Church at Union Station because that's what everyone called us. Long story short, the manager informed us that the movie theaters were shutting down. As if that weren't enough of a sucker punch, she said that the next Sunday would be our last Sunday! How do you move a congregation—numbering more than a thousand people at that point—in one week? My mind started spinning at 7,000 rpm.

It felt like we were trapped between the Red Sea and the Egyptian army, but that's when I preached the promise in Exodus 14:13. Of all the sermons I've preached, that one may be the most memorable and meaningful for me. Why? I needed a word from God, and I got one! "I don't know what we're going to do," I said to our congregation, "but I know what we're not going to do. We're not going to panic! We're going to stand still, and we're going to see the deliverance of the Lord." And we did.

When God closed that door at Union Station, it prompted us to look for property. It was right after the recession in 2008, which proved to be an opportune time to look for real estate because developers had hit the brakes in DC. NCC found a piece of property on Capitol Hill with an entire block of frontage on the 695 expressway. Are you kidding? Right around that time, we received a $3 million gift. What? Then a few years later, we purchased an entire city block right across the street for $29 million. National Community Church now owns half a dozen properties worth $75 million, and we own them debt-free. Only God.

Truth be told? We'd still be meeting in the movie theaters at Union Station if I had my way! I was downright depressed when they closed. I actually wondered whether our best days were behind us. Can I offer an exhortation that I hope is encouraging? Don't get too discouraged by closed doors. They often have a domino effect that you will someday thank God for as much as the open doors.

When we experience a setback, we don't take a step back, because God is already preparing our comeback. Isn't that what God said to Moses? "I have planned this in order to display my glory."[8] God is setting you up, but here's the catch. The right time often feels like the wrong time, and the right place often feels like the wrong place. That's when and where you have to kiss the wave and do it scared. You have to trust God's will, God's way, and God's timing.

"When a train goes through a tunnel and it gets dark," said Corrie ten Boom, "you don't throw away the ticket and jump off." What do you do? You do what the woman who survived a Nazi concentration camp said: "You sit still and trust the engineer."[9]

How do I make it a habit?

Drop the anchor!

A few years ago, the San Francisco Exploratorium did a survey. Randomly selected guests were asked two questions:

1. Is the height of the tallest redwood more or less than 1,200 feet?
2. What is your best guess about the height of the tallest redwood?

A second group of participants was asked the same question with a different number:

1 Is the height of the tallest redwood more or less than 180 feet?
2. What is your best guess about the height of the tallest redwood?

The two heights—1,200 feet and 180 feet—are called anchors, and they had a profound effect on the answers of each group. Those who were given the high anchor of 1,200 feet guessed an average height of 844 feet. Those who were given the low anchor of 180 feet guessed an average height of 282 feet. That's a 562-foot difference![10]

Remember the focusing illusion from day 10? The anchoring effect functions in much the same way. Simply put, a first impression leaves a lasting impression. Once we anchor to that first fact, that first feeling, it becomes our baseline.

In case you're curious, redwoods rank as the tallest tree species on the planet. Their root systems go down 13 feet, with 80-foot radii. They can measure up to 22 feet in girth and 360 feet in height and live up to two thousand years! Few things are as awe inspiring as standing at the foot of one of those giant redwoods and gazing upward.

The anchoring effect influences us every day in a thousand ways. It's employed by retailers who mark things up, then mark things down to make you feel better about the sale price. It's employed by parents when negotiating curfews. A word to the wise? No matter what time you want your kids home, always start an hour or two earlier!

The anchoring effect has significant implications and applications when it comes to making and breaking habits. You break bad habits by anchoring yourself to good habits—habit switching. You cultivate hard habits by anchoring them to easier habits—habit stacking. You can also anchor yourself with a commitment device, which we explored on day 5. Let me introduce one more technique that I call *dropping the anchor.*

In the book of Acts, the apostle Paul found himself in a perfect storm. What did the crew do when all seemed lost? "They dropped four anchors from the stern and prayed for daylight."[11] When I'm caught in a storm—a season of suffering, a season of grieving, a season of discouragement—I kiss the wave by dropping four anchors.

The first anchor is Isaiah 55:9: "As the heavens are higher than the earth, so are my ways higher than your ways and my thoughts than your thoughts." Theologically, this is ground zero. The distance from one side of the universe to the other is ninety-three billion light-years. According to this anchor, that's the distance between His thoughts and our thoughts.[12] So here's my thought: even on our best day, our best thought underestimates how good and how great God is by a factor of ninety-three billion light-years!

The second anchor is Romans 8:28: "All things work together for good to those who love God, to those who are the called according to His purpose" (NKJV). It doesn't say that all things are good. Bad things happen to good people. Why? We live in a broken world, a fallen world. Life is not fair, but God is good. God can recycle your pain for His purposes. That doesn't make it any less painful, but it's not for naught. If you kiss the wave, God will translate your pain into someone else's gain.

The third anchor I drop in tough times is Romans 8:31: "If God is for us, who can be against us?" There are 1,741 *ifs* in the Bible, but this is my favorite. Why? The favor of God is the X factor in our lives. It doesn't matter whether the odds are against you. Is God for you? That's all that matters! In the words of Frederick Douglass, "One and God make a majority!"[13]

The fourth anchor is Ephesians 3:20–21: "To him who is able to do immeasurably more than all we ask or imagine, according to his power that is at work within us, to him be glory in the church and in Christ Jesus throughout all generations, for ever and ever! Amen." In a nutshell, all bets are off. All things are possible. Why? God is able!

When you find yourself in crisis situations, you have to go back to basics. When all else fails, you need fallback positions. You need stopgaps. If you find yourself in one of those seasons, drop anchor! This too shall pass. And even if it doesn't get easier, you will get stronger.

Do it scared!

Day 13

Walk the Wire

Live a life worthy of the calling you have received.
—EPHESIANS 4:1

On June 15, 2012, Nik Wallenda walked a tightrope that was suspended over Niagara Falls. That 1,500-foot steel wire could not be stabilized, so it swayed back and forth. It also dipped thirty-five feet in the middle, so Wallenda walked downhill, then uphill, on a soaking wet wire that was six centimeters wide. Fun fact? He carried his passport with him and presented it to border guards on the Canadian side!

Nik Wallenda holds eleven world records, including a wire walk over the Grand Canyon. But Niagara Falls presented a unique challenge because it's an ecosystem unto itself. The waterfall produces a constant mist. There are sixty-miles-per-hour updrafts and side drafts. Plus, there is the deafening sound of six hundred thousand gallons of water cannonballing 167 feet per second.

To prepare for this particular stunt, Wallenda used airboats to produce ninety-miles-per-hour wind gusts and fire trucks to hose him down while on the wire. Somehow he pulled off what may be his most impressive high-wire act. He inched his way across that slippery wire, praying and praising Jesus Christ with each step he took.[1] If you've watched one of Nik Wallenda's stunts, that's not an exaggeration. His voice is a little off key, but that doesn't keep him from making a joyful noise unto the Lord. Nothing like worship to keep you from falling off the wire!

I get asked this question all the time: "How do you balance family and work?" The short answer is that I don't. Nobody does. To be clear, *I want to be famous in my home!* And if I have to choose between the two, *family comes first.* Those are a couple of my core convictions, and I try to establish boundaries accordingly. I don't take more than seven overnight speaking trips in a year, and the one thing I try to be religious about is my day off.

When someone asks me the balance question, I often answer it by standing on one foot. Then I ask this question: "Am I balanced?" It's a trick question of sorts. In one sense, I'm balanced because I'm not falling. But upon closer evaluation, I'm actually counterbalancing. How? The muscles in my ankles are constantly twitching.

Life is like that, isn't it? I don't think any of us ever achieve perfect balance. We're always counterbalancing our jobs, our marriages, our kids, our hobbies, and our habits. It feels like walking the wire, doesn't it?

"There are problems to solve and tensions to manage," said Andy Stanley.[2] Discerning the difference is critical. You don't manage problems—you solve them. And you don't solve tensions—you manage them. Building off that idea, bad habits are problems to solve. Good habits are tensions to manage.

I live by a little maxim: *Truth is found in the tension of opposites!* Why? "True wisdom has two sides."[3] It's awfully easy to retreat to our echo chambers in a day and age like ours. Social media algorithms are designed to help us do just that. It's awfully easy to fall into dualistic thought patterns that create false dichotomies. When we think of problems in either-or categories, it's hard to come up with both-and solutions. There is a third way, the Jesus Way.

Remember the man who was born blind? The disciples created a false dichotomy with their binary thinking: "Who sinned, this man or his parents, that he was born blind?" It had to be A or B, right? Wrong! "This happened," Jesus said, "so that the works of God might be displayed."[4] Not only did Jesus help them see a third way, but He is the third way. He is the Son of Man and the Son of God.

"When the unstoppable bullet hits the impenetrable wall, we find religious experience," said Robert Johnson. "It is precisely here that one will grow."[5] It's called the unstoppable force paradox, and I like to think of the unstoppable bullet as God's sovereignty and the impenetrable wall as people's free will. What happens when those two things collide? It's as mysterious as the basal ganglia, but that's where we make and break habits. It's a tag team. It happens only with the help of the Father, Son, and Holy Spirit.

If you want God to do the super, you've got to do the natural. You can't just pray like it depends on God—you also have to work like it depends on you. Do I believe in supernatural healing? How can I not after God healed my lungs? Go ahead and pray for healing, but you have to participate in your own healing as well. When God healed my lungs, I didn't start smoking. That would have been counterproductive. I exercised my lungs by training for a marathon. I chose to walk the wire rather than sabotaging the blessing.

Kissing the wave is refusing to take the easy way out. Instead of retreating to your echo chamber, you stand in the gap. How? You listen with both ears. You keep one ear tuned to the still, small voice of the Holy Spirit. You keep the other ear to the ground. What did Daniel do after becoming a prisoner of war in Babylon? He spent three years learning their language and literature. Why? So he could influence the culture from the inside out.

With the rise of highly polemicized and highly publicized cultural conversations, it's not easy keeping our emotional, relational, or political balance. How do we walk that wire? There is a passage that functions like a tightrope suspended over Niagara Falls. It's a great way to interrupt the pattern of polarization while keeping our eye on the prize.

I urge you to live a life worthy of the calling you have received. Be completely humble and gentle; be patient, bearing with one another in love.[6]

Reverse engineer these verses, and there are three cardinal virtues that help us navigate the issues, challenges, and difficult decisions we face. They also help us make and break habits. We walk the wire with humility, gentleness, and patience.

The first virtue is humility.

Humility isn't thinking less of yourself, as in low self-esteem. It's thinking of yourself less. It's getting past the preoccupation with me, myself, and I. Simply put, *it's not about me.* It's a predecision to put other people first. Humility doesn't ask, *What's in it for me?* It asks the opposite question: *How can I add value to your life?* Humility's default setting is *listening and learning* from others. Why? In the words of Ralph Waldo Emerson, "Every man I meet is my superior in some way. In that, I learn of him."[7] That kind of humility fosters a holy curiosity about other people.

The second virtue is gentleness.

Words matter, now more than ever, but so does tone. According to psychologist Albert Mehrabian, when it comes to credibility, we assign 55 percent of weight to body language, 38 percent to tone, and 7 percent to words! In my experience, no one wins a shouting match. The louder you talk, the less people listen. People don't care how much you know until they know how much you care. Let's not win intellectual arguments and lose relationships because we'd rather be right than righteous! "A gentle answer turns away wrath."[8] How? It's the law of reciprocation. If you want to de-escalate a situation or break a vicious cycle, try lowering your voice and softening your tone.

The third virtue is patience.

I live in a city whose rhythm is determined by the election cycle. We have hundreds of congregants whose jobs are on the line every two years. Can I offer a timeless reminder? Administrations come and go, but the kingdom of God is forever! We are here for such a time as this, no doubt. But we've got to widen our aperture. We think right here, right now. God is thinking nations and generations. Remember day 8? Remember the future!

Patience is playing the long game. It's long obedience in the same direction. *Do It for a Day* may sound like a temporal mindset, but it's putting things in eternal perspective. It's living like it's the first day and last day of your life, but it's doing things that will outlast your life. It's living like you'll die tomorrow and dreaming like you'll live forever.

How do I make it a habit?

There you are!

My friend and spiritual father, Dick Foth, says that there are two kinds of people in the world. The first kind of person walks into a room internally announcing *Here I am*. Their ego barely fits through the door. It's all about *me, myself, and I*. The second kind of person walks into a room internally announcing *There you are!* They check their ego at the door, and it's all about everyone else! They treat everyone as their superior, and they are always looking to add value.

Which kind of person are you? *Here I am*? Or *there you are*?

We live in a culture that operates in sound bites, buzzwords, and trending hashtags. We flip that script and kiss the wave by operating in the opposite spirit. What does that mean? It's the Golden Rule—do unto others as you would have them do unto you. It sees people for who they really are—the image of God—and treats them accordingly. Can I let you in on a little secret? The way you *get respect* is by *giving it*. The same goes for love and joy and a thousand other things.

When we walk the wire, we see every person as invaluable and irreplaceable. That's how you love people who don't look like you, think like you, or vote like you. Even if you don't like them, you're called to love them. It's a theology of dignity that underwrites the sanctity of life from womb to tomb and overrides the differences that divide culture. "If you destroy a single life, it's as if you have destroyed an entire universe," says the Talmud. "If you save a life, it's as if you have saved an entire universe."

It's not easy to make or break a habit. It feels a lot like walking the wire! You've got to have grace under fire. You've got to counter-balance all the time. How? You shift the atmosphere with humility, gentleness, and patience. I've said it before, but let me say it again: We don't make and break habits simply for our sake. We do it for those we love! The epitome of unselfishness is breaking bad habits that hurt others. It's making habits that add value to others. Either way, it's one way we say *There you are!*

Walk the wire!

Day 14

Connect the Dots

Daniel handled the situation with wisdom and discretion.
—DANIEL 2:14, NLT

In 2009, a dendrologist named Dr. Martin Gossner was research-ing the resilience of tree bark. As part of that study, Dr. Gossner sprayed the oldest tree in the Bavarian Forest National Park with an insecticide called pyrethrum. All the organisms that were living on or in the bark of that tree fell to the earth. Want to venture a guess as to how many specimens Dr. Gossner discovered?

To the average eye, a tree is a tree is a tree. The reality? A tree is an ecosystem. Did you know that trees communicate with one an-other by releasing chemicals into the air? They form community through their root systems, a wood-wide web. And not only do they feed microorganisms in the soil that surrounds their trunks, but they also turn carbon dioxide into the oxygen that you and I breathe.

Dr. Gossner collected 2,041 insects, animals, and other organ-isms belonging to 257 species.[1] A tree, you see, is not just a tree. It's an ecosystem unto itself, and so are you! I try to live and lead by a simple mantra: "Always think ecosystem." Every decision you make, every action you take, has a domino effect in a hundred directions. Habit formation is connecting the dots by identifying prompts and patterns and prizes. It's seeing the forest through the trees, pun in-tended.

Hold that thought.

A few years ago, I had the privilege of attending the Welcome

Conference in New York City. It was a gathering of professionals who eat, sleep, and breathe hospitality. Lots of chefs and restauranteurs and, I'm guessing, one pastor! One of the speakers was farm-to-table trailblazer Dan Barber. He founded Blue Hill at Stone Barns, made famous by *Chef's Table,* season 1. Barber told a story that is *almost* on par with the parables!

The French chef Alain Ducasse is the Michael Jordan of chefs. The first chef to own restaurants with three Michelin stars in three cities, Ducasse heard about Blue Hill at Stone Barns and decided to pay a visit. Dan Barber was incredibly flattered and more than a little anxious. What do you serve your culinary hero for breakfast?

Blue Hill has an all-pasture dairy, which means the cows don't get any grain. Barber decided to go old school and show off his butter by serving it on some freshly baked bread. Ducasse ate awfully slow, and he didn't say a single word. At one point, he took off his glasses and closed his eyes. Dan Barber was dying a slow death the entire time. *Does he like it? Not like it?* When Ducasse finally finished, he told Barber it was great, but Dan Barber wasn't buying what Alain Ducasse was selling. He said "great," but he didn't mean "great." So Barber asked a bold question: "Mr. Ducasse, how could the butter be better?"

Ducasse answered his question with a question: "Has it been raining often at Blue Hill Farm?" Ducasse had no way of knowing, having just gotten off a plane from Japan, but Hurricane Irene had just hit the East Coast, resulting in record rainfall. Alain Ducasse could *taste the weather.* The butter was washed out.

As Ducasse was about to leave, he turned around and asked another question: "Was the butter churned by hand or made in an electric mixer?" Barber was a little insulted. Blue Hill would never use an electric mixer! It ruins the viscosity by whipping in too much air. Then Ducasse posed one final question: "The butter that I ate, was it from cows near the barn or far away?" Barber told him that they pasture their cows near the barn, and that was that.

A few days after Ducasse's visit to Blue Hill, Barber was in the pastry kitchen when he caught an intern churning butter with—you guessed it—an electric mixer! "Chef," she innocently exclaimed, "I can make the butter much faster in a mixer!" Not only could Ducasse *taste the weather,* but he could also *taste the mixer!* But wait—there's more.

A week later, Barber was looking out on the pastures around Blue Hill and he couldn't see any cows. He asked a farmhand where they were. "I'm trying an experiment," said the farmhand. "I'm pasturing the cows in field seven, the field furthest away from the barn." When Barber asked why, the farmhand said, "It's full of weeds."

"It's humbling to think about what he could taste intuitively," said Barber. Alain Ducasse could taste the rain, the electric mixer, and the weeds in field seven!

Kissing the wave is seeing past the surface of the situations we find ourselves in. It's connecting the dots a little differently. How? By asking questions. By divergent thinking. By looking for interrelationships. By contemplating unintended consequences. By considering cause and effect. By identifying what's happening in field seven!

In the sixth century BC, King Nebuchadnezzar and the Babylonian army laid siege to the city of Jerusalem. They broke through the wall, plundered the temple, and took captives from the creative class and upper class back to Babylon. Among them was a teenager named Daniel, who would rise to power by unconventional means.

Daniel spent three years learning the language and literature of the Chaldeans. After learning their language, he flipped the script with a rather unique anointing. Daniel had the ability to solve impossible problems supernaturally. Daniel was a solutionary![2] "A problem cannot be solved," said Albert Einstein, "from the same level of consciousness that created it." That's when and where and why we need prophetic imagination.

When Arioch, the commander of the king's guard, had gone out to put to death the wise men of Babylon, Daniel spoke to him with wisdom and tact.[3]

The Hebrew word translated *tact* means "taste." Think sommelier. Did you know that 80 percent of a wine's taste comes from its aroma?[4] A well-trained sommelier can taste the tannin—the element that adds texture, complexity, and balance. A sommelier can taste the soil, the altitude, the age, and the weather too!

The prophet Daniel was an expert at ecosystems. His ability to perceive things beyond his five senses is almost unparalleled. Yes, he was highly educated. But the X factor, the *it* factor, is something called prophetic imagination. It's seeing the invisible, hearing the inaudible, and perceiving the impossible. We think of prophets as people who have *supernatural foresight,* and that's certainly one dimension of prophetic imagination. It's seeing *further* than others see. It's seeing *before* others see. That said, two other dimensions are less recognized but equally important.

The second dimension is *supernatural insight.* It's seeing past presenting problems and recognizing root causes. It's identifying unintended consequences before they happen. It's seeing the way different parts of an ecosystem affect one another. It's tasting the weather, the mixer, and the weeds in field seven! This is critical when it comes to hacking habits. It's hard to interrupt the pattern if you don't see it.

The third dimension of prophetic imagination is *supernatural hindsight.* It's making sense of who, what, when, where, why, and how. "You can't connect the dots looking forward," said Steve Jobs in his now-famous commencement address at Stanford University. "You can only connect them looking backward."[5] Remember the advice on day 8? Look both ways! The further backward you look, the further forward you will see.

"In decisive hours of history," said the Jewish theologian Abraham Heschel, "it dawns upon us that we would not trade certain lines in the book of Isaiah for the Seven Wonders of the World."[6] I'm not sure whether Heschel was referring to the ancient wonders or the natural wonders. Either way, we need a word from God. I'd rather have one God idea than a thousand good ideas. Good ideas are good, but God ideas change the course of history!

Prophetic imagination gives us the moral courage to live counterculturally, like Daniel. It's refusing to bow to the powers that be. It's speaking truth to power, creatively and lovingly.

It's exegesis of our lives from a divine perspective. "The task is reframing," says Walter Brueggemann, "so we can re-experience the social realities that are right in front of us, from a different angle."[7] But prophetic imagination is not just sanctified explanations; it's sanctified expectations.

In the spring of 1884, the French artist George Seurat began painting *A Sunday on La Grande Jatte*. That painting, seven feet tall and ten feet wide, hangs in the Art Institute of Chicago. In the late nineteenth century, impressionism was in vogue. Seurat broke with tradition and used a novel technique called pointillism. Instead of painting with brushstrokes, Seurat employed different colored dots.

If you stand a few inches from Seurat's magnum opus, it's anything but art. You're too close to see it for what it is! It looks like a hodgepodge of dots. The same could be said of the circumstances you find yourself in. But if you back up, the dots form a masterpiece. If you stand at the right distance and stare long enough, you'll feel like a Parisian in a park on the banks of the river Seine.

Life is like that painting, isn't it? It's awfully easy to lose perspective if you're too close to it. You need to zoom out. You need to widen your aperture. Then, and only then, will you see the metanarrative God is writing.

How did David defeat a giant named Goliath? He cultivated a compensatory skill with his slingshot, which involved lots of deliberate practice. But even more impressive than his skill set was his mindset. David was mentally tough. He connected the dots between what God had done and what God was about to do:

The Lᴏʀᴅ who delivered me from the paw of the lion and from the paw of the bear will deliver me from the hand of this Philistine.[8]

David looks back at God's past-tense providence and connects the dots with present-tense circumstances, and it produces faith for future-tense challenges. The Lions and Bears were like preseason games, preparing David to play the Giants. Testimony is prophecy! If God did it before, He can do it again. Our future-tense faith is grounded in God's past-tense faithfulness. That is where holy confidence comes from. We live at the intersection of two theologies, two realities. The faithfulness of God is pursuing us from the past. The sovereignty of God is setting us up for the future. We live at the intersection of *so far so God* and *the best is yet to come.*

How do I make it a habit?

Always think ecosystem!

Sir Richard Branson, the serial entrepreneur, lives by a simple maxim: *A-B-C-D—always be connecting the dots.*[9] You connect the dots by asking the question, *What have you come to teach me?* Ask it of every person you meet. Ask it of every situation you find yourself in. If you take a learning posture toward life, it will teach you lessons you can't learn any other way.

Can I make one more recommendation? Keep a journal to record those lessons. When I meet with people, I always try to have my journal handy. Why? I have something to learn from them, and if I don't write it down, the lesson will be lost on me.

Many years ago, Dr. Catherine Cox did a thorough study of three thousand biographical sources, researching 301 of history's greatest geniuses. Along with assessing sixty-seven character traits, she retroactively gave them an IQ grade.[10] She also discovered one common denominator among them—all of them recorded their thoughts and feelings, their ideas and insights, their observations and reflections in a journal of one kind or another.

A gratitude journal connects the dots between blessings, turning moments into memories. A dream journal connects the dots between experiences, marking your trail. A prayer journal connects the dots between cause and effect and ensures that you give God the glory when He answers those prayers!

A-B-C-D is the difference between learning from our mistakes and repeating them. It's the way we explain our experiences. Great leaders connect the dots a little differently, a little better. If you want to break a habit cycle or make one, you have to connect the dots between prompt, pattern, and prize. That takes no small measure of prophetic imagination.

Connect the dots!

Habit 3—Eat the Frog

If you want God to do the super,
you've got to do the natural.

"If you ever have to eat a live frog," Mark Twain is purported to have said, "it's best done first thing in the morning."[1] Why? Because you can go through the rest of the day knowing that the hardest task is behind you. That scenario is awfully unlikely, but it's good advice nonetheless. How you start the day sets the tone, sets the pace.

Well-begun is half-done! Of course, the opposite is true too. If your day gets off to a bad start, it's hard to course correct. On that note, all of us have at least 127 bad days per year. All right, I totally made up that statistic. I aimed high because of the anchoring effect. You felt better, if even for a second, didn't you?

Speaking of the anchoring effect, we're living on a planet that is speeding through space at nearly sixty-seven thousand miles per hour. So even on a bad day, a day when you don't get much done, you did travel 1.6 million miles through space. So there's that.

Remember the study done by Duke University? On average, 45 percent of our behavior is automatic. I daresay that the percentage is a little higher first thing in the morning. Why? We're still waking up! And if you wake up late, I bet it's even higher. You don't have time to think about anything except getting dressed and getting out the door!

At the halfway point of our thirty-day challenge, it's time to do a little deconstruction. I want you to evaluate your morning routine. What time do you get up? And why? If you don't ask why, it's awfully easy to go through the motions! What is the first thing you do? And why? Keep a time log of everything you do from the second you wake up to the moment you walk out the door. Now ask these questions: Does your routine align with your goals? Is it in sync with who you're trying to become and what you're trying to accomplish?

Remember the growth mindset from day 2? *Harder is better!* Eating the frog adds a time stamp—*harder sooner!* And it's not just "getting it out of the way" or "checking it off the list." It's an approach to life that embraces challenge! Eating the frog doesn't shirk responsibility or shrink from danger. It doesn't handicap hardship. It's a mindset that welcomes resistance as a form of resistance training. Of course, there's nothing wrong with adding an element of fun along the way!

Mark Twain and Teddy Roosevelt were contemporaries and, in many ways, cut from the same cloth. They didn't get along, politically speaking. But both of them approached life with a no-nonsense, no-excuses, no-*ifs*-*and*s-or-*but*s-about-it pragmatism that is to be applauded. That approach to life is epitomized by one of Roosevelt's favorite pastimes, something he called a point-to-point hike.

Teddy Roosevelt took no pleasure in hiking trails that had already been blazed. He loved getting off the grid, off the map. The point-to-point hike involved one simple rule: *upon setting out for a particular destination, you may not alter course!* You had to hike in a straight line, no matter what. If you came to a wall, you climbed over it. If you encountered a stream, you swam across it. Instead of going around, you had to go through.

Sounds a lot like kissing the wave, doesn't it?

The obstacle is not the enemy; the obstacle is the way!

One day President Roosevelt invited the French ambassador on one of those point-to-point hikes. "What the President called a walk was a run," said Jean Jules Jusserand. During that hike, they came across Rock Creek. I have a hunch this was very much planned. Roosevelt took off his clothes, right down to his skivvies. The French ambassador, with great reluctance, followed suit. "I too, for the honor of France, removed my apparel, everything except [for] my lavender kid gloves." Why not the gloves? "If we should meet ladies."[2] I can think of some other things you might want to keep covered, but I'm not French. I can't prove this, but I wonder whether this is where the old saying comes from: "I see London; I see France; I see the ambassador's underpants." Just a theory, mind you.

Habit formation is a point-to-point hike. You cannot allow yourself shortcuts or detours. You cannot do an end run around tough times or tough conversations. Eating the frog is having the courage to go through them and coming out the other side with a testimony. How else are you going to cultivate mental toughness?

What makes us think we can become like Jesus without being betrayed by Judas, denied by Peter, scoffed at by Pharisees, mocked by Roman soldiers, or tempted by the Enemy himself? That's how we grow up, spiritually speaking.

It's time to eat the frog!

Day 15

Do It Difficult

I have worked much harder.
—2 CORINTHIANS 11:23

On October 14, 1912, Teddy Roosevelt was on the campaign trail when he was shot point-blank by a would-be assassin. With a .32-caliber bullet lodged in his chest, he got up and gave the speech anyway. "The bullet is in me now," he said, "so that I cannot make a very long speech." Roosevelt spoke for ninety minutes, while blood from the bullet wound soaked through his shirt.[1] Of course, that was par for the course. Roosevelt was part Renaissance man, part wild man. He earned every one of his nicknames—the Bull Moose, the Rough Rider, the Man on Horseback, the Dynamo, the Trust Buster, the Happy Warrior, and the Hero of San Juan Hill, just to name a few.

Roosevelt once rode a moose bareback, flew a Wright brothers' airplane, scaled the Swiss Alps, worked as a ranch hand in the Dakotas, took down an armed cowboy during a barroom brawl, crossed a frozen river to apprehend boat thieves, went on month-long African safaris, explored the Amazon River, led the charge up Kettle Hill during the Battle of San Juan, and went skinny-dipping in the Potomac River. Think of that last one as a century-old ice bucket challenge.

Fun fact? Roosevelt set up a boxing ring in the White House where he would spar with anyone brave enough to get into the ring.

One of his aides, Dan Tyler Moore, actually blinded the president's left eye with a right hook. Roosevelt concealed the fact that he had lost his sight to protect the reputation of the man who detached his retina! "Could you ask for any better proof of the man's sportsmanship," said Moore, "than the fact that he never told me what I had done to him?"[2]

Teddy Roosevelt gave his fair share of memorable speeches, including the one in Milwaukee I mentioned above, but my personal favorite was delivered on April 10, 1899, at the Hamilton Club in Chicago. It reads more like a sermon than a speech. By my count, Roosevelt used the word *preach* four times and the word *doctrine* five times. He advocated what he called the strenuous life:

> I wish to preach, not the doctrine of ignoble ease, but the doctrine of the strenuous life, the life of toil and effort, of labor and strife; to preach that highest form of success which comes, not to the man who desires mere easy peace, but to the man who does not shrink from danger, from hardship, or from bitter toil, and who out of these wins the splendid ultimate triumph.[3]

Remember the growth mindset? This is that—the doctrine of the strenuous life. It's the essence of eating the frog. When given the option between the elevator and the stairs, *take the stairs!* In other words, take the path of *most* resistance. It is the road less traveled.

Teddy Roosevelt may have coined the phrase *the doctrine of the strenuous life,* but the apostle Paul set the standard. When he looked back on his life, what did Paul underline with a yellow highlighter? "I am out of my mind to talk like this," he said. "I have worked much harder, been in prison more frequently, been flogged more severely, and been exposed to death again and again." But wait—there's more!

"Five times I received from the Jews the forty lashes minus one. Three times I was beaten with rods, once I was pelted with stones, three times I was shipwrecked, I spent a night and a day in the open sea." How many scars did Paul have? And what about PTSD? "I have been in danger from rivers, in danger from bandits, in danger from my fellow Jews, in danger from Gentiles; in danger in the city, in danger in the country, in danger at sea; and in danger from false believers." Anything else? "I have labored and toiled and have often gone without sleep." Is that it? "I have known hunger and thirst and have often gone without food." Oh, I almost forgot. "I have been cold and naked."[4]

Remember the idea of downward counterfactual thinking from day 10? Maybe you're having a bad day, got stuck in rush-hour traffic. I know that's frustrating. I really do. Stop-and-go traffic is stressful. But Paul's résumé is a reality check, is it not? Again, *it beats a covered wagon!*

At the end of our lives, what will we remember most? It won't be the times when we had nothing to do. "Look at a day when you are supremely satisfied at the end," said the former British prime minister Margaret Thatcher. "It's not a day when you lounge around doing nothing; it's a day you've had everything to do and you've done it."[5]

The same could be said of life, could it not? If we want to one day look back at lives that have been supremely satisfying, they won't be lives of ignoble ease. We'll remember the frogs we ate! We'll remember the moments that pushed us past our limits and out of our comfort zones.

Have you ever noticed the way octogenarians remember tough times with a touch of nostalgia? Polls suggest that the London Blitz, the bombing raids that terrorized Britain for many sleepless nights during World War II, was for many Londoners the happiest time of their lives.[6] Wait—what? Why? Because we remember the tough times for what they produce. In that instance, hard-fought freedom!

It's even true of childbirth, right? After that kind of pain, followed by many sleepless nights, how does anyone have more than one child? All right, sex has something to do with it. But for many women, it's a conscious choice. Why? They forget the pain and re-member the gain.

How did Jesus endure the cross? By focusing on the joy that was set before Him![7] He approached it as a point-to-point hike. "Not my will," Jesus prayed in the Garden of Gethsemane, "but yours be done."[8] That is the key to willpower, which is one key to habit for-mation. Jesus imagined the prize—you and me.

If kissing the wave is *doing it scared,* eating the frog is *doing it difficult.* And, I might add, *doing it now.* When I was in the eighth grade, I wore ankle weights to school almost every day. Why? I dreamed of dunking a basketball. I weighed myself down so I could elevate my game.

If you want to grow stronger, you have to add resistance. Then what? Add more resistance. There is no other way to win the day! It doesn't get easier. You get stronger. How? You have to subscribe to the doctrine of the strenuous life. You can't circumvent tough times, tough questions, tough decisions, or tough conversations. Those are the things that produce mental toughness.

Remember the concept of desirable difficulty? Eating the frog is where the rubber meets that road. It's a predecision—a decision you make before you have to make a decision. It's choosing the stairs before you have a choice. It's choosing the high road, which hap-pens to be the hard road. It doesn't shrink from sacrifice or flee from danger, or handicap hardship.

How do I make it a habit?

Conquer your soul.

On Halloween in 1900, a ten-year-old boy named Ike wanted to go trick-or-treating with his older brothers. When his parents told him he was too young, he flew into a fit. He ran out the front door and punched an apple tree until his knuckles were raw. Ike was sent to his room, where he was still sobbing into his pillow an hour later. That's when his mother walked into his room, sat down on a rocking chair next to his bed, and flipped the script with Proverbs 16:32:

He that conquereth his own soul is greater than he who taketh a city.

In 1915, Ike graduated from West Point Military Academy. For the record, he ranked 125th out of 164 for discipline. Self-control did not come naturally. Of all his siblings, his mother told him that he had the most to learn about controlling his passions. As she bandaged his hands, she warned him that anger only injures the person who harbors it.

At seventy-six years of age, Ike would look back over the landscape of his life and identify this teachable moment as a turning point. It was a day when decades happened. "I have always looked back on that conversation as one of the most valuable moments of my life."[9] Why? That scripture became his script.

Before serving as the supreme allied commander of Operation Overlord during World War II, General Dwight D. Eisenhower had to conquer his own soul. Before leading America during his two terms as president, he had to lead himself.

By the end of the war, Eisenhower smoked four packs a day. Then one day he quit cold turkey. How? "I simply gave myself an order."[10] Well, there's an idea! At some point, enough is enough. Is there an executive order you need to issue to yourself? What do you need to stop cold turkey? What do you need to start on a dime? And what are you waiting for? Delayed obedience is disobedience!

How do you conquer your own soul? You wage war with your sin nature until you subdue it. Or maybe I should say, until it's subdued by a higher power. You have to take every thought captive and make it obedient to Christ. You have to take up your cross daily and deny yourself.[11] It's the best way to break a bad habit.

Leadership starts with self-leadership, and self-leadership starts with self-control. The hardest person to lead, hands down, is you. That's why habits are so hard to make and break. But if you want to conquer a city, you have to conquer yourself first.

Do it difficult!

Day 16

Make Decisions Against Yourself

"Everything is permissible,"
but not everything is beneficial.
—1 Corinthians 10:23, BSB

In 1972, a psychologist named Walter Mischel conducted a series of studies on delayed gratification, known as the Stanford marshmallow experiment.[1] It was done at Bing Nursery School with children ages three to five.[2] Each child was asked to choose between a marshmallow and a pretzel. If the child could wait for a certain amount of time, he or she could eat the preferred snack. If the child couldn't wait, he or she had to eat the other snack.[3]

A hidden camera allowed the researchers to observe the way children responded to that situation. Some kids grabbed a snack the second the researcher left the room. Others mustered as much willpower as they could, employing a wide variety of techniques. They sang songs, played games, covered their eyes, and even tried going to sleep.

Years later, a follow-up study determined whether the children's ability to delay gratification correlated with long-term academic achievement. The academic records of the children who participated in the study were tracked all the way through high school. When the longitudinal results were cross-referenced with delayed-gratification times, researchers found that the children who had delayed gratification longer were more academically accomplished.

On average, they scored 210 points higher on the SAT. The marsh-mallow test was twice as powerful a predictor of academic achieve-ment as IQ. The delayed-gratification kids were also more self-reliant and socially competent. They took initiative more frequently and handled stress more effectively. Four decades later, another follow-up study revealed higher incomes, stronger marriages, and more fulfilling careers.[4]

Countless studies have confirmed what the marshmallow exper-iment indicated. Delayed gratification is the key. The key to what? Almost everything! And most definitely habit formation. It goes by another name, *willpower*. It's mind over matter. It's nurture over na-ture. It's the old adage *Where there's a will, there's a way!*

One way to eat the frog is by not eating at all. It's called fast-ing. There are lots of physical benefits to intermittent and short-term fasting. It resets the immune system.[5] It purifies toxins, especially if you drink water or bone broth. It recalibrates your me-tabolism. And it renews your appreciation for food once you re-introduce it.

Fasting has physical benefits, but the biggest payout is willpower. If you can give up food, you can give up anything! Am I right? Few things are harder to resist than hunger pangs. In that sense, fasting exercises willpower.

There are two Greek words that are translated as "power" in the New Testament, and they have a yin and yang relationship. *Duna-mis* is the power to do things beyond your natural ability. It's where we get our word *dynamite*. *Exousia* is the power not to do some-thing that is within your power. It takes *dunamis* to bench-press two hundred pounds. It takes *exousia* to eat only one Oreo!

The human body has more than six hundred skeletal muscles. In case you care, they have the combined potential of lifting twenty-five tons if they were all leveraged at the same time, the same way! The hardest-working muscle is the heart, pumping blood through sixty thousand miles of veins, arteries, and capillaries every day. The largest muscle is the gluteus maximus. And the strongest muscle is the masseter in your jaw, which can exert two hundred pounds of force on your molars.[6]

Those muscles exert *dunamis,* giving you the strength to do what needs to be done. How is *exousia* exercised? I like to think of it as "the no muscle." It's the muscle you flex when you say no to dessert. It's not as easy to exercise as your pectorals, but one of the best ways to bench-press willpower is via fasting. It'll help you break bad habits by interrupting the pattern, but it's key when it comes to making habits too. Why? Discipline in one area of our lives begets discipline in all other areas of our lives!

When it comes to willpower, Jesus set the bar. It's no coincidence that His first temptation involved food. Jesus fasted for forty days, and the Enemy hit Him where it hurt. He told Jesus to turn stones into bread, which seems harmless enough. Jesus leveraged every ounce of willpower in His possession. He resisted the temptation by identifying the prompt and interrupting the pattern. He went back to the script: "Man shall not live on bread alone."[7]

Eating the frog is all about delayed gratification. *Wait—I thought it was eating the frog first?* It is! Delayed gratification is doing the hardest thing first. It piggybacks off the idea that *harder is better* and adds a time stamp—*harder sooner.* When the hardest task is prioritized, everything else seems easy by comparison.

Several years ago, I hiked to the top of Half Dome in Yosemite National Park. It's not the hardest hike I've ever done, but it was the scariest. The last leg involves an extreme angle, especially if you're scared of heights like me. I did it scared. And facing that fear gave me a newfound confidence.

When I reached the top of Half Dome, I spotted a rock with writing etched into it. I have no idea how long it took to carve, but someone scribbled a life-altering message on that rock: *If you can do this, you can do anything.* That rock proved to be a prompt. It flipped my script, flipped my switch. At the time of the hike, I was suffering from severe plantar fasciitis because I was twenty-five pounds over my optimal body mass index. I made a decision right then, right there. I gave myself three months to tip the scales at sub-two-hundred.

I had just faced my fear of heights and conquered it. If I could conquer that fear, I could certainly lose twenty-five pounds! You need to do it scared, do it difficult, and do it now. How? By making decisions against yourself. Why? To prove to yourself what's possible! That's the essence of eating the frog.

"Everything is permissible," but not everything is beneficial.[8]

The distinction between *permissible* and *beneficial* is the difference between good and great. If you settle for what's permissible, you'll never tap your potential. The enemy of good is not bad; it's *good enough*. It reminds me of the maxim that Academy Award–winning film director James Cameron is purported to have used as motivation while producing *Avatar—Good enough isn't.*

When I was in my twenties, I spent a week with Jack Hayford at his School of Pastoral Nurture. That week transformed the trajectory of my ministry. Two decades later, I reconnected with Jack at a gathering of pastors in the DC area. An octogenarian by then, Jack shared one secret to his longevity, productivity, and, I might add, integrity.

His secret sauce? *Make decisions against yourself.* Well, that doesn't sound like fun! I know it doesn't, but hear me out. Making decisions *against yourself* is making decisions *for yourself.* It's as counterintuitive as breaking down your muscles to build them up and just as effective. The good news? Nothing compounds interest like delayed gratification!

Is there something you need to say no to? In many instances, abstinence is easier than moderation. Why? It requires less willpower because you rely on a strong predecision. Moderation is a slippery slope. In my experience, it's harder to eat one Oreo than no Oreos! If you feed a craving, it grows. If you starve it, it atrophies. If you want to break a bad habit, try abstinence.

For two hours Jack detailed some of the defining decisions—

difficult decisions—he had made. Some were right-or-wrong decisions, like resisting temptation. Others were matters of personal conviction. They wouldn't have been wrong for anyone else, but they would have been for Jack. Why? He would have been compromising his convictions. In some ways, defining decisions equate to an Old Testament vow. They are voluntary, not mandatory. But once you make the vow, it's inviolable. It's not unlike the commitment device employed by the marathon monks on day 101 of their thousand-day challenge.

When Jack was in his forties, he decided to give up chocolate. No, not for Lent. As far as he knew, it was forever. If that doesn't qualify as making a decision against yourself, I'm not sure what does. That seems like cruel and unusual punishment. Jack would be the first person to say there is nothing wrong with chocolate. Can we take a moment to thank God for chocolate? Praise God for hot chocolate, Hershey's Kisses, and molten chocolate lava cake!

For more than four decades, Jack Hayford has abstained from eating chocolate. For whatever reason, he felt like God wanted him to steer clear. Jack made a decision against himself, and it had a domino effect. How so? If you can say no to chocolate, you can say no to almost anything! Am I right, or am I right? When you exercise willpower in one area of your life, it has a domino chain reaction. Physical discipline begets spiritual discipline and vice versa. Eating the frog is a domino habit.

If you want to get out of debt, you have to make decisions against yourself financially. It's called budgeting. If you want to lose weight, you have to make decisions against yourself physically. It's called dieting. If you want to write a book or get a graduate degree or train for a marathon, you have to make decisions against yourself chronologically. It's called calendaring. You don't *find time*. You have to *make time*. How? By setting your alarm clock a little earlier in the morning.

What decision do you need to make against yourself? What are you waiting for?

Remember my thesis? *Almost anyone can accomplish almost anything if they work at it long enough, hard enough, and smart enough.* The key is delayed gratification. It's making decisions against yourself. When? Today. Why? So you can reap the dividends tomorrow! It takes starting power, but it also takes staying power, which is a function of willpower.

How do I make it a habit?

Make your body!

Remember the doctrine of the strenuous life from day 15? You didn't think it was one and done, did you? No way was I going to let us off that easy! The strenuous life is rise and shine, rain or shine. It's the daily grind. It's a point-to-point hike.

As a child, Teddy Roosevelt was the quintessential hundred-pound weakling. He suffered from severe asthma, which I empathize with. Of course, Roosevelt didn't have an albuterol inhaler at his disposal like I did. Asthma limited his outdoor activities and curbed his athletic pursuits. So how did he become such a proponent of physical fitness? The tipping point was tough love. It often is, isn't it?

When Teddy was young, Theodore Roosevelt Sr. threw down the gauntlet and said to his son, "Theodore, you have the mind, but you have not the body." Teddy's father flipped the script and challenged him to eat the frog: "Without the help of the body, the mind cannot go as far as it should. I am giving you the tools, but it is up to you to make your body." Those three words—"make your body"—changed the trajectory of Teddy Roosevelt's life. Without hesitating, he said, "I will make my body!"[9] From that day forward, Teddy Roosevelt began a regular exercise routine that included boxing, wrestling, hiking, and horseback riding. He took up tennis, eventually forming his infamous "tennis cabinet." He even tried his hand at jujitsu, never reaching a rank.

Teddy Roosevelt started exercising, and he never stopped. Even when he struggled with his weight later in life, he didn't quit on himself. At the age of fifty-eight, Roosevelt did a two-week stint at Jack Cooper's Health Farm. His goal? Losing thirty-five pounds. My point? There is no finish line. You have to keep making decisions against yourself until the day you die!

When it comes to physical fitness, I'm acutely aware of hereditary factors. More than four hundred genes have been implicated when it comes to being overweight or obese. Depending on the person, genetic influence is responsible for 25 percent to 80 percent of the predisposition to be overweight.[10] My advice? Don't use genetics as an excuse; use it as motivation. Focus on inputs, and leave the outcome to God. While you're at it, quit playing the comparison game. Regardless of body type, you can control the calories you consume. I'm not minimizing hereditary factors. I believe in both nurture and nature. But when push comes to shove, I believe in nurture over nature just like I believe in mind over matter!

Gerald Schattle serves as principal of the Kenneth R. Knippel Education Center—an alternative education program for students who have violated the code of conduct at their own public schools. Schattle has battled obesity most of his life. A few years ago, he tipped the scales at 397 pounds. That's when he set a God-sized goal—run a marathon. Schattle had to lose eighty pounds before he even started running. When he reached his target weight, he started running prayer circles around the eighty-two campuses in his school district. Not only did Schattle run a marathon, but he also lost nearly half his body weight. And inspired his students to go after their goals in the process!

Is there a goal that seems impossible from where you stand right now? With the right daily habits, it's not impossible. It's inevitable! Will it take willpower? Absolutely. But if you do the *natural,* God will do the *super.*

Make decisions against yourself!

Day 17

Live Not by Lies

We are not unaware of his schemes.
—2 CORINTHIANS 2:11

On February 12, 1974, Aleksandr Solzhenitsyn was arrested by the KGB and charged with treason. He had won the Nobel Prize in Literature in 1970, but Solzhenitsyn was more than an ivory tower intellectual. He had spent eight years in the Russian gulag. Why? He was one of those rare souls who muster the moral courage to stand against what's wrong and stand up for what's right. He refused to bow to power, to propaganda, and to the intimidation tactics used against him and his family.

On the eve of his exile, Solzhenitsyn published one final plea to the Russian people. The title speaks for itself: "Live Not by Lies." "It will not be . . . an easy choice for the body," he said, "but [it is] the only one for the soul."[1]

Before I tell you what *living not by lies* is, let me tell you what it isn't. It's not just giving lip service to make yourself look or feel better. That's called virtue signaling—a subtle form of self-righteousness that is heavy in speech but light in action. Living not by lies is anything but cheap talk.

Living not by lies is refusing to bow to cultural idols and ideologies that fail to pass the truth test. It's living according to your convictions while showing compassion to those who don't believe the way you do. It's risking your reputation for that which you believe to be good and right and true. It's speaking truth to power, and it's speaking the truth in love. Living not by lies is a conscience taken captive by the Word of God, by the Spirit of God.

"Be as shrewd as snakes," said Jesus, "and as innocent as doves."[2] It's a two-sided truth. Once again, true wisdom has two sides. Being innocent as a dove speaks to the motivation behind our actions. If you do the right thing for the wrong reasons, it doesn't even count in the kingdom of God. We need to check our motives while we check our ego at the door. But we also have to outsmart the Enemy, who happens to be the "shrewdest of all."[3] In other words, we have to beat the Enemy at his own game!

There is an old adage: *The best defense is a good offense.* I believe that's true, spiritually speaking. The best way to stay out of trouble is *not* by focusing on staying out of trouble. Remember the Jolly Green Giant and the idea of the double bind? Goodness is not the absence of badness! You can do nothing wrong and still do nothing right.

The best way to stay out of bad trouble is by getting into good trouble! You need a vision that's bigger and better than the temptation you face. It's one method of habit switching. The best way to break a bad habit is by building a good habit. That's how we interrupt the pattern and alter the habit cycle.

The best defense may be a good offense, but we can't afford to let down our guard either. All the Enemy wants is a foothold, because footholds turn into strongholds. If you give the Enemy an inch, he'll take a mile. Again, abstinence is one of the most effective ways to interrupt the pattern. You eliminate the option altogether! Abstinence doesn't always mean *forever.* You can give things up for a set amount of time. Whole 30 is a great example. So is Lent. So is a CrossFit boot camp. You have to define your start date and end date, and then you have to be explicit about what it is you're giving up. You can't allow loopholes if you want to form a new habit loop.

No sugar means *no sugar.*

No alcohol means *no alcohol.*

No social media means *no social media.*

I'm not sure what habit you're trying to make or break, but how is it going? If you've gotten derailed, hit the reset button. Consider this your mulligan! Habit formation always involves a few false starts. It's time for a fresh start.

On day 5, we explored the idea of awareness training. It's taking inventory of our triggers. "It seems ridiculously simple," said Nathan Azrin, "but once you're aware of how your habit works, once you recognize the cues and rewards, you're halfway to changing it."[4]

When it comes to breaking bad habits, you've got to identify the prompts. In the words of the apostle Paul, "We are not unaware of his schemes."[5] Along with self-awareness, we need to cultivate situational awareness. It requires the prophetic imagination we discussed on day 14—*always think ecosystem!*

There is an old acronym: *HALT.* It stands for *hungry, angry, lonely,* and *tired.* Can I let you in on a little secret? The Enemy is an opportunist. All he wants is a foothold, and HALT moments are some of the easiest footholds. Remember, what you tolerate will eventually dominate. The good news? We are not unaware of his tactics! We've got game film going all the way back to the Garden of Eden.

The Enemy goes by a few names, and those monikers reveal his methods. One of his signatures is *accuser of the brethren.* The Enemy has been blackballing since the beginning of time. He tries to steal, kill, and destroy future-tense vision by getting us to focus all our energy on past-tense guilt. You've got to identify the false accusations that lead to false identities and false narratives.

A second signature is *angel of light.* The angel of light uses smoke and mirrors to distract us. And if that doesn't work, he blurs the line between right and wrong. Remember the first temptation of Christ? "Tell these stones to become bread," Satan said. That seems innocent enough. What's wrong with that proposition? After all, Jesus would miraculously feed five thousand with five loaves and two fish! The problem with that proposition is that Jesus would have been proving His identity the wrong way.

The third signature is *father of lies*. Whenever you lose hope, you have believed a lie of the Enemy. His native tongue is fake news! He is always redefining right and wrong. He is always rewriting true and false. Many of our bad habits are based on false assumptions. You've got to analyze those assumptions. Is there a lie you have believed to be true? Once you identify it, you have to renounce it like Aleksandr Solzhenitsyn did.

In the gospel of John, there is a man who hadn't walked in thirty-eight years. He went to the pool of Bethesda every day, waiting for the waters to be stirred. Why? A superstition had grown up around the stirring. People believed it was caused by an angel. The first one in the water was the winner, winner, chicken dinner. I'm not sure which is worse: *unbelief* or *false belief*. Either way, it was superstition that got in the way of this man experiencing the supernatural. His greatest handicap wasn't physical; it was spiritual—a false belief based on a false assumption.[6]

We make the same mistake, don't we? We keep trying what isn't working! Please hear me: your system is perfectly designed for the results you're getting! That's why we need tough love. We need someone who cares enough to confront. We need someone to ask the honest question: "How's that working for you?"

If you want to live counterculturally, you need a counternarrative. I love a good pep talk, but that isn't good enough. A TED Talk isn't good enough either. We need a metanarrative that rises above cultural talking points and trending hashtags. What is our counternarrative? It's the Sermon on the Mount. Jesus rewrote the rules in a way that is as radical now as it was then.

At the heart of habit formation is the art of breaking *and* making rules, and no one did it better than Jesus. He broke the rules of religiosity by eating with sinners, touching lepers, and celebrating Samaritans. In doing so, Jesus established a *rule of life* for those who follow in His footsteps.

Many of us have an adverse relationship to rules. The word conjures up negative connotations. Please hear me when I say that *the right rules are your best friends.* Imagine how many accidents would happen without the rules of the road. Imagine a game of football without an out-of-bounds, offside, or pass-interference penalty. You couldn't even play the game! The same goes for every game, including the game of life.

We have rules for just about everything, right? There is a mnemonic rule for spelling: i *before* e *except after* c. There is a rule for crossing the street: *look both ways.* I have a rule for the staff at NCC: *if you can't laugh at my jokes, we can't work together.* I don't just believe in the theory of fun; it's a rule of life.

On that note, I love fun facts. Do you know the name of the robe worn by Benedictine monks? It's called a habit. I also love double entendres! The habit worn by Benedictine monks symbolizes the seventy-three habits that make up their rules of life.

In the sixth century, Benedict of Nursia abandoned his studies in Rome, moved into a cave outside Subiaco, Italy, and lived as a hermit for three years. Another fun fact? Benedict is the patron saint of speleologists, a fancy name for those who chose spelunking as a career!

Saint Benedict would found twelve monasteries, including Monte Cassino. That is where the Rule of Saint Benedict would be composed. Consisting of seventy-three chapters, the Rule of Saint Benedict gave those monks guidelines and guardrails in their everyday lives. The intent was to foster spiritual growth and Christian community by implementing rules of life. My favorite rule? If you're fasting and someone visits you, you can employ Benedictine rule number fifty-three and eat with your guest. Hospitality trumps your fast.[7] Quit judging me! I'm a pastor, not a monk!

The Latin word for "rule" is *regula,* and it refers to the trellis on which plants grow. A trellis is often employed by gardeners or vintners to lift limbs, and its purpose is twofold. It keeps limbs off the ground, protecting them from predators. It also maximizes fruitfulness by keeping the limbs straight.

A rule of life consists of the daily routines that undergird growth.

It's an expression of the growth mindset, protecting us against temptation and pointing us toward growth. It's the framework for the habits that help us grow physically, intellectually, relationally, emotionally, and spiritually.

How do I make it a habit?

Rewrite the rules!

In the practice of law, there is a concept called the bright-line rule. It's a clearly defined rule that eliminates the need for decision-making. Why? The precedent has already been set. It's a lot like the predecisions we made on day 4. Here are a few of my bright-line rules:

> I want to be famous in my home.
> Playing it safe is risky.
> Truth is found in the tension of opposites.
> Criticize by creating.
> Let God be as original with others as He is with you.
> Brag about people behind their backs.
> Check your ego at the door.

When it comes to establishing priorities and establishing boundaries, bright-line rules are critically important. You need to write them down and put them in visible places. You need to say them out loud over and over again. Why? We tend to believe what we hear ourselves say out loud.

I love the bright-line rule Mister Rogers put on a piece of paper and carried in his wallet: "There isn't anyone you couldn't love once you've heard their story."[8] It might be worth writing down and putting in your wallet. Like Fred Rogers, I try to keep written reminders front and center. When our kids were young, it was a Post-it note on the bathroom mirror: *Choose your battles wisely.* I have a piece of Emily Dickinson poetry hanging in my office: *Dwell in Possibility.*[9] I have a note card in my Bible that says, *Whatever keeps me from my Bible is my enemy, however harmless it may appear to be.*[10]

What rules do you need to make?

What rules do you need to break?

Live not by lies!

Habit 4—Fly the Kite

How you do anything is how you'll do everything.

O n November 9, 1847, a civil engineer named Charles Ellet Jr. was commissioned to build a bridge across the Niagara Gorge. The greatest challenge was getting the first cable across an 825-foot chasm with 225-foot cliffs on either side. Enter Theodore Graves Hulett, a local ironworker who suggested—get this—a kite-flying contest. Of course!

A fifteen-year-old boy named Homan Walsh won the ten-dollar cash prize for flying the first kite across the chasm. The day after that successful flight, a stronger line was attached to that kite string and pulled across. Then an even stronger line. Then a rope. Then a cable consisting of thirty-six strands of ten-gauge wire.[1] The bridge would eventually become the world's first railway suspension bridge. It would connect two countries, and it was strong enough to support a 170-ton locomotive. And it all started with a single kite string! Don't despise the day of small beginnings.

Do not despise these small beginnings, for the LORD rejoices to see the work begin, to see the plumb line in Zerubbabel's hand.[2]

Plumb line, kite string—same difference! A plumb line was an ancient architectural device. It was a vertical reference line ensuring that a structure was centered. Stop and think about this. God was rejoicing *before* they even broke ground. All they'd done was find the center of gravity, and God was giving them a standing ovation.

We want to do amazing things for God, but that isn't our job. God is the one who does amazing things for us. We fly the kite, and God is the one who can build the suspension bridge! Our job is to consecrate ourselves to God, one day at a time. If we do our job, God will do His.

We are easily overwhelmed by the size of our dreams. It's so hard to take the first step, but you can't finish what you don't start. My advice? Start small. We need to set stretch goals, but we need to reverse engineer them into small wins. If you do little things like they're big things, God will do big things like they're little things!

Remember my hike to the top of Half Dome? Before we started the hike, I looked up at the top, and a thought fired across my synapses: *How in the world are we going to get all the way up there and all the way back down before sunset?* You know the answer: one step at a time!

You get in shape one workout at a time.

You get out of debt one dollar at a time.

You run the marathon one mile at a time.

You write the book one page at a time.

You build the relationship one date at a time.

You build the business one sale at a time.

When it comes to habit formation, you have to break it down!

Even a pie gets sliced into pieces!

In 1952, Winston Churchill was serving as chancellor of Bristol University when he was tasked with the honor of laying the foundation stone of a new building on campus. As he picked up the silver trowel to lay the ceremonial stone, he said, "The stone isn't level."[3] The very embarrassed officials produced a plumb line to double-check. Sure enough, Churchill's dead reckoning was right.

That incident raises the question, How did a professional politician have that kind of eye for architectural detail? The answer is the summer of 1928. Under tremendous pressure as the chancellor of the exchequer, a position he held from 1924 to 1929, Churchill desperately needed rest. The prime minister, Stanley Baldwin, gave him a leave of absence. "Do remember what I said about resting from current problems," Baldwin wrote. "Paint, write, play." Churchill added one exercise to that list—laying bricks! He retired to the countryside, where he built a cottage for his daughter.

During that sabbatical, the future prime minister of Britain regained his sense of perspective. Writing to the current prime minister, Churchill said, "I have had a delightful month building a cottage and dictating a book: 200 bricks and 2000 words a day."[4]

Two hundred bricks.

Two thousand words.

Flying the kite is all about consistent consistency. It's the department of redundancy department. It's making marginal progress every day—two hundred bricks, two thousand words! It's compound interest. It's 1 percent improvement. It's getting better every day.

Very few athletes rival the longevity and productivity of Kobe Bryant. His NBA career spanned 1,346 games over twenty seasons. He scored 33,643 regular-season points, the fourth most of all time. That includes sixty points in his final game! Bryant won five NBA championships and two Olympic gold medals, among many other awards and accolades.

How did he do it? Success isn't one dimensional, so there isn't one answer. Bryant ate the frog with his "biblical workouts."[5] But he also flew the kite with film study. "I went from watching what was there to watching for what was missing and should have been there." That's next level. That's flying the kite! "Film study eventually became imagining alternatives, counters, options, in addition to the finite details of why some actions work and others don't work."[6] If we had a fraction of that kind of focus, it would be game on!

It's time to fly the kite!

Day 18

Do It Small

Little by little I will drive them out.
—Exodus 23:30

In July 2018, I was invited by Coach John Harbaugh to speak to the Baltimore Ravens on their opening day of training camp. I gave a talk based on my book *Chase the Lion,* and that title became their team theme that season. After my talk, Coach Harbaugh took the time to take me on a tour of their training facility. They have the latest and greatest technology, including a biometric scale that measures body fat. I will neither confirm nor deny stepping on that scale, nor will I reveal the results.

The most impressive piece of technology may have been a computer algorithm that uses electromyography to measure muscle pathology. The biofeedback from that machine gives the strength-and-conditioning coaches a quick read on biomechanical deficiencies. It enables them to identify weaknesses that need to be strengthened, as well as tendencies that need to be counterbalanced. The technical term is *gait analysis,* and the goal is helping athletes move more efficiently, more effectively.

A key component of self-leadership is self-evaluation. We've got to do our own gait analysis. How? By going through the three-step cycle we keep coming back to—identify the prompt, interrupt the pattern, and imagine the prize. We may not be able to hook ourselves up to a machine that provides real-time biofeedback, but we can deconstruct a habit cycle if we know what we're looking for.

If it helps, do a SWOT analysis. It's often employed by organizations for strategic planning purposes, but it works just as well for individuals. *SWOT* stands for *strengths, weaknesses, opportunities,* and *threats*. A SWOT analysis may help you reverse engineer the habit cycle.

I have a friend who used to work in the front office of an NFL franchise, and he shared a fascinating five-year study that used regression analysis to isolate and identify key factors that led to the success or failure of NFL franchises. In statistics, regression analysis is used to determine whether two sets of data are related. It differentiates between causation and correlation. It identifies the variable that makes the biggest difference.

From 2009 to 2013, teams that ended the season with a top-ten differential in turnovers finished 521–278–1. That translates to a 65.1 percent winning percentage, averaging 10.4 wins per season. Conversely, teams that ended in the bottom ten in turnover differential finished 287–512–1. That equates to a 35.9 percent winning percentage and 5.7 wins.

The bottom line? It's really hard to win if you're turning over the ball! It's true in football, and it's true in life. It's the unforced errors that hurt the most. But it's not single mistakes that sink the battleship. It's single mistakes that we allow to turn into losing streaks. Footholds that we let become strongholds. Bad decisions that we allow to become bad habits.

Like a stop-loss order in the world of finance, you need safeguards against compounding mistakes! Of course, the opposite is necessary as well. You have to turn small wins into winning streaks by repeating them over and over again.

If you were to do a regression analysis on your habits, what would it reveal? Good or bad, our smallest habits can have a domino chain reaction. You don't have to make major changes. You need to identify the little habits that are high leverage—the domino habits.

Did you know that the average person checks their phone ninety-six times a day?[1] And I bet some of you are above average! In one sense, smartphones save us time and energy. But not if it adds up to three hours and forty-three minutes of screen time![2] We complain about not having enough time for this, that, and the other thing. The reality? We could be buying back that screen time for other things. Or at the very least, using that screen time to habit stack!

When it comes to imagining the prize, you've got to play the long game. Simply put, *there is no finish line.* It's the Japanese concept *kaizen,* an unconditional commitment to continual improvement. It's about getting a little better every day in every way. That mindset is the key to every habit—*do it small.*

There is a three-word phrase in the book of Deuteronomy that produces mixed emotions for me. "Little by little I will drive them out before you," God said, "until you have increased enough to take possession of the land."[3] Did you catch it? "Little by little."

Let me set the scene, and then I'll explain the mixed emotions. The Israelites were about to occupy the promised land, but it didn't come on a silver platter. God told them they would have to plant the crops they wanted to harvest, dig the wells they wanted to drink from, and build the houses they wanted to live in. It's the law of measures all over again. You'll get out of it what you put into it—nothing more, nothing less.

Then God told them that it wouldn't happen overnight. It would happen "little by little." On one level, this is discouraging. Why? We want God to do it in a day! News flash: it might take as long to break the bad habit as it did to make it. Now let me flip the script. The encouraging fact is that anybody can *do it small.* It's the mundanity of excellence. Again, if you do little things like they're big things, God will do big things like they're little things!

Remember day 2? *Harder is better!*

How about day 3? *Slower is faster!*

What about day 5? *Smaller is bigger!*

When it comes to making and breaking habits, those are the subplots. The process will be harder than you hope and longer than you like. Simply put, it will happen little by little. That's how God grows us, promotes us, and often heals us.

I'm certainly not suggesting that God cannot deliver you in a day. He can do more in one day than you can accomplish in a thousand lifetimes. He can do it as easily as He turned water into wine! But more often than not, deliverance is a process. More specifically, a three-step process called the habit cycle. Even if God does deliver you in a day, you have to back up that deliverance with daily habits.

The goal is not the goal.

The goal is the process!

I believe in setting God-sized goals. Go after a goal that is impossible without divine intervention. But the goal isn't accomplishing the goal. It's who you become in the process. God uses big dreams to make big people. Why? They keep us on our knees! They force us to exercise faith. They make us make sacrifices.

Flying the kite is all about focusing on inputs. Yes, you have to identify the goals you're going after. But then you need to reverse engineer them into small wins that will help you get there. That's how you build suspension bridges to the future. The bigger the goal, the more attention you need to pay to details!

After retiring from coaching, John Wooden was asked what he missed most. I'll give you a hint: It wasn't the games. It wasn't the trophies or the championships either. I love his one-word answer: "Practice."[4]

There is an old axiom: *Practice makes perfect.* That's not false, but it's not entirely true either. You have to practice the right way! It goes back to the equation I introduced on day 3:

Deliberate Practice + Desirable Difficulty = Durable Learning

If you practice the wrong way, you cultivate bad habits. Anders Ericsson called it naive practice.[5] Deliberate practice is paying attention to the details. Why? *Perfect practice makes perfect.* It's true whether you're practicing scales, practicing a crossover dribble, or practicing spiritual disciplines. Just as you have to do the right thing for the right reason, you have to do it the right way. That is the Jesus Way.

During his illustrious career as a composer, Johann Sebastian Bach wrote 256 cantatas. Three of his compositions cracked *The 50 Greatest Pieces of Classical Music*, which ranks him right behind Mozart and Beethoven.[6] Bach doesn't get invited to many weddings anymore, but he crashes the party all the time. How? "Jesu, Joy of Man's Desiring" still ranks as the most-played piece of music at traditional weddings.

Any guess as to how Bach composed all those cantatas? One note at a time! I know it's starting to sound like a broken record, pun intended. And point made! It's the mundanity of excellence, applied to music.

Upon completing those compositions, Bach would inscribe three letters in the margin of the music—*SDG*. Those three letters stood for the Latin phrase *soli Deo gloria*—"to the glory of God alone." It was one of the rallying cries of the Protestant Reformation, but Bach employed it as a means of giving credit where credit is due. The prize was God's glory!

How do I make it a habit?

Start small.

Go ahead and dream big, but you have to start small and think long. You have to fly the kite a little higher, a little longer every day. Over time, the ceiling becomes the floor! "You cannot jump to the second floor from the pavement," said Emil Zátopek. "Step by step, though, a man will come to the fifth floor."[7]

That's how Zátopek won three gold medals at the 1952 Helsinki Olympics. That's how he won sixty-nine races in a row. That's how he became the greatest runner of all time, at any distance. Emil

Zátopek ran a total of fifty thousand miles—the equivalent of two laps around the earth!

Remember the law of measures? If you cheat the system, you're cheating yourself. If you cut corners, you're short-circuiting your own success and shortchanging God's glory! The way you create a habit loop is by not giving yourself any loopholes.

How's your habit going?

Is it still measurable, meaningful, and maintainable?

Have you reverse engineered it little by little?

You've got to turn those life goals into daily habits.

What's the one little step you need to take *today* to make that little-by-little progress?

For Kobe Bryant, flying the kite was studying game film.

For Winston Churchill, flying the kite was laying two hundred bricks and writing two thousand words per day.

For the marathon monks, it was circling Mount Hiei every day.

For me, it was reading three thousand books before writing one.

Do it small!

Day 19

Exercise Your Authority

*When Jesus woke up, he rebuked the wind
and said to the waves, "Silence! Be still!"*
—MARK 4:39, NLT

On October 14, 1947, a B-29 bomber took off from an airstrip in Southern California. Attached to the belly of that bomber was a much smaller plane, the Bell X-1. That plane is now suspended from the ceiling of the National Air and Space Museum. In the world of aviation, the common assumption was that the speed of sound, Mach 1, was an unbreakable barrier. But much like records, barriers were made to be broken!

At twenty-five thousand feet, the B-29 bomber dropped the Bell X-1. It fired its engines, ascended to forty-three thousand feet, and accelerated to 500, 600, 700 miles per hour. At .965 Mach, the control panels on the dashboard went haywire. At .995 Mach, the g-force blurred Chuck Yeager's vision and turned his stomach into knots. Just when it felt like that plane would implode, there was a sonic boom.

At 761 miles per hour, the Bell X-1 broke the sound barrier, and the air pressure that had been pounding the front of that plane shifted to the tail. It was as if the perfect storm became the perfect calm—absolutely still, absolutely silent. Why? At supersonic speeds, the plane was traveling faster than the sound waves it produced. The Bell X-1 reached 1.07 Mach, Chuck Yeager cut the engines, and the rest is history.

In the Gospels, there's a story about Jesus crossing the Sea of

Galilee with the disciples. He was actually taking a nap, which I love. That's all the justification I need to nap, but let me add a sidebar—a study done by NASA found that a twenty-six-minute nap increases productivity 34 percent.[1] It's good stewardship, and it's good science. If I ever ran for public office, one plank in my platform would be a national nap time. No, I'm not announcing my candidacy. And the nap would be optional. I just think we'd be a kinder, happier, and healthier nation if we had a nap time!

As Jesus napped, a furious storm started rocking their boat, sort of like the headwind that battered the Bell X-1. This kind of storm was not uncommon. The Sea of Galilee is seven hundred feet below sea level, but it's surrounded by hills and mountains. The Golan Heights, which were called the Decapolis in Jesus's day, were 2,500 feet above sea level. That topography made the Sea of Galilee susceptible to very sudden, very violent storms.

Do you remember what happened next? The disciples, some of whom were professional fishermen, were scared to death. They woke Jesus up with these words: "Teacher, don't you care if we drown?"[2] Really? Jesus was taking a nap, which meant He somehow didn't care? Talk about a rush to judgment.

Our reactions reveal a lot about us, don't they? It's much easier to *act* like a Christian than it is to *react* like one. In crisis situations, we're awfully quick to assign blame. We're awfully quick to assume the worst. We're awfully quick to judge motives, even our friends'. If you take the time to change news channels, you'll notice that everyone is blaming everyone else for almost everything. Can I remind us? No one wins the blame game!

Now let me flip the script. What did Jesus do when they woke Him up? Did He panic? Did He start bailing out the boat? Did He grab an oar and start rowing? No, no, and no! Jesus stood up in the boat like the karate kid and did the crane! At least that's how I envision this moment.

Who rebukes the wind?

Who speaks to the waves?

I'll tell you who—the One who made them! He exercised His spiritual authority over the physical elements the same way He turned water into wine, the same way He cursed the barren fig tree, the same way He called Lazarus out of the tomb![3]

I'm not sure what habit you're trying to make or break, but you're going to have to exercise your spiritual authority! How? First, you need to hold your peace in the midst of the storm. You have to keep calm and carry on. You have to maintain a nonanxious presence. How do you do that? By interrupting the anxiety prompt with a pattern of prayer. Holding your peace is holding space. It's being fully present. It's embracing the tension of now but not yet. It's confronting the brutal facts with unwavering faith. Second, you need to speak your peace! I'm not sure what challenges you face, but you need to speak peace to your spouse. Speak peace to your kids. Speak peace to your friends. Speak peace to racial tension and political polarization. How? By operating in the opposite spirit.

As a Christ follower, I am obliged to call injustice on the carpet. Caring for the marginalized is the Jesus Way. We lament with those who suffer injustice, but we don't play the victim card. We don't play possum either. We exercise our authority as more than conquerors.[4] We step up, we step in, and we stand in the gap as peacemakers, grace givers, and tone setters.

In 1913, Josiah Royce founded a community that he called the Fellowship of Reconciliation. Their goal was to become a beloved community. That fellowship would accept into its membership Dr. Martin Luther King Jr., who would champion this idea of beloved community and cast vision for it. The goal of the civil rights movement wasn't just civil rights. The goal was becoming a beloved community where people would be judged not by the color of their skin but rather by the content of their character.[5] The goal was the creation of a community whose love was so strong that it transformed opponents into friends. "It is this love," said Dr. King, "which will bring about miracles in the hearts of men."[6]

It's hard to change individual habits. It's even harder to change cultural habits. "This will require a qualitative change in our souls," said Dr. King, "as well as a quantitative change in our lives."[7] We need to take personal responsibility while putting pride and prejudice on the altar. We need to sacrifice for the greater good while being unoffendable.

Most people live their lives at .965 Mach. The control panels are going haywire. The cockpit is out of control. Some people make it to .995 Mach. Blurred vision. Stomach in knots. It feels like your marriage or your mental health could implode at any moment. You may be closer to a breakthrough than you think! Don't cut the engine just yet.

If you're going to make or break a habit, you've got to exercise your authority. You've got to rebuke the wind and the waves. At some point, you have to stop talking to God about your problems and start talking to your problems about God. You have to declare His power, His presence, His promises. Yes, there are lots of things you can't control. But you can take response-ability.

We're so good at telling God all about our problems. We *explain* them as if He doesn't know what's wrong. We *complain* about them as if He doesn't care. We *remind* Him as if He has forgotten. My advice? Exercise your authority. Doubt is letting your circumstances get between you and God. Faith is letting God get between you and your circumstances!

How do I make it a habit?

Shift the atmosphere.

On Good Friday 1963, Dr. Martin Luther King Jr. was jailed for a peaceful protest without a permit. When criticized for his timing and his tactics, Dr. King wrote an open letter from a jail cell in Birmingham, Alabama:

There was a time when the church was very powerful—in the time when the early Christians rejoiced at being deemed worthy to suffer for what they believed. In those days the church was not merely a thermometer that recorded the ideas and principles of popular opinion; it was a thermostat that transformed the mores of society.[8]

Are you a thermometer or a thermostat? Are you regurgitating the news channels you watch and the social media you follow? Or are you taking your cues from the script of Scripture? Are you conforming to culture? Or are you interrupting the pattern with faith, hope, and love?

Thermometers reflect the temperature—body temperature, water temperature, air temperature. Most people surrender to their circumstances, no questions asked. Remember day 7 and the staged elevator experiment? They face the rear rather than facing the front! They give in to groupthink. They live down to the least common denominator. They allow their environment to determine how they feel, how they think, how they act. As Christ followers, we're called to a higher standard. We shift the atmosphere by operating in the opposite spirit. That's how we exercise our authority!

We must represent the kingdom of God with so much love, so much joy, so much hope that it provokes questions for which the gospel is the answer. How do we do that? When we love our enemies, pray for those who persecute us, and bless those who curse us, it provokes questions for which the gospel is the answer. When we turn the other cheek, go the extra mile, and give away the shirts on our backs, it provokes questions for which the gospel is the answer.[9]

We counter hate with love.

We counter pride with humility.

We counter cursing with blessing.

We counter lies with truth.

We counter racism with reconciliation.

We counter cancel culture with grace and peace.

That's how we rebuke the wind and the waves. And when we do, it provokes questions for which the gospel is the answer! That's how breakthroughs happen. We don't fight fire with fire. As thermostats, we shift the atmosphere with joy unspeakable, a peace that passes understanding, and an extra measure of grace.

You have more authority than you can imagine! You have the authority to stop storms. You have the authority to heal diseases. You have the authority to move mountains. How? With mustard seeds of faith. Spiritual authority is like any muscle that has to be exercised, and we exercise our authority with humility! But don't be shy about it. Stand up like Jesus in the storm. Stand in the gap as a peacemaker, grace giver, and tone setter!

Where you have experienced victory in your life, you have authority. Your testimony is someone else's prophecy. Your breakthrough is someone else's blessing. The church is a faith community. When we elevate each other's faith, we experience herd immunity against things like fear and shame and hate.

You aren't doing God any favors if you operate at less than full authority. You are discounting the price Jesus paid on Calvary's cross! Quit living like Jesus is still nailed to the cross. The only thing nailed to the cross is your sin. The Enemy is a defeated foe. It's time to live like it.

Exercise your authority!

Day 20

Enough Is Enough

What are you, mighty mountain?
—Zechariah 4:7

On November 7, 2020, Chris Nikic became the first person with Down syndrome to finish the Ironman Triathlon. Nikic swam 2.4 miles, biked 112 miles, and ran 26.2 miles in sixteen hours and forty-six minutes. "Goal set and achieved," he said the next day. "Time to set a new and bigger goal." Chris Nikic is a kite flyer! "Whatever it is, the strategy is the same," he said. "1 percent better every day."

It's so easy to use our weaknesses as crutches, isn't it? To submit to the mistakes we've made or the odds against us. Try taking a cue from Chris Nikic! He didn't use Down syndrome as an excuse—he used it as motivation! Nikic added one more thing to the mix: "I did the work, but I had angels helping me."[1]

I love that mindset—it's a growth mindset coupled with a God mindset. It's recognizing the role that God's favor plays, but it doesn't diminish personal responsibility. It's praying like it depends on God while working like it depends on you. It's doing the *natural* and trusting God to do the *super*. It's the place where our grit meets God's grace!

In 536 BC, a man named Zerubbabel led a Jewish remnant back to Jerusalem to rebuild the temple that was in ruins. It was a God-sized vision, but Zerubbabel is staring at a pile of rubble. That's when you need a word from God, and Zeb gets one: "This is the word of the LORD to Zerubbabel: 'Not by might nor by power, but by my Spirit,' says the LORD Almighty."[2] Can I let you in on a little secret? God wants to do things in you and through you that are beyond your ability, your resources, your education, your experience, and your expertise. Why? So you can't take credit for them! How? By His Spirit. The Holy Spirit is the *x* factor, the *it* factor, the *wow* factor.

Then the Lord said, "What are you, mighty mountain? Before Zerubbabel you will become level ground."[3] I have no idea what mountain is staring you in the face—the mountain of anxiety or anger or addiction, the mountain of injustice or unforgiveness, the mountain of depression or doubt or fear. Even if it's a mountain range, the One who made the mountains can make them level ground.

He is still the God who makes sidewalks through the sea.

He is still the God who makes the sun stand still.

He is still the God who turns water into wine.

He is still the God who makes iron ax-heads float.[4]

God is still in the business of moving mountains. How? With mustard seeds of faith! Don't despise the day of small beginnings. Or 1 percent improvements!

After breaking his neck playing college football, Chris Norton was given a 3 percent chance of ever moving again. That's when 97 percent of people give up! But Chris Norton is cut from the same cloth as Chris Nikic—all grit, no quit. One of his doctors told Norton, "You'll never walk again." A lot of people would have accepted that diagnosis and taken the cue to quit trying. Norton didn't get sad; he got mad. A few days later, he wiggled his big toe!

I was on a Zoom call with Norton the night before the documentary film about his life debuted. It's appropriately titled *7 Yards* because it took seven years for him to walk seven yards! That was the length of the aisle on his wedding day. How did he do it? He never lost faith, and, I might add, he never lost his sense of humor.

Remember the theory of fun? Chris Norton is a subscriber!

When he realized he could wiggle his toe, he asked his dad to give his toe a pep talk. His dad obliged by doing his best Matt Foley motivational talk. That's when Norton wiggled his toe!

Well played, Chris Norton! Well played.

There comes a moment in all our lives when we reach the end of our rope. It's the end of the line, or is it? Lazarus was four days dead, but it's not over until God says it's over. Don't put a period where God puts a comma.

At some point, *enough is enough*. Remember yesterday's challenge? You have to stop talking to God about your problems, and you have to start talking to your problems about God. The same goes for mountains. That's how you flip the script and fly the kite. You declare His goodness—"Surely goodness and mercy shall follow me all the days of my life."[5] You declare His faithfulness—"He who began a good work in you will carry it on to completion."[6] You declare His sovereignty—"All things work together for good to those who love God, to those who are the called according to His purpose."[7] You declare His favor—"If God is for us, who can be against us?"[8]

That's what I did on July 2, 2016. I prayed a bold prayer, and God healed my lungs. Yes, it's got to be God's will, God's way. Every prayer has to pass a twofold litmus test—it has to be in the will of God and for the glory of God. If it's not, it's a nonstarter. But if it is, you'd better buckle your seat belt and keep your arms and legs inside the ride at all times!

I have a piece of art sitting in my office. It's the opening line from an Emily Dickinson poem. By all accounts, Emily Dickinson was a recluse. She lived in relative isolation, rarely leaving her bedroom. The friendships she did have were maintained by correspondence. Her physical world was incredibly small, but her spirit soared when she penned poetry. That's how she flew the kite. Three words she wrote sit enshrined in my office—*Dwell in Possibility*. I admit it—I'm an eternal optimist. How can I not be? I believe in the resurrection of Jesus Christ, and the same Spirit that raised Christ from the dead dwells in me. That means all bets are off and all things are possible!

On December 23, 2011, I was doing a chapel for the Minnesota Vikings when I met All-Pro running back Adrian Peterson. I remember that meeting for two reasons. One, Peterson's handshake is rather infamous because of the size and strength of his hands. His handshake is like a submission move! The other reason is that Peterson experienced a devastating knee injury the next day. He tore the ACL and MCL in his left knee. That kind of injury has ended many NFL careers, but Peterson would bounce back to win Comeback Player of the Year and Most Valuable Player honors the next season. He rushed for 2,097 yards, just 9 yards shy of the NFL single-season record. How did he do it? The short answer is lots of rehab! He turned the mountain into level ground by running hill sprints! Adrian Peterson may be a freak of nature, but his work ethic is nurture over nature. And his mental toughness is a testament to mind over matter. Instead of using his injury as an excuse, he used it as motivation.

Not long after the injury, Peterson's trainer, James Cooper, was asked how long he thought Peterson could play. Instead of answering the question directly, Cooper shared a personal story. A fitness fanatic himself, Cooper was competing at a USATF Masters meet for athletes thirty-five and up. During the hundred-meter dash, Cooper felt, in his words, "this old man right next to me." The old man was Bill Collins, who, at forty-six years of age, ran 10.58 seconds!

Cooper, who was much younger than Collins, was so blown away by Collins's performance that it flipped the script and wound the clock in one defining moment. "It taught me that forty is not the age to submit," said James Cooper. Then he upped the ante: "Fifty is not the age to submit." His point? Age is relative! And it's not just true of athletes like Adrian Peterson or Bill Collins.

If we take our cues from Caleb, eighty-five is not the age to submit either. "Here I am today, eighty-five years old!" said Caleb. "I am still as strong today as the day Moses sent me out."[9] I know this seems impossible, physiologically speaking. But I have no reason to doubt Caleb's self-assessment. I think Caleb could squat as much at eighty-five as he could at forty. The question, of course, is, How? There are lots of factors, but a fraction of our physical strength is a function of mental toughness. Positive thoughts can increase physical strength by 42 percent. If you don't believe me, check out *Win the Day*.[10] I shared a study about the power of suggestion that substantiates mind over matter. "Whether you believe you can do a thing or not," said Henry Ford, "you are right."[11]

Time takes a toll on all of us. Skin wrinkles. Metabolism slows. Muscles atrophy. The last time I checked, time is undefeated. But the toll that time takes varies from person to person, and mindset makes all the difference in the world. If you don't believe me, you haven't been to a high school reunion twenty years in the making!

Did you know that there is only one way for a doctor to ascertain your age? It can't be measured like heart rate or blood pressure. A doctor determines your age the same way everyone else does—by asking your birth date!

For the love of time, *own your age*. After all, you earned it. Own your age, but *don't let age own you*! As long as you're going after a God-sized vision, you're never past your prime. As long as you're pursuing a God-ordained passion, you never age out.

Here's the bottom line: *don't submit to age*. While we're on the subject, don't submit to addiction, temptation, or other people's expectations. Don't submit to fear, hate, or self-doubt. Don't submit to the labels placed on you by others or the lies of the Enemy. There's only one thing you should submit to, and that's the will of God. Submit to God, and all those things will submit to you. That's not name it, claim it. It's exercising your authority as a child of God.

I've said it before, but let me say it again: what you tolerate will eventually dominate. You don't have to tolerate anything less than God's good, pleasing, and perfect will.[12] Don't tolerate abuse. Don't tolerate a bad attitude. Don't tolerate a seed of bitterness. Don't tolerate entitlement. Don't tolerate ingratitude. Is there something you've submitted to that is not the will of God? At some point, *enough is enough.*

How do I make it a habit?

Change your number!

You don't have to submit to a doctor's diagnosis. Did you know that? I promise you, I love and respect doctors! Medicine has saved my life more than once. But autopsies reveal that doctors misdiagnose their patients 40 percent of the time. Despite tremendous advances in medical science, the misdiagnosis rate has hardly changed in the last hundred years.[13] And even if the diagnosis is right, you don't have to submit to it.

You don't have to submit to a bad review, bad grades, or bad luck.

You don't have to submit to false assumptions or false prophecies.

When Suzanne was in high school, her mom told her the number she should weigh. In Suzanne's words, "I never achieved that number." Even while running cross-country in college, she was eleven pounds over that number. Even after running eight marathons, Suzanne was twenty pounds over that number. Even after completing her three hundredth Peloton session, she was thirty pounds over that number.

The number Suzanne's mother gave her was her mother's own weight. The issue with that is this: her mother is less than five feet tall and very petite! Many decades later, Suzanne came to terms with a simple fact: "It wasn't my number to achieve. It was never my number." She stopped submitting to impossible expectations, and it set her free. "I exercise today not to beat myself up," she said, "or to achieve an impossible goal set by someone else." Why does she exercise? "I love strengthening the awesome muscles God gave me."

Remember 3M? Your habits have to be measurable, meaningful,

and maintainable. When you set a number goal, make sure it's *your* number! Going after someone else's goal is a recipe for disappointment.

Let me add one more thing to the mix. When I was training for my marathon, I had more than one time target. I had a whisper number that would have required my best run on my best day. I had another time that represented a stretch goal. I knew it would push my pace and give me the best chance of finishing the race. Set a stretch goal and then target 1 percent improvement every day. Whatever habit you're trying to make or break, it's go time!

Enough is enough!

Habit 5—Cut the Rope

Playing it safe is risky.

In 1853, America hosted its first World's Fair in New York City. The organizers built an exhibition hall to showcase the latest and greatest inventions. That is where a man named Elisha Otis stole the show with a unique sales pitch. The inventor of the elevator safety brake was having a hard time selling his idea to safety-first skeptics. What did he do? He gave the OG elevator pitch.

Standing on a platform high above the exhibition hall, Otis positioned an axman above the elevator shaft. Then he yelled, in a voice loud enough for everyone in the exhibition hall to hear, "Cut the rope!" The crowd held its collective breath as the elevator fell—a few feet. Otis announced, "All safe, gentlemen, all safe."[1]

The safety brake worked, as did the elevator pitch. When Elisha Otis cut the rope, only a few buildings in New York City were taller than five floors. Why? No one wanted to take the stairs! In 1854, Otis installed an elevator in a building on Broadway. By 1890, ten buildings were taller than ten stories. By 1900, sixty-five buildings were taller than twenty stories. By 1908, 538 buildings in New York City qualified as skyscrapers.

Fast-forward a hundred years.

According to the Otis Elevator Company, the equivalent of the world's population rides an Otis elevator or escalator every three days![2] Not only did Elisha Otis turn the world upside down, but his idea also influences the everyday lives of billions of people 150 years later. Of course, I still stand by the advice offered on day 2—*take the stairs!*

If you want to build a suspension bridge, fly a kite.

If you want to build a skyscraper, cut the rope.

Fly the kite—habit 4—is all about starting small. Over time, those small wins add up to winning streaks. Cut the rope—habit 5—is about cutting the ribbon. It's going public, which is a powerful commitment device. Like Elisha Otis, go big or go home! Cutting the rope is throwing down the gauntlet in a way that marks the moment.

In the winter of 2000, Reed Hastings and Marc Randolph got onto an elevator at the Renaissance Tower in Dallas, Texas. I'm not sure whether it was an Otis elevator, but they were about to cut the rope. After exiting the elevator, Reed whispered to Marc, "Blockbuster is a thousand times our size."[3]

They exited the elevator on the twenty-seventh floor, walked into a cavernous conference room, and made their elevator pitch. At the time, Blockbuster was a $6 billion giant that dominated the home entertainment business with almost nine thousand retail stores. Hastings and Randolph suggested that Blockbuster purchase their start-up company called Netflix, and Netflix would run their online video rental arm—blockbuster.com.

You know what Netflix has become. You've probably binge-watched a few of their original series. When Netflix made this pitch, they were a two-year-old start-up with an unorthodox business model. People could order their movies on Netflix's website and receive those DVDs through the mail. They had three hundred thousand subscribers at the time, but their net losses that year would total $57 million.

Blockbuster took a hard pass! Why? They didn't see the future. They were stuck in the past. Unwilling to change their business model, which is a lot like interrupting the pattern, they missed out on an opportunity to buy Netflix for $50 million. That price might seem steep for a start-up, but it represented three days of revenue for Blockbuster.

In 2000, only 1 percent of homes in the United States had a broadband internet connection. Hard to remember, right? Actually, if you ever had a dial-up internet connection, you'll never forget that sound, will you? By 2010, broadband connections had skyrocketed to 62 percent.[4] That changed the game, and the name of the game was video streaming.

You know the rest of the story. Blockbuster would file for bankruptcy, and Netflix is now worth an estimated $125 billion![5] Of course, it didn't have to be that way. Blockbuster played it safe, and playing it safe is risky.

In the world of economics, there are two kinds of cost—*actual cost* and *opportunity cost.* An actual cost is an expenditure that shows up on your balance sheet as a liability. An opportunity cost is a hidden cost. There is an old adage—*Count the cost*—and it's a two-sided coin. You have to count the actual cost like an accountant—do your homework, do your legwork, do your groundwork. You also have to count the opportunity cost, which is a very different calculus.

When Amazon stock went public in 1997, I thought long and hard about investing in it because I was buying books from Amazon every other day. It wasn't a huge amount of money, but I decided to invest elsewhere. Failing to invest in Amazon didn't cost me a dime in terms of actual cost. No harm, no foul. I recently calculated how much that investment would have been worth today, and it was a painful exercise. In terms of opportunity cost, I lost a small fortune!

It sounds contradictory, but the greatest risk is taking no risks. Not only does it maintain the status quo, but it's also a recipe for regret. More specifically, inaction regret. According to psychologist Tom Gilovich, there is a difference between short-term and long-term regret. In the short term, we tend to regret the mistakes we've made. In the long term? We regret the opportunities we've missed more than the mistakes we've made by a margin of 84 percent to 16 percent.[6] We all experience failure, and it can be incredibly painful. But at the end of our lives, our greatest regrets will be the things we would have, could have, and should have done.

It's time to cut the rope!

Day 21

Change the Routine

This is the LORD's battle, and he will give you to us!
—1 SAMUEL 17:47, NLT

In June 1976, a massive explosion leveled half a city block in Los Angeles and killed nine people. It was caused by an eighteen-inch miscalculation. While excavating the 9500 block of Venice Boulevard, someone cut into a petroleum pipeline, releasing thousands of gallons of pressurized gasoline. It wasn't the first or last accident of its kind, but the enormity of that tragedy led to the use of color-coded utility markings.

If you live in an urban area, you've seen sidewalks spray-painted with red and yellow and green markings. To be honest, those markings were a mystery to me most of my life. In fact, I found them a little irritating. You get a new sidewalk, and the next thing you know, it's got graffiti all over it. I now know why, and it makes common sense.

Those aboveground markings map the underground network of pipes, tubes, and wires that crisscross every city in America. In case you care, I'll decode the colors. Red represents electric. Yellow denotes gas. Orange is telecommunications. And green signifies sewer. Those color-coded utility markings help excavators steer clear of subsurface hazards.

Remember the Duke University study? Forty-five percent of our behavior is automatic. In other words, it's subconscious. Those habits are the wires that crisscross our cerebral cortex. You could even call them trip wires. If you're going to deconstruct and reconstruct your habit cycles, you have to identify those subsurface hazards.

When I was in graduate school, I was introduced to the work of an eccentric psychologist named Milton Erickson. His therapeutic methods are quite legendary and, I might add, nontraditional. His genius was identifying and interrupting patterns of behavior.

One day an overweight man came to Dr. Erickson for counseling. His self-assessment? "I'm a retired policeman—medically retired. I drink too much, I smoke too much, eat too much. . . . Can you help me?" Dr. Erickson asked him a series of questions. "Where do you buy your cigarettes?" The man said, "There is a handy little grocery store around the corner from where I live." Dr. Erickson asked, "How do you buy your cigarettes?" The man said, "Usually three cartons at a time." Dr. Erickson continued his questioning: "Where do you shop?" The policeman said, "At a handy little grocery around the corner." Dr. Erickson continued: "Where do you dine out?" The man said, "At a very nice restaurant, around the corner." And finally Dr. Erickson asked, "Now the liquor?" The man said, "There's a handy little liquor store around the corner."

Do you know why bad habits are hard to break? They're too convenient. What did Dr. Erickson do? He interrupted the pattern by changing the man's routine. "You are an ex-policeman and you want to correct your blood pressure and your obesity, emphysema, and you buy your cigarettes three cartons at a time," said Dr. Erickson. "Now your therapy isn't going to require very much." His prescription?

You can do all the smoking you want. Buy your cigarettes one package at a time by walking to the other side of town to get the package. As for doing your own cooking, well, you haven't much to do so shop three times a day. Buy only enough for one meal but no left-overs. As for dining out, there are a lot of good restaurants a mile or two away . . . that'll give you a chance to walk. As for your drinking . . . I see no objection to your drink-

ing. There are some excellent bars a mile away. Get your first drink in one bar, your second drink in a bar a mile away. And you'll be in excellent shape before very long.[1]

That sounds almost like reverse psychology, doesn't it? I'm not sure I would put the stamp of approval on harmful habits, but the prescription worked. How? By interrupting the pattern. If you want to break a bad habit, make it less convenient. Once again, *harder is better!*

You have to turn your habits inside out and upside down. You have to reverse engineer them. Sometimes the solution is as simple as changing the sequence. Other times it requires interrupting the pattern by changing tactics altogether.

Few phrases are more famous than *David versus Goliath.* It's the quintessential mismatch, the classic underdog story. The irony is that we read this story the wrong way. We think David was the one at a disadvantage. If they'd been engaging in hand-to-hand combat, yes! There is no way David could have defeated Goliath in a cage match. But David's perceived disadvantage, in terms of size and experience, turned out to be his greatest advantage.

Goliath was infantry. All he had was a ground game. David was artillery. He used the skill set he had cultivated as a shepherd. Remember Kenny Sailors and his patented jump shot? David took a jump shot with his slingshot, and Goliath didn't even see it coming!

In his book *David and Goliath,* Malcolm Gladwell cited a study by Eitan Hirsch, a ballistics expert with the Israel Defense Forces. According to Hirsch, an average-size stone hurled by an expert slinger could travel the length of a football field in three seconds flat. At that velocity, it's got the same stopping power as a .45-caliber handgun.[2] Goliath's spear may have been the size of a weaver's beam, but he still just brought a really big knife to a gunfight.

David was not the underdog! Goliath was a sitting duck! Goliath's strength proved to be his weakness, and David's weakness proved to be his strength. Remember the giant Blockbuster? They didn't adapt to evolving technology, and it cost them their company. An upstart company called Netflix used a slingshot called streaming to interrupt the pattern and deliver movies wirelessly!

David's victory was not improbable; it was inevitable. Sure, David looked a little foolish going to war with a slingshot. But there is no way artillery loses to infantry! Of course, you have to cut the rope. How? At some point, *enough is enough*. You need to pick up a few rocks from the brook Elah and put them in your pouch.

Israel had been held captive by Goliath's taunting long enough. The same goes for the bad habits that taunt us. If you measure them against your ability, you come out on the short end of the stick. If you measure them against God, it's no contest. To the Infinite, all finites are equal. There is no big or small, easy or difficult, possible or impossible.

How big is your God? Is He bigger than your biggest problem, your worst mistake, your greatest challenge? "How much happier you would be, how much more of you there would be," said G. K. Chesterton, "if the hammer of a higher God could smash your small cosmos."[3]

I know, giants are big. I know, giants are scary. But the bigger they are, the harder they fall. "You come against me with sword and spear and javelin," said David. Can't you see him wagging his finger like Dikembe Mutombo? Or wiggling his big toe like Chris Norton? "But I come against you in the name of the LORD Almighty, the God of armies of Israel, whom you have defied."[4]

Sometimes the solution is *more*, but more of the same doesn't solve every problem. Instead of trying harder, you need to try different. Remember habit 3, eat the frog? If you want God to do the super, you've got to do the natural. Let me push that envelope and cut that rope. *If you want God to do something new, you can't keep doing the same old thing.*

In the Sermon on the Mount, Jesus interrupted the pattern by reconditioning reflexes. When someone curses you, what is your natural reaction? You curse back! Of course, all that does is per-petuate the problem. It escalates the situation by creating a vicious cycle. In a dog-eat-dog world, Jesus issued a counterintuitive com-mand: "Bless those who curse you."[5] That is easier said than done, but there is no defense against it. Try it.

Remember day 19? We shift the atmosphere by operating in the opposite spirit. We stop vicious cycles by exercising grace. We start virtuous cycles by exercising faith, hope, and love. Either way, it provokes questions for which the gospel is the answer.

One key to making habits is establishing routines. But once the routine becomes routine, you have to change it. It's called the law of requisite variety. If you always work out the same way, eventually that workout loses effectiveness because your body adapts to the routine. You have to confuse your muscles by interrupting the pat-tern. The same is true spiritually, relationally, emotionally, and in-tellectually. The good news? If you tweak your routines, a 1 percent change can make a 99 percent difference!

The next time someone insults you, return that volley with a compliment. Don't be surprised if you see a confused look on the person's face. It will throw him for a loop, a habit loop. It may not stop the bad behavior, but it will stop him in his tracks.

If you fight fire with fire, all it does is escalate the situation. No one wins a shouting match. No one wins the blame game. When God wants us to change, do you know what He does? He doesn't issue threats. He shows us kindness.[6] If that doesn't work? He shows us more kindness! It's a counterintuitive tactic, but it's awfully effec-tive. It has the potential to break a vicious cycle and start a virtuous cycle.

In the eighth century BC, the Israelites and the Arameans were like the Hatfields and the McCoys. They were constantly at war until the prophet Elisha interrupted the habit cycle. How? He lured the Aramean army into Israel's capital city, and he could have killed them. Of course, that would have escalated the conflict to another level. What did he do? He threw them a surprise party! With full stomachs and confused minds, Elisha sent them home. The result? "Aram stopped raiding Israel's territory."[7]

Was it a risky strategy? Absolutely! But that's how you break the cycle, break the habit. Who do you need to throw a party for? What are you waiting for? In the words of Pink's 2001 classic hit, "Get the party started."

One of the best ways to win the day is by making someone's day! You can interrupt the pattern with a single smile. You can shift the atmosphere with a single compliment. One act of kindness can break the cycle and have a domino effect that changes generations. Let me connect the dots, *A-B-C-D* style.

Long before David challenged Goliath to a duel, his great-great-grandmother cut the rope with an act of kindness. What was it? She saved the lives of some Jewish spies, with one request: that her family would be shown mercy when Israel conquered Jericho.[8] That one act of kindness didn't just save her life; it set the table for future generations. She married Salmon and had a son named Boaz, who had a son named Obed, who had a son named Jesse, who had a son named David.[9] Make it your mission to make someone's day. It could change the course of history!

How do you make it a habit?

Try different.

In 1894, the *Times* of London ran a feature article about an impending crisis that threatened civilization itself. In a word, *manure*. The population of London had topped one million people, and more people meant more horses—fifty thousand to be exact. Do the math. The average horse poops thirty pounds per day. That adds up to 1.5 million pounds of poop per day! The *Times* estimated that London would be buried under nine feet of manure in fifty years.[10] London, we have a problem! And New York City was even worse.

There were vacant lots with manure piled sixty feet high. Experts forecast that the Big Apple would be up to its third-story windows in manure by the year 1930.

In 1898, urban planners met in London to try to solve the problem. The first conference was scheduled to last ten days. The organizers called it quits after three days with no solution in sight. Why? They were trying to solve today's problems with yesterday's solutions. They were thinking incremental instead of dreaming exponential.

Meanwhile, a man named Henry Ford was thinking different. The best way to reduce horse emissions? A horseless carriage, of course. The solutions to our biggest problems are very rarely less or more of the same. You have to break the rules. You have to change the game. You have to jump the curve.

If you're struggling with making or breaking a habit, maybe it's time to try different. After all, as I've said before, your system is perfectly designed for the results you're getting. Try reverse engineering your routines and then reconstructing them a little differently. How? Add a prompt. It doesn't have to be complicated. It can be a deep breath to reset yourself. It can be a stretching routine that allows you to warm up or cool down. It can be a simple thought or prayer that you put on repeat. Before I speak, I pray this prayer: *Lord, help me help people.* It shifts my focus from self-consciousness to others-consciousness—*There you are!*

Change the routine!

Day 22

Pick a Fight

Villagers in Israel would not fight;
they held back until I, Deborah, arose.
—JUDGES 5:7

On November 5, 1872, Susan B. Anthony cast a ballot in the presidential election in her hometown of Rochester, New York. She was arrested, indicted, tried, and convicted of voting illegally. At her two-day trial in June 1873, she was assessed a one-hundred-dollar fine. "I shall never pay a dollar of your unjust penalty," said Anthony.[1] And she never did.

Susan B. Anthony devoted fifty years of her life to a cause that was once considered a crime—a woman's right to vote. She didn't live to see the Nineteenth Amendment passed, but her courage was a catalyst in that cause. A century later, the image of the woman who refused to pay that one-hundred-dollar fine was emblazoned on the one-dollar coin—the Susan B. Anthony dollar.

On the occasion of her eighty-sixth birthday, Anthony gave a speech at Church of Our Fathers in Washington, DC. She deflected praise and gave credit to all those who had committed their lives to the cause of women's suffrage. These would prove to be her final public words: "With such women consecrating their lives, failure is impossible!"[2]

I love that mindset—*failure is impossible.* Remember our thesis? *Almost anyone can accomplish almost anything if they work at it long enough, hard enough, and smart enough.* It might not happen in your lifetime, but legacy is the things that outlive you. It's doing things that will make a difference a hundred years from now. It's growing fruit on other people's trees!

Susan B. Anthony never lost faith in the end of the story, but every movement starts with a single step of faith. Remember Nahshon? He had to wade into the water up to his nostrils. He wasn't just kissing the wave; he was cutting the rope. How? With a grand gesture! For Susan B. Anthony, it was casting a vote. For Rosa Parks, it was refusing to give up her seat on the bus. For Katherine Johnson, the human computer who inspired *Hidden Figures* and helped calculate the flight path for Apollo 11, it was asking for a seat at the table reserved for men.

All those women remind me of a woman named Deborah who rose to power in the thirteenth century BC. A vicious cycle repeated itself in the days of the judges. The people would do what was right in their own eyes. Then God would raise up judges, twelve of them, to help Israel find their way back to God. The fourth judge was a woman named Deborah who led the nation for sixty years. She wasn't just a judge; she was a poet and a prophet. According to Jewish tradition, she was one of seven prophetesses. Last but certainly not least, Deborah was a mom.

The nation of Israel was experiencing a financial recession, as well as military oppression. What were they doing? Cowering in fear! "Villagers in Israel would not fight." Not only had they lost their way, but they had also lost their will to fight. It wasn't a pretty picture, but there is a plot twist that deserves a drumroll: "They held back until I, Deborah, arose."[3]

There is a timeless truism: *The only thing necessary for the triumph of evil is for good men to do nothing.* Of course, I would add "good women" to the equation! All it takes is for one person to take a stand. All it takes is for one person to wade into the water. All it takes is for one person to cast a vote.

If you reverse engineer watershed moments in history, there is always a recognizable tipping point. It's the point of no return—the point at which a single domino starts a chain reaction. Malcolm

Gladwell said it this way: "The tipping point is that magic moment when an idea, trend, or social behavior crosses a threshold, tips, and spreads like wildfire."[4]

I love the way Deborah went third person: "Deborah arose as a mother for Israel."[5] In the words of Martin Lawrence, "You go, girl." This was a day when decades happened. At some point, *enough is enough.* You have to go third person. What does that mean? It's approaching your problems with a third-party perspective. It's seeing your life as a laboratory. It's seeing yourself as a scientist and your habits as an experiment.

Leonardo da Vinci journaled until the day he died, and I mean that literally. It's how he connected the dots. While on his deathbed, Leonardo described his symptoms in great detail.[6] Why? For posterity! A third-person approach to habit formation means putting yourself under the microscope. Or in the case of Evan O'Neill Kane, putting yourself on the operating table.

Dr. Kane performed more than four thousand surgeries during his distinguished career as chief surgeon at Kane Summit Hospital, but his greatest contribution to medicine was pioneering the use of local anesthesia. Dr. Kane believed that general anesthesia was an unnecessary risk for patients with heart conditions and allergic reactions, so he set out to prove his point by performing major surgery using nothing more than a local anesthesia. On February 15, 1921, his patient was prepped for surgery and wheeled into the operating room. After local anesthesia was administered, Dr. Kane cut the patient open, clamped the blood vessels, removed the patient's appendix, and stitched the wound. Two days after surgery, the patient was released from the hospital. It was pretty easy for Dr. Kane to monitor the patient's recovery since the patient was none other than Dr. Kane himself, and his self-surgery changed standard operating-room procedure.

Let me double back to Deborah.

Israel was held captive by the Canaanite king, Jabin, and his general, Sisera. According to rabbinic tradition, Sisera's voice was so powerful that it could shake walls and make wild animals stop in their tracks![7] Deborah was unshaken. She led the Israelites into battle like Joan of Arc and helped them win their independence.

I love what happened next. I'm not sure whether it was a midlife crisis or newfound passion but Deborah launched her musical career with a song that topped the ancient charts. We don't have the chords, but we do have the lyrics. There is a footnote at the end of that song: "Then there was peace in the land for forty years."[8]

What made that peace possible? A woman arose! Deborah broke the glass ceiling in more ways than one. She proves our thesis: *almost anyone can accomplish almost anything if they work at it long enough, hard enough, and smart enough.* Of course, you'll have to cut the rope like Deborah did. How? She declared war! I don't mean that literally. But figuratively speaking, you need to come out of your corner fighting for your good habits. It's the only way. At some point, you need to declare war on your bad habits.

In *Rocky III,* Rocky Balboa gets a rematch with Clubber Lang after getting knocked out in their first fight. A few rounds into the rematch, Rocky is getting clobbered by Clubber once again. That's when he starts taunting Clubber, like David trash-talking Goliath. "You ain't so bad," says Rocky. "You ain't so bad." After Rocky takes a few too many punches, Apollo Creed says, "He's getting killed." But Paulie knows better! "He's not getting killed; he's getting mad!"[9]

A few years ago, I was part of a panel at the National Prayer Breakfast with Bob Goff. Bob said something that has become a mantra of mine: "Pick a fight." It's getting into good trouble, as the late John Lewis would say. Pick a fight with poverty. Pick a fight with injustice. Pick a fight for any kingdom cause you care about. If you're willing to fight, you have a fighting chance. The same goes for making and breaking habits. Don't take defeat sitting down! Pick a fight with your shadow side.

When we self-identify as the hands and feet of Christ, do we think about the implications? Do you remember what happened to the hands and feet of Jesus? They were nailed to a cross with nine-inch nails. What makes us think we're exempt from pain and suffer-ing? But when you suffer for righteousness' sake, the gain is worth the pain!

One of the best ways to win the day is to make someone's day. In the same vein, one of the best ways to solve your problems is to help someone else reverse engineer theirs. Reflecting on his work as a psychiatrist, Carl Jung discovered a fascinating truth about seem-ingly insurmountable problems. They can't be solved. They can only be outgrown.[10] We have to discover something more important than the problem. When we do, the problem eventually loses its power and goes away.

Just as happiness is an indirect by-product of blessing others, habit formation is not a self-centered endeavor. Some problems are solved only by helping others! Not only does it put your problems in perspective, but your problems also lose power.

How do you make it a habit?

Fight one more round!

On September 7, 1892, a boxer named Gentleman Jim Corbett got into the ring with arguably the greatest boxer of all time, John L. Sullivan. Sullivan was the last heavyweight champion of bare-knuckle boxing and the first heavyweight champion of gloved box-ing. In fifty fights, Sullivan was undefeated. The only fight he would ever lose was this one!

Corbett knocked Sullivan out in the twenty-first round, becom-ing the heavyweight champion of the world. But in my nonprofes-sional opinion, that wasn't his most impressive fight. The year before, Corbett had sparred with his crosstown rival, Peter "Black Prince" Jackson. Their fight went sixty-one rounds and—get this—ended in a draw! For the record, professional bouts are now limited to a maximum of twelve rounds.

How do you come out of the corner sixty-one times?

Gentleman Jim Corbett lived by a motto: "Fight one more round."

When your arms are so tired that you can hardly lift your hands to come on guard, fight one more round. When your nose is bleeding and your eyes are black and you are so tired that you wish your opponent would crack you one on the jaw and put you to sleep, fight one more round . . . the man who fights one more round is never whipped.[11]

In his first letter to the Corinthians, the apostle Paul did a little bare-knuckle boxing: "I do not fight like a boxer beating the air. No, I strike a blow to my body."[12] Remember Teddy Roosevelt? *Make your body!* This sounds an awful lot like that, doesn't it? Paul was preaching the doctrine of the strenuous life. In his second letter to Timothy, he said, "I have fought the good fight."[13] In his letter to the Ephesians, it sounds like he had gone sixty-one rounds: "Put on the full armor of God, so that when the day of evil comes, you may be able to stand your ground, and after you have done everything, to stand."[14]

I have no idea whether the apostle Paul was a flyweight, feather-weight, or heavyweight. But he certainly carried his weight, didn't he? He keeps coming off the ropes, out of the corner! How are you doing with the habit you're trying to make or break? I told you from the get-go, it won't be easy. Why? You're picking a fight.

Can I challenge you to fight one more round?

Can I challenge you to keep coming out of the corner?

Pick a fight!

Day 23

Do It Now

Perhaps the LORD will act in our behalf.
—1 SAMUEL 14:6

In the summer of 1957, twelve-year-old Ed Catmull was on a cross-country trip with his family, driving on a very crooked canyon road with no guardrails. A car driving in the opposite direction zigged into their lane, and Catmull's dad zagged in the opposite direction. Their car came two inches from driving off that cliff.

That's how close we came to never seeing *Cars, The Incredibles,* or *Up.* Why? Ed Catmull is the cofounder of Pixar Animation Studios. No Catmull means no *Toy Story, Toy Story 2, Toy Story 3,* or *Toy Story 4.* Hard to imagine, isn't it? Looking back on that close call, he made this observation: "Two more inches—no Pixar."[1]

It's two-inch events that change the trajectory of our lives, isn't it? Two-inch event, two-inch domino—same difference. Life turns on a dime! It's not just Pixar's films that would have gone missing. Catmull observes, with great satisfaction, how many Pixar employees have met and married and had what he calls Pixar kids. "All of those Pixar couples . . . have no inkling of the two inches that could have kept them from meeting or their children from being conceived."[2]

Life is a game of inches! It's full of close calls and course corrections. In my experience, life's detours have a way of rerouting us. So do disappointments. In fact, a disappointment can turn into a divine appointment.

Edgar Bergen is considered the greatest ventriloquist to ever throw his voice. He's also the father of award-winning actress Candice Bergen. How did he get interested in ventriloquism? As a boy, Bergen ordered a book on photography but received a book on ventriloquism instead. Naturally, he was disappointed. But it was that mix-up that led to his life calling!

"I find it endlessly fascinating that a reserved man, a man who had difficulty expressing his feelings, fell into the profession of a ventriloquist on radio," said Candice Bergen. "And that the person he created was this devil-may-care, no-holds-barred, take-no-prisoners dummy."[3] The dummy, by the way, was a wooden puppet named Charlie McCarthy.

When I was a sophomore in high school, I gave a speech that doubled as my first sermon. I just didn't know it at the time. My mom gave a copy of that speech to my grandmother, who gave it to her Bible study teacher, who asked a question: "Has Mark ever thought about ministry?" That question got relayed to my mother, then to me. Honestly, I had never thought about it. Until that moment, that is! It was an inception moment, an inciting incident. An innocent question planted a seed in my spirit, three levels down.

When it comes to making and breaking habit cycles, we have to start by identifying the prompt. That includes the prompting of the Holy Spirit. If you don't obey His prompting this time, you'll be less likely to obey next time. Why? Disobedience hardens our hearts and our hearing.

Delayed obedience is disobedience! My advice? *Do it now!* Remember the old adage? *Don't put off until tomorrow what you can do today!* The longer you wait, the harder it will get.

We're so good at delay tactics, aren't we? If you want to write a book, you have to give yourself a deadline. Then you have to reverse engineer how many words you need to write every day, based on your end date. I promise you, the hardest step is the first step. Why? You have to overcome inertia.

During the tenth century BC, the Israelites were engaged in a conflict with their archenemies, the Philistines. Shocking, I know!

The feud never seemed to end, but there were a few moments of peace in that plotline. The catalysts for those moments of tranquility were often acts of courage. Let me set the scene:

> Saul was staying on the outskirts of Gibeah under a pomegranate tree in Migron. With him were about six hundred men.[4]

I know this seems rather unremarkable, and that's the point. Instead of picking a fight, like we talked about yesterday, the king of Israel was snacking on seeds in the shade of a pomegranate tree. This single snapshot is a pretty good indication of his character, isn't it? He should have been the one to challenge Goliath, but he deferred to David. He should have been on the front line fighting the Philistines, but he was on the sideline.

Now let me flip the script. Saul's son Jonathan was as different from his dad as different can be. It's hard to believe he came from the same gene pool. The pomegranate fell pretty far from the tree! Saul played defense, while Jonathan played offense. Saul played not to lose, while Jonathan played to win. Saul let fear dictate his decisions, while Jonathan operated by faith. Jonathan's mindset is revealed by one of my favorite verses:

> Perhaps the LORD will act in our behalf.[5]

Most people operate out of the opposite mindset: perhaps the Lord *won't* act on my behalf. They play it safe because they let fear dictate their decisions. More specifically, they fear failure. They're content to live under a pomegranate tree on the outskirts of Gibeah! Can I offer an exhortation? *Quit living as if the purpose of life is to arrive safely at death!*

Jonathan had a bias for action, which is part and parcel of cutting the rope. It's refusing to sit still or stand down. Why? There is a sin of silence. It's not saying what needs to be said. There is a sin of toleration. It's not doing what needs to be done. But Jonathan climbed a cliff and proactively picked a fight with the Philistines.

Few people were better at picking a fight than Dr. Martin Luther King Jr. Like Jonathan, he was driven by a holy urgency. "We are now faced with the fact, my friends, that tomorrow is today," said Dr. King. "We are confronted with the fierce urgency of now."[6] There is a difference between anxious urgency and the urgency of conviction. Remember what Jesus said? "Don't you have a saying, 'It's still four months until harvest'? I tell you, open your eyes and look at the fields! They are ripe for harvest."[7] Once again, delayed obedience is disobedience!

If you wait until you're ready, you'll be waiting until the day you die! At some point, you have to go, set, ready! Remember Nahshon, the patron saint of plodders? You have to take that first step of faith. When? Now! Quit trying to win the lottery, and start winning the day! Don't wait for something to happen. Make something happen.

According to Parkinson's Law, the amount of time it takes to complete a task depends on how much time is allotted. In other words, it'll take two months if you're given two months. It'll take two weeks if you're given two weeks! The term was coined by Cyril Northcote Parkinson in an article for *The Economist* in 1955, and it's as relevant today as it ever was![8]

There is a sin of presumption—it's getting ahead of God. There is also a sin of procrastination—it's getting behind God. If you struggle with procrastination, it's hard to tie off the umbilical cord on anything. The same is true of perfectionism. Why? There is always room for improvement. At some point, you need to just climb the cliff like Jonathan. If I hadn't leveraged my thirty-fifth birthday as a writing deadline, I would still be working on my first book. If I hadn't cast the vision for multiple campuses, we'd still be daydreaming.

What idea do you need to initiate?

What are you waiting for?

How do I make it a habit?

Give yourself a start date!

The challenge on day 18 was *start small.* Let me time-stamp that challenge: *start now!* If you're going to make or break a habit, you have to give yourself a start date and a deadline. Then you have to do the math. How? Reverse engineer the number of pounds you want to lose, the number of pages you want to write, or the number of miles you want to run! You can't just wish upon a star. You have to start the clock, like in a game of speed chess.

Remember the concept of commitment devices? We may not think of it this way, but one of the most common commitment devices is called an alarm clock. What time do you set your alarm clock for? And more importantly, why? If we're being honest, lots of people get up at the last second possible. That's no way to attack the day. Don't just get up in time to get dressed and get out the door. Get up to go after a goal. When? That's up to you, but why not start now by making a predecision about tomorrow morning?

Victor Hugo ranks as one of history's bestselling authors. He wrote nineteen novels, including *Les Misérables,* while living in exile on the isle of Guernsey. That sounds prolific, but Hugo had a natural proclivity toward procrastination. How did he overcome that tendency? You guessed it—a grand gesture. You could even call it a master class in commitment devices!

In the summer of 1830, when Hugo should have been writing, he became consumed with everything but writing. His publisher gave him a deadline of February 1, 1831. With less than six months to write his promised novel, Hugo knew it would take a minor miracle. What did he do? He collected all his clothes and had them locked away in a large chest. With nothing left to wear but a large shawl, he remained in his study for days on end. During the fall and winter months, he wrote fast and furious.

On January 14, 1831, Victor Hugo beat his deadline and completed *The Hunchback of Notre Dame*. That 940-page novel has been adapted dozens of times by Broadway and by Hollywood. It has sold tens of millions of copies. When the Notre-Dame Cathedral caught fire in 2017, Hugo's book became a number one bestseller all over again.

You make only a few major decisions. You spend the rest of your life managing those decisions. I'm not recommending a grand gesture every other day. They are few and far between, but they are the two-inch dominoes that determine our destiny. They are the days when decades happen. Sometimes it's breaking a bad habit, cold turkey. Enough is enough! Like Dwight D. Eisenhower on day 15, you give yourself an order. Sometimes it's making a good habit. Either way, you interrupt the pattern with grand gestures.

If you want to compete in a triathlon, register. The grand gesture is the admission fee. Now you've got skin in the game! And that goes for any goal. If you want to write a book, put together the proposal. Once you've invested blood, sweat, and tears, it's harder to quit on yourself.

Do it now!

Habit 6—Wind the Clock

Time is measured in minutes;
life is measured in moments.

When Dr. Tony Campolo was a professor at the University of Pennsylvania, he turned an ordinary lecture into an unforgettable lesson. He asked a student sitting on the front row, "Young man, how long have you lived?" The unsuspecting student answered his age. "No, no, no," said Dr. Campolo. "That's how long your heart has been pumping blood. That's not how long you have lived."

That's when Dr. Campolo told the class a story about one of the most memorable moments of his life. In 1944, his fourth-grade class took a field trip to the top of the Empire State Building—the tallest building in the world at the time. When he got off the elevator and stepped out onto the observation deck overlooking New York City, time stood still. "If I live a million years," said Dr. Campolo, "that moment will still be part of my consciousness, because I was fully alive when I lived it."

Dr. Campolo turned back to the student and said, "Now, let me ask you the question again. How long have you lived?"

"When you say it that way," the student said, "maybe an hour; maybe a minute; maybe two minutes."[1]

Let me ask you two questions.

One, how old are you?

Two, how long have you lived?

It's easy calculating age. Quantifying life is much more difficult. Why? Because time is measured in minutes, while life is measured in moments. When was the last time that time stood still? Some of those moments are as unplanned as a joke that makes your beverage shoot out your nose! Others can be as planned as our predecisions. Either way, we've got to recognize those moments and steward them. How? By making the most of them.

Habit formation happens in real time, but it's heavily influenced by the past and the future. We've been conditioned by past-tense cues. We're driven by future-tense rewards. Winding the clock is remembering the past and remembering the future. It's managing the minutes and the moments.

Nagin Cox is a NASA engineer who lives on Earth, but she works on Mars time. Cox served as the deputy team chief of the engineering team that has landed three land rovers on Mars. The most recent rover was named *Perseverance* by seventh grader Alexander Mather. That's precisely what it takes to innovate the technology necessary to fly a rover 140 million miles to Mars!

A Mars day is called a sol, and it's almost forty minutes longer than an Earth day. So Cox and her team have to adjust their body clocks forty minutes every day. How? They start work forty minutes later every day. Eventually the middle of a Mars day is the middle of an Earth night. Confused? That's why Cox and her team wear Mars watches! The weights have been mechanically adjusted to run slower. Those Mars watches keep them on Mars time.[2]

In a sense, we all wear two watches. The first is a *chronos* watch, and it's the way we manage minutes. In the words of a popular Broadway musical, "Five hundred twenty-five thousand six hundred minutes."[3] You can hear it in your head, can't you? All of us are allotted the same amount of time every day—1,440 minutes. Time is the great equalizer.

The other watch is a *kairos* watch, and it's the way we get off the clock. It helps us recognize moments when we need to stop and smell the roses. One way to do that is by keeping the Sabbath. Of course, that's easier said than done! When it comes to *kairos,* you don't *find time;* you *make time.* You have to be intentional about establishing priorities and boundaries. I won't serve on more than three boards simultaneously. Why? I know my tendency to spread myself too thin. If I try to be all things to all people, I won't be any good to anybody! And that includes myself.

If you want every day to count, you have to count the days! The psalmist said, "Teach us to number our days."[4] How do we do that? You can do it literally, and I'll unpack that on day 25. But I will offer one idea at the outset. My friend Reggie Joiner is the founder of a wonderful organization called Orange. They empower parents and kids to live their best lives. How? By making every day count. Reggie suggests using a jar filled with marbles to make the point. When your child is born, fill a jar with 936 marbles. Then remove a marble every week, and that's how many weeks are left until your child turns eighteen.

It's a visual reminder that the clock is ticking. Our kids aren't under our roofs forever. And let's be honest—that's a good thing! But you've got to make every day count. The jar of marbles is a visual reminder that we're playing for keeps. Somehow find a creative way to make every day count.

If you don't control your calendar, your calendar will control you. When was the last time you did an audit of your time? If time is money, we owe it to ourselves to do an audit. In the very first sermon I preached at National Community Church, I cited a sociological study of fifty people over the age of ninety-five that involved one question: "If you had to live your life over again, what would you do differently?" Three answers emerged as a consensus.

One, they'd *risk more.*

Two, they'd *reflect more.*

Three, they'd *do more things that would live on after they die.*

It's time to wind the clock!

Day 24

Tip the Cap

Tie them as symbols on your hands.
—DEUTERONOMY 6:8

In 1931, America was in the depths of the Great Depression. A young entrepreneur named Conrad Hilton wasn't just staring foreclosure in the face. He was borrowing money from bellhops to make ends meet. People weren't traveling, and his hotel chain was suffering. That's when Hilton came across a photograph of the Waldorf Astoria in New York City.

The icon of luxury, the forty-seven-story Waldorf Astoria ranked as the world's largest and tallest hotel from 1931 until 1963. It had six kitchens, two hundred chefs, five hundred waiters, and 2,200 rooms. It even had its own private hospital and railroad station.

After clipping the photograph of the Waldorf Astoria, Hilton placed it under the glass top of his desk so it stared him in the face. It stared him in the face every day! I'm not sure who insured his hotels, but that photograph ensured that he never lost sight of his God-sized goal.

Remember the habit cycle? It starts with a prompt—a trigger that flips a switch in your brain so it goes into automatic mode. The second step is a pattern—physical, mental, emotional, spiritual, or relational. The third step is the prize. The bigger the prize, the more sacrifices you're willing to make and the more risks you're willing to take.

For Conrad Hilton, the Waldorf Astoria was the grand prize. Not only did he keep a photograph front and center, but he also tipped his cap every time he walked by or drove by. It was his way of remembering the future and reminding himself of the ultimate goal. In October 1949, having tipped his cap hundreds of times, the reward became reality when he purchased 249,024 shares of the Waldorf Corporation. Hilton finally crowned his collection of hotels with the Queen, as he called her.[1]

Remember John Heywood, the English playwright? He is famous for saying, "Rome wasn't built in a day."[2] That's one of many axioms that have stood the test of time. He also coined this one: *Out of sight, out of mind.*[3] And it's key when it comes to habit formation. The technical term is *object permanence,* and it's part of Piaget's theory of human development.

Object permanence is understanding that things still exist even though they can't be seen. Young children don't have this fully formed cognitive capacity until they are about eight months old, which is why peekaboo is so much fun! Children eventually develop object permanence, but we never outgrow the tendency to forget that which isn't front and center. That's why we need to clip the photo and tip the cap!

While we're on the subject, *a picture is worth a thousand words.* Actually, that math is a little off. The brain is able to process print on a page at a rate of fifty bits per second.[4] The brain's ability to process pictures goes way beyond that. The brain can recognize an image in as little as 13 milliseconds.[5] And it can process pictures at a much higher volume. Of course, that depends on size. According to one estimate, a wallet-size photo is worth 324,000 words while an 8" x 10" is worth 4.3 million.[6] Either way, 1,000 words is a gross understatement!

If you walked into SpaceX headquarters, you'd see two posters of Mars. One shows a cold, barren planet. The other looks a lot like Earth. That second poster represents Elon Musk's life purpose—colonizing Mars. "I'd like to die on Mars," said Musk, "just not on impact."[7] If that's not shooting for the moon, I'm not sure what is!

That poster is Elon Musk's way of tipping his cap to Mars. It's his jar of marbles.

When Jim Carrey was a struggling actor, he had a routine that he repeated many nights. Not unlike Conrad Hilton tipping his cap, Jim Carrey would drive to the top of Mulholland Drive and look out over the city of Los Angeles. "Everybody wants to work with me," he'd say to himself. "I'm a really good actor. I have all kinds of great movie offers." It was Carrey's way of flipping the script and winding the clock. "I'd just repeat those things over and over, literally convincing myself that I had a couple movies lined up. I'd drive down the hill, ready to take on the world."

Jim Carrey did one more thing, an epic example of imagining the prize. He wrote himself a check for $10 million. He scribbled "for services rendered" on the memo line, and he postdated that check five years into the future! Carrey kept that check in his wallet for many years. He would eventually get his $10 million payday, plus a few hundred million! He has starred in more than forty films, which have grossed more than $2.5 billion at the box office.[8] His net worth is estimated to be $180 million.[9]

At this juncture, let me offer a little reminder. "What will it profit a man," Jesus said, "if he gains the whole world, yet forfeits his soul?"[10] A $10 million payday isn't worth one red cent if you lose your soul in the process! Having said that, Aristotle said this: "The soul never thinks without an image."[11]

Remember habit 1, flip the script? If you want to change your life, change your story. While you're at it, change the picture you're painting! Winding the clock is all about imagining the prize, and pictures are a powerful way of doing that.

A single snapshot has the power to jog your memory and release a flash flood of emotions. It can also exercise your imagination by painting a picture of your preferred future. Either way, you've got to find a way to stay focused on your goals.

When it comes to trust, David Horsager wrote the books. He is author of *The Trust Edge* and *Trusted Leader*. In the course of a recent conversation, he shared the backstory behind him losing fifty-two pounds in five months. Why fifty-two pounds? He wanted to get back to his high school weight, but there is more to it than that.

Remember 3M? Our habits have to be measurable, meaningful, and maintainable. Getting back to his high school weight made his goal meaningful, but the real inspiration was his parents. When his mom and dad celebrated their fiftieth wedding anniversary, they fit into the same clothes they had worn on their wedding day! His mom still weighed 117 pounds, and his dad still weighed 150 pounds. Horsager took a prompt from his parents, and it helped him lose fifty-two pounds by projecting himself into the future.

One way to make or break a habit is by taking cues from others. Do you know why I get up early in the morning? I credit my father-in-law, Bob Schmidgall. He had an early-morning prayer habit that I wanted to emulate. I was also inspired by one paragraph in a biography about D. L. Moody. Moody felt a twinge of guilt if he heard the blacksmiths hammering before he was up studying the Bible.[12] My goal? On workdays, I try to get up before the sun is up!

Whose habits are you hacking? As a Christ follower, I pattern my life after the person of Jesus Christ. I hack His habits to change mine. I take my cues from His life, death, and resurrection. When I have a hard time forgiving people, I think of what Jesus said about those who nailed Him to the cross: "Father, forgive them, for they know not what they do."[13]

If Jesus can forgive those who nailed Him to the cross, I can forgive those who have wronged me or said wrong things about me. The way you tip the cap to Jesus is by being unoffendable! You forgive seventy times seven. You see other people for who they really are—the image of almighty God—and treat them accordingly.

One way we wind the clock is by redeeming the time. Remember Saint Benedict and his rule of life? Along with the seventy-three rules he created, Saint Benedict divided the day into eight prayer periods called the daily office. You don't need to check into a monastery to put this idea into practice, and it doesn't have to be eight. My recommendation? Establish a prayer routine in the morning or the evening or both. There is no better way to tip the cap to God— and to God-sized goals—than a regular prayer rhythm.

If it helps, employ a few simple rules. Hit your knees when you get out of bed in the morning or go to bed at night. Turn your phone off on your day off. Read your Bible before you check your phone. Any one of those prompts can interrupt the pattern and keep you focused on the prize!

How do I make it a habit?

Posterize your priorities!

When it comes to habit formation, we need visible reminders. It can be a photograph of the Waldorf Astoria, a poster of Mars, or marbles in a jar. When our daughter, Summer, was a teenager, we created a poster with nine adjectives that were descriptive and prescriptive. Those nine adjectives were who we believe Summer to be—present tense and future tense. For the Israelites, it was symbols that they wore on their hands and their foreheads. God also told them to posterize their homes with ritual reminders called mezuzahs.

The Shema is an ancient prayer that the Israelites recited twice daily. It begins like this: "Hear, O Israel: The LORD our God, the LORD is one."[14] The Shema functioned as a prompt—the first words spoken in the morning and the last words spoken at night. It was a reaffirmation of God's rule. It was the way an observant Jew received the kingdom of heaven on the daily.

The opening cue is followed by a command to love God with all one's heart, soul, and strength. The original context of the Shema also imagines the prize. God promised the Israelites houses they didn't build, wells they didn't dig, and vineyards they didn't plant.

Between the prompt and the prize, God gave them explicit instructions related to their daily routines. Again, habit stacking and habit switching are nothing new! They are as old as the Shema.

In August 1996, I did a 4.7-mile prayer walk around Capitol Hill. It proved to be a day when decades happen. Twenty-five years later, we own half a dozen properties worth $75 million right on that prayer circle. I had that prayer walk posterized, and it sits outside my office. Why? As a sacred reminder of that prayer prompting. It's the same reason I have hanging in my office a picture of the cow pasture where I felt called to ministry.

You need to posterize your priorities, posterize your goals, and posterize your values. You can do it on a shirt. You can do it on a wall. You can do it on a bathroom mirror or computer screen. Somehow you've got to keep those things front and center!

Tip the cap!

Day 25

Do the Math

Teach us to number our days.
—PSALM 90:12

In 1948, Korczak Ziolkowski was commissioned by Lakota chief Henry Standing Bear to design a mountain carving that would honor the famous Native American leader Crazy Horse. Ziolkowski devoted more than three decades to carving the larger-than-life statue. For the record, it's nine times larger than the faces on Mount Rushmore. When Ziolkowski died in 1982, the Ziolkowski family carried on his vision and continues to carve. The projected completion date is 2050, just shy of the century mark!

"When your life is over," said Korczak Ziolkowski, "the world will ask you only one question." What is it? "Did you do what you were supposed to do?"[1] If you want to wind the clock, you have to answer that question.

There never has been—and never will be—anyone like you. That's not a testament to you. It's a testament to the God who created you. The significance of that is this: no one can lead like you or for you. No one can love like you or for you. No one can worship like you or for you. Simply put, no one can take your place. That makes you invaluable and irreplaceable.

Are you doing what you are supposed to do? If you can't answer that question posed by Korczak Ziolkowski, it may be time for a time-out. You have to define success, as we talked about on day 8.

You have to define your purpose and your priorities. You have to define the values and virtues that you want to be known for.

If you pursue habit formation for selfish reasons, you're short-changing yourself, and the habit will be short lived. You have to imagine the prize by aiming at the endgame. You have to know *who you are* and *why you are*. You have to live for something bigger and better and longer and stronger than self-interest.

Remember David Horsager, who lost fifty-two pounds? His father is still farming in his nineties. When Horsager asked him why he was planting things he may never get to harvest, he didn't skip a beat: "Somebody will enjoy it someday."

Do you have any life goals that will take a lifetime to achieve?

If you don't, it's time to dream a little bigger and think a little longer.

Have you ever stopped to consider the size and scope of Noah's ark? It ranks as one of the largest and longest construction projects in the ancient world. From start to finish, it took 43,800 days! The ark measured three hundred cubits in length, fifty cubits in width, and thirty cubits in height. In the Hebrew system of measurement, a cubit was the equivalent of seventeen and a half inches. That means the ark was the length of one and a half football fields. Not until the late nineteenth century did a ship that size get constructed again, yet the 30:5:3 design ratio is still considered the gold standard for stability during storms at sea.[2]

The volume of the ark was 1,518,750 cubic feet—the equivalent of 569 boxcars. If the average animal was the size of a sheep, the ark had the capacity for one hundred and twenty-five thousand animals.[3] To put that into perspective, there are two thousand animals from four hundred species at the Smithsonian's National Zoo in Washington, DC. You could fit sixty National Zoos on board Noah's ark!

Noah deserves a lifetime achievement award, but let me reverse engineer his process. Do you know how he started building the boat? According to rabbinic tradition, the first thing Noah did was to plant trees.[4] Why? Given the size of the boat, he knew he'd need plenty of planks! Winding the clock is doing the math, and it's one key to imagining the prize.

Remember the two watches that we wear? Chronos and kairos. We can make great time and waste our lives away. If we succeed at the wrong thing, we've failed. We've got to make sure we're doing the right thing, the right way, at the right time.

The average person spends 145 minutes on social media every day.[5] Are you above average or below average? That adds up to 15 percent of our waking hours. Is that how you want to spend 15 percent of your life? Quit living vicariously and start actually living. Make predecisions that will help you manage the minutes and moments better.

I live by a little maxim: *Don't accumulate possessions; accumulate experiences.* I haven't met many people possessed by a demon, but I've met lots of people possessed by their possessions. Quit accumulating possessions and start accumulating experiences. One way I put this into practice is by doing an annual challenge or going on an annual adventure. Calendaring is choice architecture, is it not? It's one way we imagine unborn tomorrows.

There is a word in the dictionary that gets used about as much as *Beamonesque.* It's the word *Micawberish,* and you probably have no idea what it means unless you majored in English literature. It's taken from the Charles Dickens novel *David Copperfield.* One of the characters, Wilkins Micawber, has a catchphrase: "If anything turns up." On the verge of getting out of debtors' prison, he says, "I shall, please Heaven, begin . . . to live in a perfectly new manner, if—in short, if anything turns up."[6]

Juxtapose that with this.

I have a friend named Marcus Bullock who made a mistake as a teenager, a big mistake. Marcus carjacked someone when he was fifteen, he was tried as an adult, and he spent the next eight years in prison. But Marcus took the opposite approach to Micawber. He read books. He learned computer languages. Marcus was released when he was twenty-three, but he had a hard time getting a job because of the felony on his record.

Marcus applied for forty-one jobs. All of them asked whether he had a felony, and he gave an honest answer. Finally he applied for a job that asked whether he'd committed a felony in the previous seven years. Marcus had been locked up for eight, so the honest answer was no. He got a job at a paint store, and he parlayed that into his own contracting company.

Marcus is now the founder of Flikshop, a company that helps families send picture postcards to loved ones in prison.[7] Why? Because it was the pictures his mom sent him that helped him keep his sanity. Those pictures wound the clock. How? She sent him a picture of a hamburger and said, "Someday you'll eat this on the outside." She sent him a picture of a mattress and said, "Someday you'll sleep on this."

Objectively speaking, those pictures may not be as remarkable as the Waldorf Astoria, but they are just as meaningful. And they served the same function. Those pictures helped Marcus tip the cap and wind the clock. They kept his focus—getting out of prison— front and center.

There are two kinds of people in the world: those who *let things happen* and those who *make things happen*. There are those who find time and those who make time. There are those who waste time and those who wind the clock. Are you Micawber? Or are you Marcus?

There is an old adage: *Time is money.* Which do you spend more carefully—time or money? Truth be told? A lot of us waste a lot of time, so let's do a little audit. The average life span is seventy-nine years, which equates to 28,835 days. The average person spends twenty-six years in bed and an additional seven years trying to fall asleep. My advice? Get a good mattress! We spend 4,821 days at work; 4,127 days looking at screens; 1,583 days eating; and 368 days socializing. Fun fact? We spend 115 days laughing![8]

According to researchers at the University of California, the average worker is interrupted every eleven minutes.[9] Those same workers regain focus after twenty-five minutes. Do the math, and it adds up to a focus problem. Of course, some of those interruptions are self-inflicted. Again, we check our phones ninety-six times per day! Did you know that your phone has a "do not disturb" function? Use it or lose it.

Part of time management is identifying time wasters. They're the barren fig trees you need to curse. Why? They aren't producing fruit. What are those barren fig trees? Unnecessary meetings that produce sideways energy. An overwhelming number of emails that make you feel like you're sinking in quicksand. A lack of priorities that results in more commitments than you can keep. Most of us are guilty on all three counts!

The psalmist said, "Teach us to number our days."[10] That principle has lots of applications. If you want every day to count, count the days. One way I do that is by numbering the days I've been inhaler-free! As I note in *Win the Day*, Buzz Williams keeps track of the number of days he's held his current coaching position. Whatever habit you're trying to make or break, counting the days helps you keep track of the winning streak!

How do I make it a habit?

Audit your time!

I'm often asked how long it takes to write a book. There isn't an easy answer, especially if you count reading as research. But let me try to reverse engineer my process. I use my birthday, November 5, as a start date. I use Super Bowl Sunday as a deadline. I usually bracket that writing season with a three-day writing retreat on the front end and back end. I still wear my pastor hat, but I do less teaching and I don't take meetings that aren't NCC related. I average four writing days per week, and I get ten to twelve hours of writing in. That adds up to approximately 550 hours of writing time. Of course, that doesn't include reading or research.

Let me add one more thing to the mix. During a writing season, I set my alarm clock a little earlier in the morning. It's not easy getting up before the sun is up, but that's when I do the math. As I see it, the books I author are my way of spending about five or six hours with anyone, anytime, anywhere. *The Circle Maker* ranks as my bestselling book. If you multiply the number of copies sold by average reading time, it adds up to 1,741 years. We're approaching two millennia of reading time, which is a pretty good return on an investment of 550 hours. Doing the math motivates me to get up early! It helps me establish boundaries and priorities. Doing the math is more than a Jedi mind trick; it's good stewardship!

All of us trade our time for something. You trade time for a paycheck. You trade time for relationships. You trade time for the experiences you accumulate. Along with figuring out the barren fig trees, you have to identify the money trees! By *money trees*, I mean the things that produce the greatest return on time investment. For me, one of those things is writing.

There is an old axiom: *A place for everything, and everything in its place.* The same is true of time. That's why I designate different days for different purposes. Tuesday is a meeting day. Wednesday and Thursday are study days if I'm speaking. Monday is a rest day, my Sabbath. It's not a perfect science—I promise you that. And I get interrupted as much as everyone else! But designating certain days for certain functions gets me into the right mindset and helps me focus on the task at hand.

If I check email too early in the day, it feels like that's all I do all day long! Sure, there are days when I need to empty out my inbox in order to clear my mind. But I also try to clear my calendar. That allows me to follow different ideas, wherever the rabbit trail takes me. During a writing season, I turn those rabbit trails into chapters.

We all manage time a little differently, but there is one common denominator among those who actually get things done—intentionality. They don't *spend* time. They *invest* time like it's their 401(k).

Do the math!

Day 26

Play the Long Game

With the Lord a day is like a thousand years,
and a thousand years are like a day.
—2 Peter 3:8

On December 31, 1759, Arthur Guinness opened a brewery in Dublin, Ireland. He found a four-acre piece of property at St. James's Gate, the western entrance to the city. It was the site of the annual fair, where ale was the bestseller, but there was one other factor that Guinness took into account. He knew that city planners intended to build Ireland's Grand Canal adjacent to St. James's Gate, which would give his brewery a built-in shipping lane.

Guinness had an eye for opportunity, and he must have had a knack for negotiation too. Somehow he managed to secure a nine-thousand-year lease.[1] You read that right. That must be a Guinness world record, pun intended. Arthur Guinness put down one hundred pounds as a down payment and agreed to pay forty-five pounds per annum.

Let me ask the obvious question: Who signs a nine-thousand-year lease? The short answer is someone who is playing the long game. For the record, Guinness is older than America! When it comes to decision-making, Guinness employs this policy: *considering long and acting quickly.*[2]

That two-sided coin is a good rule of thumb when it comes to winding the clock. We need to keep one eye on our long-term goals. We also need to act quickly, act decisively. When it comes to making and breaking habits, you have to strike while the iron is hot.

Motivation is a form of energy. As such, it tends to dissipate over time. That's why you need life goals that take a lifetime to achieve. They force you to wind the clock by thinking long!

How do you play the long game?

If you're going to dream big, you have to start small. That was the challenge on day 18. The challenge on day 26 is *think long*. The bigger the dream, the longer it's going to take to accomplish it. So be it. I say, go big or go home!

One of the best examples of thinking long is the mysterious forest of oak trees that populate the Swedish island of Visingsö. Their origin was unknown for many decades. In 1980, the Swedish navy got a letter from the forestry department reporting that their requested ship lumber was ready. The navy didn't know they had ordered any, because the order had been placed in 1829! That's the year that the Swedish parliament voted to plant twenty thousand trees on Visingsö and have them protected for the navy.[3]

For the record, the lone objector was the bishop of Strängnäs. He didn't doubt that there would still be wars to fight at the end of the twentieth century, but he believed that ships might be built of different materials by then! The moral of the story? We need to think long, but we also need to think different.

Let me offer a little reminder at this juncture: *time is a human construct.* "With the Lord a day is like a thousand years," said the apostle Peter, "and a thousand years are like a day."[4] That makes no sense within the four dimensions of spacetime, but God doesn't exist within the spacetime dimensions He created. There is no past, present, and future! God is here, there, and everywhere—all at the same time! He is God most high and God most nigh. He is the Ancient of Days, and He is the Eternal Now.

Creation was God's way of winding the clock, the chronos clock. Eternity is kairos time. We think of heaven as a future-tense destination, but heaven is invading earth right here, right now. Eternity is invading time every second of every minute of every hour of every day!

We count up, but God is counting down. We live our lives forward, but God is working backward. Remember the Day of Pentecost? God poured out His Spirit on day 10 of the disciples gathering in the upper room.[5] The disciples were counting up, but I think God was counting down—10, 9, 8, 7, 6, 5, 4, 3, 2, 1.

Teleology is a fancy word in philosophy. It's the second habit of highly effective people: *begin with the end in mind.*[6] That's who God is. That's what God does. For us, the arrow of time moves in one direction—past, present, future. Then Jesus showed up and said, "Before Abraham was, I AM."[7] Wait—what? He winds the clock in a very different way. Simply put, *God is counterclockwise.*

There are moments in Scripture when God wound the clock in a unique way. He made the sun and the moon stand still over the Valley of Aijalon. He turned back time for King Hezekiah—the shadow on the sundial moonwalked ten degrees backward.[8] My favorite example may seem less mysterious, but it is no less miraculous. Before the Israelites started circling Jericho, God said, "I have delivered Jericho into your hands."[9]

That verb tense doesn't make sense, because it hadn't happened yet. Right? It should be future tense, but the verb tense God used reveals a sacred sequence. Simply put, *everything is created twice.* The first creation is internal. It's mind over matter. That's especially true when it comes to habit formation! The second creation is physical.

Remember the 4.7-mile prayer walk I did around Capitol Hill? It was a Jericho march of sorts. Twenty-five years later, we own half a dozen properties on that prayer circle including a city block that was built as the Navy Yard Car Barn in 1891. I didn't have a category for a city block when I did that 4.7-mile prayer walk. And I definitely didn't have a category for the $29 million price tag. At the time, we had fewer than twenty people and our monthly income as a church was $2,000!

Guess what? Prayer is writing history before it happens! It's one way we wind the clock. It's no coincidence that we signed the contract on that piece of property exactly eighteen years from the day of that prayer walk. It was providence. In fact, I'll take it one step further. God put a futures contract on that piece of property the day I circled it in prayer!

Playing the long game is all about long obedience in the same direction. It's doing things that will make a difference long after we are gone. And it doesn't have to be big things. Again, it's starting small and thinking long.

In 1964, Dick Foth was a graduate student at Wheaton College, working on his master's thesis. He now laughs at the long title: "An Exploratory Investigation of the Transition from Missionary to National in the Administration of Latin American Bible Schools." Needless to say, not many books on that subject! His professor and adviser, Lois LeBar, asked Dick whether he and his wife, Ruth, were going to attend InterVarsity's Urbana conference as part of his primary research. Dick said he couldn't afford it. Lois LeBar excused herself, walked into another room, and came back with five twenty-dollar bills.

More than half a century after the fact, Dick gets emotional about that moment: "That one gift totally changed the trajectory of my life." It totally changed mine, too, and I'll explain how in a moment. Then Dick laughingly said, "And I'm not overstating it, because sometimes I overstate things." I couldn't help but hear Ruth chuckling in the background. Because of that one-hundred-dollar gift, Dick and Ruth attended Urbana. Eighteen months later, they would return to Urbana, Illinois, to plant a church.

Let me connect the dots, A-B-C-D. If Lois LeBar hadn't given Dick that gift, he wouldn't have planted Urbana Assembly of God. If he hadn't planted that church, he wouldn't have met my father-in-law and fellow church planter, Bob Schmidgall. If he hadn't met my father-in-law, I never would have meet Dick Foth. My point? Lois LeBar changed my life by changing Dick's life! I'm a secondary beneficiary of her generosity. Not only were Dick and Ruth Foth part of our original core group of nineteen people, but Dick has also been a friend, mentor, and spiritual father to me for more than twenty-five years!

You never know how a one-hundred-dollar gift will change the course of history! But here's what I know for sure: Your legacy is not what you accomplish. Your legacy is what others accomplish because of you.

My life verse is Ephesians 2:10: "We are his workmanship, created in Christ Jesus for good works, which God prepared beforehand."[10] Did you catch it? The good works you're destined to do are already prepared. God is setting you up! God is counting down! That's where holy confidence comes from. That redefines what it means to imagine the prize. It's already been accomplished in the spiritual realm!

How do I make it a habit?

Make it a game!

Breaking bad habits is serious business. That said, you can't afford to forget the theory of fun. No matter how hard the habit is to make or break or how long it takes, you have to add an element of fun. How? Turn it into a game.

On June 6, 1985, Joe Simpson and Simon Yates set out to summit Siula Grande. With an elevation of 20,814 feet, it ranks as the tallest mountain in the Southern Hemisphere. The western face had never been climbed, until Simpson and Yates did just that. Of course, what goes up the mountain must come down, and that's when 80 percent of mountain-climbing accidents occur.

On the morning of June 8, Simpson slipped on the ice, fell fifteen hundred feet into a crevasse, and shattered his leg. It seemed like a death sentence since rescue teams weren't able to reach him. For most people, it would have been game over. But Joe Simpson was cut from the same cloth as Chris Nikic and Chris Norton—all grit, no quit.

After using his climbing rope to descend farther into the crevasse, Simpson somehow found a way out. On one leg, he managed to climb 130 feet at a forty-five-degree angle. Did I mention that his fingers were black from frostbite? Even after escaping that ice coffin, he was six miles from base camp. He couldn't feel his fingers, while his leg pulsed with pain. But Joe Simpson survived.

"In the most dangerous, high-stakes situation imaginable," said author Eric Barker, "he did the craziest thing." What's that? "He made it a game." How? "He started setting goals: *Can I make it to that glacier in twenty minutes?*"[11] Sounds like the question that frames this entire book, doesn't it? *Can you do it for a day?*

Joe Simpson managed to climb and claw and crawl all the way back to base camp. His mantra? "Keep playing the game."[12] Turning difficult situations into a game may sound trivial, but it's a powerful way to keep your perspective. You can't use obstacles as an excuse; you have to use them as motivation!

Falling the equivalent of fifteen stories is not fun and games. It's life or death. But turning the situation into a game is a metacognitive mind trick that only humans are capable of. Remember day 10 and the idea of cognitive reappraisal? This is that, and it's incredibly important in crisis situations. Kids are naturals at cognitive reappraisal. Just ask their imaginary friends! When they get bored, they imagine alternate realities like taking the last-second shot in the championship game.

Making it a game combines multiple habits—flip the script, kiss the wave, eat the frog, and wind the clock. I know that gaming the system has negative connotations, but let me redeem that phrase. In *Win the Day,* I shared the story of Frank Laubach and "the game with minutes."[13] He leveraged time by turning it into an alarm clock. His goal? Thinking about God every minute of every hour of every day.

I know that sometimes spiritual disciplines feel like chores. Why not game the system? How? By interrupting the pattern and imagining the prize. I try to read the Bible from cover to cover every year. I change the routine by changing translations. Why do I do it? Because my most prized possession is a 1934 Thompson Chain-Reference Bible that belonged to my grandfather. My goal is having enough well-read, well-marked Bibles to leave to my kids and, God willing, grandkids and great-grandkids.

You can game the system by changing prayer postures.

You can game the system by fasting from things other than food.

You can game the system by keeping a gratitude journal.

If you've lost a little momentum during this thirty-day challenge, game the system! Add an element of fun. If you're crushing it, you might want to up the ante by adding a degree of difficulty.

Play the long game!

Habit 7—Seed the Clouds

Sow today what you want to see tomorrow.

On November 13, 1946, a single-propeller airplane took off from Schenectady County Airport with a rather unique payload—six pounds of dry ice. The pilot was a chemist named Vincent Schaefer who had been conducting clandestine experiments at the House of Magic, the General Electric Research Laboratory.

Prior to his historic flight, Schaefer had been using a freezer chilled to subzero temperatures to create clouds using his breath as condensation. Then he seeded those man-made clouds with the solid form of carbon dioxide. That dry ice catalyzed a chemical reaction that caused snow crystals to form in the freezer.

A few months later, it was time for a field test. Schaefer rented the aforementioned airplane, flew it into a cumulus cloud, and dumped the dry ice. Eyewitnesses on the ground said it was almost like the cloud exploded. The subsequent snowfall was visible forty miles away. The *GE Monogram* had a little fun with Schaefer's breakthrough: "Schaefer made it snow this afternoon over Pittsfield! Next week he walks on water."[1]

Seeding clouds is a marvel of modern science, but the idea is as old as the prophet Elijah. It hadn't rained in Israel for three years when Elijah climbed Mount Carmel, bowed down to the ground, and seeded the clouds with prayer seven times.[2]

The number seven is not insignificant. That's the number of days Israel circled Jericho. That's the number of times Naaman dipped in the Jordan River.[3] The number seven may not be magical, but it is biblical. It indicates completeness, and it raises these questions: What if Elijah had prayed only six times? What if the Israelites had stopped circling on day six? What if Naaman had done only six dips? The answer is obvious: they would have forfeited the miracle right before it happened.

I have no idea what habit you're trying to make or break, but I do know this: it's too soon to quit! Maybe you've had a few setbacks during this thirty-day challenge. The best baseball players on the planet get a hit only every third time. As we unpack this final habit, finish strong! Maybe even double down on that daily habit.

I wrote *The Circle Maker* almost a decade ago. The book draws its title from an ancient sage named Honi the Circle Maker who had an Elijah-like anointing. In the first century BC, there was a devasting drought, much like the drought in Elijah's day. When the people asked Honi to pray for rain, he took his staff and drew a circle in the sand. Then he knelt inside that circle and prayed this prayer: "By Your great Name I swear that I will not move from here until You have mercy on Your children."[4] When that prayer went up, rain came down! It was a prayer that saved a generation—the generation before Jesus!

According to the Talmud, Honi the Circle Maker was captivated by one line in one verse of Scripture, Psalm 126:1: "When the LORD brought back the captives of Zion, we were like those who dream."[5] That line—"we were like those who dream"—provoked a question that Honi wrestled with his entire life:

Is it possible for a person to dream continuously for seventy years?[6]

Longitudinal studies have shown that as we age, the cognitive center of gravity tends to shift from the right brain to the left brain. This is an oversimplification, but the left brain is the locus of logic. The right brain is the locus of imagination. That neurological tendency poses a problem: at some point, most of us stop living out of imagination and start living out of memory. We stop creating the future and start repeating the past. We stop living by faith and start living by logic. That is when we stop living and start dying, but it doesn't have to be that way.

Seeding the clouds is all about prophetic imagination. Remember day 14? It's living like we'll die tomorrow but dreaming like we'll live forever. Seeding the clouds is imagining unborn tomorrows, but it's not pie in the sky. It's long obedience in the same direction. It's doing things today that will make a difference a hundred years from now. It's leaving a legacy that will outlive us!

From 1934 to 1961, a British historian named Arnold Toynbee published a twelve-volume history that traces the rise and fall of nineteen civilizations. There is a question long debated by historians: *Do all civilizations follow a predictable pattern, a life cycle from birth to growth to decline to death? Or is it possible for a declining civilization to experience a rebirth?* Toynbee believed that a civilization could experience a rebirth, but the key is something he called the creative minority.[7]

According to Toynbee, the collapse of civilization doesn't happen because of outside attacks. The disintegration of civilization is caused by the deterioration of this creative minority. What is a creative minority? Toynbee cited the church as an example, but it's any minority that creatively responds to crisis. How? With prophetic imagination. With revolutionary resolve. With grace and with grit.

One last warning: Creative minorities deteriorate when they worship their former selves.[8] In other words, they stop creating the future and start repeating the past. In doing so, they become prisoners of their own past.

In the words of R. T. Kendall, "The greatest opposition to what God is doing today comes from those who were on the cutting edge of what God was doing yesterday."[9] Eventually new wineskins become old wineskins! As soon as you stop dreaming, you start dying. As soon as you stop growing, you start atrophying. As soon as you stop learning, you start reverting to bad habits.

It's time to seed the clouds!

Day 27

It Takes a Team

A cord of three strands is not easily broken.
—ECCLESIASTES 4:12, HCSB

In 1468, a fourteen-year-old boy named Leonardo, from a town called Vinci, moved sixty miles east to apprentice for an artist named Andrea del Verrocchio. Florence, Italy, wasn't a large city—only about forty thousand people. But it had a high concentration of creatives. There were more wood-carvers than butchers—eighty-three to be exact. Florence was a city of artists, and the incubators were creative collaborations called workshops. Florence boasted fifty-four of them. One of them was Verrocchio's workshop. Fun fact? Many of the pieces produced by these workshops during the Renaissance bear no signature because they weren't the work of one artist.

Art was a team sport. So is habit formation! We need people in our lives who believe in us more than we believe in ourselves. Remember Bob Beamon? He borrowed Ralph Boston's faith for six seconds and flew twenty-nine feet, two and a half inches because of it. Diana Nyad borrowed her father's faith and swam across the Straits of Florida. Marcus Bullock borrowed his mom's faith, served his sentence, and started Flikshop.

We need people who will push us past our limits. We also need people who will push our buttons when necessary. Why? "Iron sharpens iron."[1] The friction of competition is one example. The sharpening of friendship is another.

The goal of this book is to help you tap your potential. Maybe I should have mentioned this at the outset—*you can't do it all by yourself.* Habit formation is a team sport. I'm not suggesting you form friendships like a draft board, but it should involve some intentionality. Who do you want to become? Spend time with that kind of person! David had his mighty men. Elisha had the company of prophets. Even Jesus had His twelve disciples! If we're taking our cues from Christ, we'll surround ourselves with a prayerfully selected team. The bottom line? It takes teamwork to make the dream work!

After his four-year apprenticeship, Leonardo da Vinci continued working in Verrocchio's workshop. He would spend a decade working side by side with the master artist. Verrocchio and Leonardo collaborated on a masterpiece called *The Baptism of Christ.* It's worth googling! There are two angels in that painting. The angel on the right is Verrocchio's angel. The angel on the left is Leonardo's angel. I'm neither an artist nor an art historian, but the consensus is that Leonardo's angel is more angelic! In fact, Verrocchio was so awed by Leonardo's angel that he "resolved never again to touch a brush." The student had become the master![2]

That raises the question, Who was the greater genius? Verrocchio or Leonardo? If it's a measure of pure artistic talent, the answer is Leonardo, hands down. But there is a kind of genius that can spot genius. It's the genius of Jesus, isn't it? He saw potential in His disciples that no one else did. Without the genius that is able to spot genius, lots of genius goes undiscovered. Potential goes untapped, talent gets wasted, and opportunities are left on the table.

Artists need artists. Leaders need leaders. Coaches need coaches. Even long jumpers need long jumpers! I'll stop there, but there are no exceptions! Remember Ed Catmull? If he hadn't started a workshop called Pixar, the collective talent of all those animators and storytellers would have gone untapped.

As a leader, you have to see the ecosystem that every person represents. When I meet with a leader, I'm not just investing in them; I'm investing in their organization. When I spend time with a coach, I'm investing in their team. When I spend time with a father, I'm investing in his children. I even do the math sometimes. I've had meetings with people who lead companies, lead countries. In a sense, I'm meeting with every person they represent. That mindset adds value to the time invested, and it has a domino chain reaction.

In my book, success is succession. We stand on the shoulders of the generation before us, and we return the favor by passing the baton. In the Broadway blockbuster *Hamilton,* there are these lines that I love: "Legacy. What is a legacy? It's planting seeds in a garden you never get to see."[3]

I never met Lois LeBar, the professor who made a hundred-dollar investment in Dick and Ruth Foth, but she is a shareholder in everything God does in and through National Community Church. How? Dick Foth reinvested the dividends of her generosity in my life!

I've had the privilege of pastoring National Community Church for a quarter century, but I'm still an *interim* pastor. All of us are transition leaders. All of us will pass the baton sooner or later. Are you setting up the next generation? Who is your Elisha? Who are you giving your mantle to? We seed the clouds by making disciples! It's the fourth dimension of discipleship—*disciple others the way you were discipled.*

When Diana Nyad swam ashore in Key West, she said, "We should never, ever give up. . . . You are never too old to chase your dream." Then she said something I omitted until now: "It looks like a solitary sport but it takes a team."[4] Nyad had a team of thirty experts that included doctors, oceanographers, meteorologists, and shark scientists, not to mention family and friends! Once again, it takes teamwork to make the dream work.

Alex Haley, author of the Pulitzer Prize–winning book *Roots,* famously kept a picture of a turtle on a fencepost in his office. Why?

"Anytime you see a turtle on a fence post," said Haley, "you know he had some help!"[5] Any time Alex Haley was tempted to take credit for his accomplishments, he would swivel his chair and look at that turtle. Simply put, your blessings are the by-product of someone else's sacrifices. If you don't believe that, then you haven't connected the dots.

At the end of his epistle to the Romans, Paul shared a who's-who list that includes twenty-nine names. Phoebe. Urbanus. Andronicus. Olympas. Erastus. Quartus. To us, it's as boring as the begats. But these people meant the world to Paul. They were his best friends, his closest confidants. They were the ones who risked their lives for him. This was Paul's dream team!

Who's on your Romans 16 list?

When was the last time you thanked them?

Author and entrepreneur Jim Rohn is famous for saying that we become the average of the five people we spend the most time with. Can I up the ante to twelve? Let's be honest—the disciples were not first-round draft picks by anyone's standards. They were ordinary in every way, except one. They spent three years with Jesus! They had box seats to every parable, every miracle. They drank the water that was turned into wine. They ate the five loaves and two fish that fed thousands. For three years, they went hiking, camping, and fishing together!

Do you remember the way the Sanhedrin classified the disciples? They called them "unschooled." True, they may not have had academic credentials, but the Sanhedrin "took note that [they] had been with Jesus."[6] That was their JND—just noticeable difference!

Our pastor of prayer, Heidi Scanlon, doesn't have accountability partners. She has *expectability* partners. I like that language. All too often, accountability partners focus on sin management. Sure, we need people to hold us to certain standards. But we also need people who expect the best and bring out the best in us! It's someone who holds us to a higher standard. An expectability partner asks the question, *What are you expecting from God?* And those sanctified expectations need to be beyond your ability and beyond your resources!

If you surround yourself with bad examples, it's hard not to pick up bad habits. According to the science of social networks, if a friend of yours becomes obese, you are 45 percent more likely to gain weight over the next two to four years.[7] Of course, the opposite is true too! Your friends can help you become more fit. Either way, it's a function of our mirror neurons. Bad company corrupts good behavior, but good company sanctifies it.

One way you seed the clouds is by getting in the right room with the right people. The key to your success is not just *what* you know but *who* you know! Genius often happens in clusters. In sports, it's called a coaching tree. There is a Bill Walsh tree, a Bill Belichick tree, and an Andy Reid tree. In a sense, each of those coaches created a domino chain reaction. And it's true of every endeavor from business to science.

Remember Dwight D. Eisenhower? His graduating class at West Point has been called "the class the stars fell on." Of the 164 graduates in his class, 59 of them attained the rank of general.[8] How does 36 percent of a class climb the ladder to that rank? The obvious answer is the timing of World War II, no doubt. But that class rose to the occasion!

A church is a community of faith that spurs one another on toward love and good deeds.[9] How? For starters, testimony is prophecy! We borrow faith from one another, just like Bob Beamon did from Ralph Boston. We are challenged by the likes of Susan B. Anthony, Rosa Parks, and Katherine Johnson. We are convicted by overcomers like Chris Nikic and Chris Norton. A community of faith results in herd immunity against fear! It also unleashes our creativity. In a sense, a healthy church is Verrocchio's workshop!

How do I make it a habit?

Choose your friends wisely!

In the world of running, the four-minute mile was considered an unbreakable barrier by many. Then on May 6, 1954, Roger Bannister ran the mile in three minutes, fifty-nine and four-tenths seconds. As of this writing, the four-minute mile has been broken 1,497 times, and that world record has been lowered by more than seventeen seconds![10]

How did Bannister break that barrier? He didn't do it by himself—that's for sure! Bannister had pacesetters. Few people remember their names—Chris Chataway and Chris Basher. But Bannister wouldn't have broken that record without them. They pushed him past his limits by setting the pace.

Remember our thesis? *Almost anyone can accomplish almost anything if they work at it long enough, hard enough, and smart enough.* I stand by it, and Roger Bannister is evidence of it. But you need to surround yourself with the right pacesetters!

When it comes to habit formation, Benjamin Franklin is a founding father. He was fanatical about cultivating thirteen virtues, to the point of keeping a daily scorecard as noted on day 5. But Franklin knew that he couldn't reach his potential by himself. What did he do? In 1727, Benjamin Franklin formed the Leather Apron Club for the purpose of mutual improvement.[11] It was an eclectic group that included philosophers and cabinetmakers, merchants and mathematicians, printers and surveyors. They gathered on Friday nights to discuss subjects that ranged from physics to philosophy to politics.

I could cite dozens of groups like this one. They range from Count Nicholas Ludwig von Zinzendorf and his Order of the Mustard Seed to Josiah Royce and the Fellowship of Reconciliation. Those creative minorities formed communities that changed the course of history. The whole was greater than the sum of the parts.

When geese fly in V formation, overall efficiency is improved by 71 percent.[12] Enough said. Who are you flying with? Who are your pacesetters? Who is pushing you past that 40 percent rule we discussed on day 3? There is no way you can tap your full potential without the right people around you, but I'll take it one step further. At the outset of any endeavor, your daily habits are the key to your success. Over time, the key to your success is surrounding yourself with the right people. They will help you fly further, faster.

Many years ago, I added a relational element to my life goal list. Why? It's more fun crossing the finish line together, but that's not all. Those who sweat together stick together. Going after a goal is relational glue that bonds us to each other's future!

It takes a team!

Day 28

Prophesy Your Praise

We do not know what to do, but our eyes are on you.
—2 CHRONICLES 20:12

I n the spring of 1992, the capital city of Bosnia was besieged by the Yugoslav People's Army. The Siege of Sarajevo would last 1,425 days. On May 27, innocent civilians were standing in a breadline when a bombshell exploded. The blast killed twenty-two people, leaving a crater in the center of the city.

Moments after the blast, a man named Vedran Smailović ran to the scene, but he wasn't sure what to do. He wasn't a medic. He wasn't a firefighter. He wasn't a soldier. Vedran Smailović was the principal cellist in the Sarajevo Opera. All he had was his cello. For most of us, the story would have ended there. We let what we can't do keep us from doing what we can.

The day after that disaster, May 28, 1992, Vedran Smailović put on his tuxedo, grabbed his cello, climbed into the crater, sat down on a scorched chair, and played Adagio in G Minor by Albinoni. For twenty-two straight days, one day for each victim, the cellist of Sarajevo made music in craters, in cemeteries, in the rubble of bombed-out buildings. The city of Sarajevo was under siege by shells and by snipers, so why risk your life to make music? In the words of Vedran Smailović, "My weapon was my cello."[1]

What is your weapon?

I know that sounds militaristic, but the last time I checked, we were born on a battlefield between good and evil. Lots of craters all around us! We don't wrestle against flesh and blood. We're fighting against powers and principalities.[2] The good news? "The weapons we fight with are not the weapons of the world. On the contrary, they have divine power to demolish strongholds."[3]

You are here for such a time as this.

You are here for such a place as this.

All of us have a *superpower*, and I mean that literally. God is "able to do immeasurably more than all we ask or imagine." How? "According to his power that is at work within us!"[4] His power is your superpower, but there's a catch. Where is God's power made perfect? The answer, of course, is in our weakness![5] We touched on this truth on day 1. God wants to use your weak hand as well as your strong hand. Either way, we seed the clouds by climbing into craters and making music. Not only do we give God the sacrifice of praise, but we also prophesy our praise!

In the ninth century BC, King Jehoshaphat found himself in a crisis situation. The Moabites and Ammonites had declared war on Judah. Much like General McAuliffe at the Battle of the Bulge, they were surrounded by the enemy. Jehoshaphat called Judah to a fast, and then he exercised his authority by praying a prophetic prayer.

"We are powerless before this vast army that comes against us," said the king. He confronted the brutal facts, but he did so with unwavering faith! "We do not know what to do, but our eyes are upon You."[6] When Jehoshaphat finished praying, Jahaziel got a word from God: "Do not be afraid or discouraged because of this vast army, for the battle does not belong to you, but to God."[7]

Prayer is the difference between you fighting for God and God fighting for you! The same is true of praise. When we hit our knees in prayer, when we lift our voices in praise, God fights our battles for us! We don't praise God only when everything is going great. When it feels like the world is falling apart, we climb into craters and sing our songs of lament. Why? *Whatever you don't turn into praise turns into either pride or pain.*

Pay careful attention to what happened next: "[Jehoshaphat] appointed singers to walk ahead of the army, singing to the LORD and praising him for his holy splendor."[8] Permission to speak frankly? This seems like the worst battle plan ever! Instead of sending the guys with shields, let's send the sopranos! Please hear this: worship is a domino habit. "At the very moment they began to sing and give praise, the LORD caused the armies of Ammon, Moab, and Mount Seir to start fighting among themselves."[9]

"It is easy to stand around a bombed-out crater and talk about the crater—how it got there, who's to blame for it, and all its particulars," said Sara Groves. It's true, isn't it? "It is much harder to step past the edge of it, down into the middle, and say or make or do something generative."[10] We are called to be solutionaries! We climb into the craters left by pain and suffering with hope and healing. We climb into the craters left by injustice and lift our voices for the voiceless. We climb into the craters left by cancel culture and offer an extra measure of grace.

What does any of that have to do with making and breaking habits? In my experience, it's easier making habits when you're making music. Have you ever watched a movie without the soundtrack? It's not nearly as epic! In fact, a movie without a soundtrack is kind of boring. So is habit formation. Our soundtrack is worship. In fact, it's one of the most powerful weapons in our spiritual arsenal.

There is nothing the Enemy hates more than our worship. Why? When we worship, we are reminding him of who he was. Lucifer led worship in time before time. When we worship, the Enemy wants out of earshot. Now let me flip the coin. Worship reminds the Enemy of who he was, and it reminds us of who God is. When we worship, we are mirroring what is happening in heaven right now. We come into alignment with the heavenly realm, and heaven invades earth. Healing happens. Deliverance happens. Breakthrough happens. Worship is the seedbed for a thousand miracles!

I think it's safe to say that Paul's missionary journeys started a domino chain reaction that turned the ancient world upside down. They were the catalyst for almost every church we read about in the book of Acts—Corinth, Ephesus, Philippi. What was the impetus for those three missionary journeys? When and where and how did it happen? The genesis is four words—"while they were worshiping."[11] Retrace every move of God, and you'll find someone worshipping God with reckless abandon!

When I look back on my life, worship is the place where breakthrough has happened. The week after God healed my lungs, our worship team sang a song that dropped me to my knees. I had gone one week without my inhaler, and I had a holy hunch that God had healed my lungs. Then we sang this chorus: "It's Your breath in our lungs, so we pour out our praise."[12] I almost lost it as we sang. I don't know that I'd ever sung a song with more faith. I didn't just pour out my praise; I prophesied my praise! I didn't just sing those words; I exercised my spiritual authority!

There are two kinds of praise, and both of them are powerful. Past-tense praise is thanking God *after* He does it. This is when we sing "Great Is Thy Faithfulness." On that note, we may sing the same words, but each of us is singing a very different song. Why? God's faithfulness is as unique as your fingerprint. Future-tense praise is the other kind. It's thanking God *before* He does it. It's prophesying our praise by faith.

On July 23, 2000, I had emergency surgery for ruptured intestines and spent the next two days on a respirator, fighting for my life. I lost twenty-five pounds in a week, and it initiated the hardest year of my life. I could have prophesied my pain by complaining, but I made a conscious choice to flip the script and kiss the wave and wind the clock and seed the clouds. How? By worshipping my way out of that painful situation.

As I was recovering from surgery, I heard a song by Darrell Evans. These lines got in my spirit: "I'm trading my sickness; I'm trading my pain; I'm laying them down for the joy of the Lord."[13] I put that song on repeat. I sang it 437 times at least. In *Win the Day*, I wrote about the importance of signature stories.[14] That was my *signature song* for that season!

I have no idea what hardships you've had to endure, and I would never make light of them. I know people who have been to hell and back. I have a friend who was stabbed thirty-seven times during an armed robbery and lived to tell about it. Even in the worst of situations, we have a choice to make. We can choose bitterness or forgiveness. Kevin Ramsby has four feet of scars on his body, but God healed his heart. How? Kevin not only forgave the man who stabbed him, but he also befriended him.

We have two primary weapons at our disposal—confession and profession. Confession is admitting what's wrong with us. Profession is declaring what's right with God. Confession catalyzes the healing process by identifying the problem. Profession seals the deal by pronouncing the solution. In a sense, it is *imagining the prize.*

How do you make it a habit?

Cross the bridge!

On March 21, 1965, thousands of peaceful protestors gathered in Selma, Alabama. Motivated by the brutality of Bloody Sunday a few weeks before, they crossed the Edmund Pettus Bridge in an act of solidarity. They walked twelve miles a day, slept in the fields, and ultimately rallied for the right to vote in Montgomery, Alabama.

One of those who marched was Abraham Heschel, considered by many to be the preeminent Jewish theologian of the twentieth century. Why did Heschel march? When you are just a few decades removed from concentration camps that exterminated millions of Jews, you intuitively identify with what Dr. King said: "Injustice anywhere is a threat to justice everywhere."[15]

Looking back on the march, Abraham Heschel said, "I felt my legs were praying." Author and activist Frederick Douglass said something similar a century earlier: "I prayed for twenty years but received no answer until I prayed with my legs."[16] May God raise up another generation of prophets who don't just talk the talk but walk the walk. May your life be louder than your words! The key? You've got to get a word from God. How? It starts with a prophetic ear. The still, small voice of the Spirit has to be the loudest voice in your life. Then, and only then, will you have a prophetic voice. Then you use that voice to prophesy your praise!

"The prophet is human," said Abraham Heschel, "yet he employs a note one octave too high for our ears."[17] The prophet hears the silent sigh. The prophet gives voice to silent agony via the language of lament. "To the prophets," said Heschel, "even a minor injustice assumes cosmic proportions."[18]

Crawl into the crater.

Cross the bridge.

Prophesy your praise!

Day 29

Swim Upstream

The water from upstream stopped flowing.
—JOSHUA 3:16

In 1864, there were 54,543 doctors in the United States. Only three hundred of them were women, and none of those women were black. That year, Rebecca Lee Crumpler became the first black woman to earn a medical degree and the title "doctress of medicine."[1]

Dr. Crumpler moved to Richmond, Virginia, the year after graduation. Stop and think about it. A black woman moving to the capital of the Confederacy the same year the Civil War ended took tremendous courage. That qualifies as cutting the rope! She endured relentless racism with amazing grace. How? Rebecca Lee Crumpler made no distinction between medical practice and religious practice. In her words, medicine was "a proper field for real missionary work."[2] She wasn't just a doctress; she was a prophetess.

On March 3, 1865, Congress established the Freedman's Bureau to provide food and housing, education and medical care for four million slaves who were now free. The head of the bureau from 1865 to 1874 was a Civil War general nicknamed "the Christian General," Oliver Otis Howard. He helped secure the vote for emancipated slaves. He also served as president of the school that bears his name, Howard University.

When Dr. Crumpler started practicing medicine, supplies were short and doctors were few and far between. There were only 120 doctors to care for four million emancipated slaves. What did Rebecca Lee Crumpler do? She had already broken one glass ceiling, so why not break another? If slaves couldn't get the medical care they needed, she would empower them and equip them to be nurses and doctors themselves! Just as Elisha Otis turned the world upside down, Rebecca Lee Crumpler turned medicine inside out.

In 1883, she published *A Book of Medical Discourses.* That makes her the only female physician to author a book in the nineteenth century. In doing so, she made medicine accessible and available to the average person. Remember the mantra I introduced on day 14? "Always think ecosystem." Here's another one: "Always go upstream."

When it comes to habit cycles, you have to swim upstream. It's solving the problem before it happens. That's why we built the DC Dream Center in Ward 7, an underserved part of our city. It's a place where hope becomes habit. We're trying to change statistics, and that happens one child at a time. That's how you interrupt the school-to-prison pipeline. That's how you seed the clouds!

Remember the eighth wonder of the world? That's what Albert Einstein called compound interest. We overestimate what we can accomplish in a day, but we underestimate what God can do in a year or two or ten. Again, consistency beats intensity seven days a week and twice on Sunday! Give it enough time, and you can transform your body, your mind, your marriage, your finances, and your attitude.

A six-pack may be one hundred pounds from here.

A marathon may be 475 miles of training down the road.

Writing a book may be fifty thousand words away.

Debt-free may be $100,000 beyond your budget.

Restoring your marriage may be seventeen counseling sessions from now.

The good news? This can be the day when decades happen! Sixteen years from now, you'll look back on this day as the tipping point, the turning point. Sixteen years, sixteen miles—same difference! What do I mean? The Israelites crossed the Jordan River opposite Jericho, but the miracle happened sixteen miles upstream at a place called Adam: "The water from upstream stopped flowing. It piled up in a heap a great distance away, at a town called Adam."[3]

In the last two decades, National Community has taken 273 mission trips and given more than $25 million to missions. That is the result of a domino chain reaction, but the two-inch domino was the first fifty-dollar check that we gave to missions. If you swim upstream, you'll find a conviction that guides our decision-making at NCC—*God will bless us in proportion to how we give to missions and care for the poor in our city.* That is how the Jordan River parted for National Community Church.

Our worship team has produced seven albums. Those songs have been sung millions of times all around the world. We have 150 vocalists and musicians on our worship team, but it all started with a $400 drum set that we purchased for a drummer we didn't have yet. We prophesied our praise, literally! We waded into the water, and God made a sidewalk through the sea by sending our first drummer.

Remember the 4.7-mile prayer walk around Capitol Hill? I prayed that prayer a long time ago, but it started a domino chain reaction. The miracle is always upstream. Of course, so is the problem. In therapy, the presenting issue is rarely the root problem. The root issue is usually sixteen years ago, right? It's sixteen miles upstream. It's out in field seven.

Swimming upstream is reverse engineering our good habits and bad habits. If you want to break a bad habit, it helps if you understand the origins. That's how you identify the prompt and interrupt the pattern. You have to connect the dots, *A-B-C-D*. Of course, we need the help of the Holy Spirit as well. The Counselor surfaces things in our subconscious and helps us flip that script.

"When you spend years responding to problems," said Dan Heath, "you can sometimes overlook the fact that you could be preventing them."[4] Again, the solution is always upstream! Seeding the

clouds is sowing today what you want to see tomorrow. Where do
you want to be in sixteen years? I know, that's hard to imagine, isn't
it? But that's the point. Everything is created twice! You have to
imagine those unborn tomorrows if you want them to happen! If
you don't, you have nothing to tip your cap to!

Would you take a few minutes to do a stream-of-consciousness
exercise? Grab a pen and a piece of paper. Even better, we've created
a *Win the Day Journal* with prompts designed to help you harness
the power of twenty-four hours. By definition, stream-of-
consciousness writing means you start writing and you don't stop
until you answer the last question. Don't rehearse your responses.
Don't edit as you go. By the time you're done, you will have painted
a picture of your preferred future. Ready or not, here we go.

- *Where do you live sixteen years from now?*
- *What do you do for a living?*
- *What degrees have you earned?*
- *What accomplishments are on your résumé?*
- *How much money do you have in the bank?*
- *How much money have you given away?*
- *When you look in the mirror, what do you look like?*
- *When you step on the scale, how much do you weigh?*
- *What character traits have you cultivated?*
- *What is the state of your mental health?*
- *How about emotional intelligence? Relational equity?
  Spiritual maturity?*

Remember the check that Jim Carrey wrote? Instead of writing a check, write your own eulogy! I know, that seems a little mor-
bid. But it's a healthy exercise. If you want to do a little method
acting, rehearse it at a local cemetery. Of course, that exercise is
optional.

How do you want to be remembered?

It's worth thinking long and hard about that question. "Résumé

virtues are . . . the skills that you bring to the job market," said David
Brooks. "Eulogy virtues . . . get talked about at your funeral."[5]

What do you want people to say about you?

What do you want etched on your tombstone?

In 1888, Alfred Nobel had the rare privilege of reading his own
obituary. A French newspaper mistakenly thought he had died. It
was actually his brother Ludvig who had passed. Curious as to how
he'd be remembered, Alfred Nobel read the obit. It called him "the
merchant of death" and said that his invention of nitroglycerin was
responsible for the death and destruction in modern warfare. That
obituary sent shock waves through his soul, and he decided to do
something about it.

Alfred Nobel was granted 355 patents during his lifetime, but his
most famous invention was dynamite. His invention simplified the
construction of dams, railroads, canals, and tunnels. Projects that
would have taken decades took a fraction of the time. Of course, his
invention had the power to be misused.

Reading his own obituary was a ritual of reckoning. Nobel decided to rewrite his will and use his $9 million fortune to establish
one of the most coveted awards in the world. The Nobel Prize has
inspired countless discoveries and advancements in physics, chemistry, physiology and medicine, literature, and peace. The domino
chain reaction is incalculable, but it all started with imagining the
prize!

Consider this your ritual of reckoning!

How do I make it a habit?

Set God-sized goals!

On a rainy morning in 1940, a teenager named John Goddard
pulled out a piece of paper and wrote down 127 life goals. By the
time he turned fifty, Goddard had accomplished 108 of those 127
goals. These were no garden-variety goals! Here's a small sample:

✓ Milk a poisonous snake
✓ Learn jujitsu
✓ Study primitive culture in Borneo
✓ Run a mile in five minutes
✓ Retrace the travels of Marco Polo and
   Alexander the Great
✓ Photograph Victoria Falls
✓ Build a telescope
✓ Read the Bible from cover to cover
✓ Circumnavigate the globe
✓ Publish an article in *National Geographic*
✓ Play the flute and violin
✓ Learn French, Spanish, and Arabic

Honestly, I would have counted French, Spanish, and Arabic as three separate goals. And I would have counted the flute and violin as two goals, but that's me. My favorite Goddard goal? *Visit the moon.* Goddard set that goal long before *Sputnik* escaped the earth's atmosphere or the *Eagle* landed on Tranquility Base. That's aiming for the stars, literally!

"Indiana Jones, the swashbuckling fictional adventurer," said the *Los Angeles Times,* "would seem to have nothing on John Goddard."[6] For the record, Goddard didn't accomplish every goal he set. He never climbed Mount Everest, and his quest to visit every country in the world fell short by thirty countries. But if there is a lesson to be learned from John Goddard's life, it's this: *you won't accomplish 100 percent of the goals you don't set.*

I share seven steps to setting life goals at markbatterson.com, along with my list of one hundred life goals.[7] I hope it helps you seed the clouds! Here's what I know for sure: "Faith is being sure of what we hope for."[8] If your life isn't going the way you want it to, it's not too late to rewrite your future. How? By seeding the clouds with God-sized, God-honoring goals.

Swim upstream!

Day 30

Choose Your Own Adventure

He ran ahead and climbed a sycamore-fig tree to see him.
—Luke 19:4

In December 1874, a terrible snowstorm swept through the Yuba Valley. John Muir, one of the founders of the Sierra Club, was staying at a friend's cabin in the Sierra Nevada. Instead of seeking shelter, Muir sought adventure. He located the tallest Douglas fir tree he could find, and then he climbed to the top of it and held on for dear life.

This was nothing out of the ordinary for John Muir. He once charged a bear just so he could study its running gait. That's about as crazy as chasing a lion into a pit on a snowy day! Is there anything else you need to know about him? Muir once took a thousand-mile walk from Louisville, Kentucky, to New Orleans, Louisiana. Why? Why not! He explored sixty-five glaciers in the Alaska Territory, sledding down some of them for the fun of it. And, of course, Muir did all this before REI, GPS, or the Snowy Owl EX -60 sleeping bag!

John Muir loved nature or, as he called it, "the invention of God."[1] To Muir, nature was a "cathedral" with "every flower a window opening into heaven."[2] Muir took lots of field trips, but let me double back to that snowstorm in the Sierra Nevada. He climbed the tallest Douglas fir tree he could find and hugged it for several hours. The hundred-foot tree swayed up to thirty degrees from side to side. All the while, Muir feasted his senses on the sights and sounds and smells of the storm.

"On such occasions, nature always has something rare to show us," said John Muir. "And the danger to life and limb is hardly greater than one would experience crouching deprecatingly beneath a roof."[3] Most people live as if the purpose of life is to arrive safely at death, but not Muir. John Muir had a passion for life that took no prisoners.

The challenge on day 29 was *swim upstream.*

The challenge on day 30 is *go outside.*

There is a moment in the book of Genesis when God took Abram on a two-foot field trip. If you aren't careful, you'll read right past it. Abram was inside his tent when the Lord "took him outside."[4] The question, of course, is, Why? As long as Abram was inside his tent, his vision was obscured by an eight-foot ceiling. So God took him on a two-foot field trip, then told him to look up and count the stars, if he could. Why? Outside the tent, the sky was the limit. God gave Abram a visual reminder of the promise He had made. His descendants would someday outnumber the stars! Simply put, *don't put an eight-foot ceiling on what God can do!*

There are 9,096 stars visible to the naked eye. Of course, that is a small fraction of the stars in the Milky Way galaxy. Astrophysicists estimate that there are at least three hundred billion stars in the Milky Way. In light of day 25, let me do the math. There are 31,536,000 seconds in a year, so one hundred years equals 3.15 billion seconds. If Abraham had tried to count every star in the Milky Way galaxy, one star per second, it would have taken ten thousand years. If you take it literally, counting the stars might be the most difficult command in all of Scripture. And that's just one of an estimated two trillion galaxies! My point? *Don't put an eight-foot ceiling on what God can do!*

Remember this formula from day 3? *Change of pace + change of place = change of perspective.* Why not take a two-foot field trip? Go outside, look up, and do a little stargazing! Or if you prefer, climb a Douglas fir tree like John Muir!

If you want to imagine unborn tomorrows, you need to widen your aperture. How? You need to dream big, pray hard, and think long. That's how we seed the clouds, but let me add one more piece to this puzzle. Choose adventure. How? Climb the tree like John Muir or a man named Zacchaeus.

Do you remember the story from the Gospels? A flash mob formed when Jesus visited Jericho. A tax collector named Zacchaeus, who was vertically challenged, couldn't get a sight line. What did he do? Instead of using his small stature as an excuse, he used it as motivation. Zacchaeus got creative and climbed a sycamore tree. It wasn't exactly a Douglas fir during a storm, but he had to risk his reputation to do it. Zacchaeus was one of those rare people who didn't follow the crowd. He wasn't afraid of looking foolish. He wasn't afraid of nonconformity!

The result? Jesus invited him to lunch. That is when and where Zacchaeus employed a commitment device. The real act of courage wasn't climbing the tree; it was radical repentance in the form of repayment. Zacchaeus wasn't just a tax collector; he was the chief tax collector. He was making bank off the backs of the people who paid taxes.

According to Levitical law, Zacchaeus was obligated to pay back what he had stolen, plus 20 percent.[5] Zacchaeus went way above, way beyond what the law required. "Here and now I give half of my possessions to the poor," he said. "If I have cheated anybody out of anything, I will pay back four times the amount."[6]

Don't miss what he did. This is habit switching at its best. He went from stealing to giving. How? By interrupting the pattern! Tax collectors were infamous for blackmail and bribery. It was all about their bottom line. Zacchaeus didn't just flip the script; he seeded the clouds with a grand gesture. He gave back quadruple what he had taken! If that isn't evidence of repentance, I'm not sure what is!

Remember day 21, change the routine? When God wants to wake us up to a new reality, He gets us out of our regular routine. The grass isn't greener on the other side, but change is often preceded by a change in scenery. God took Abram on a two-foot field trip outside his tent. God took Moses outside the camp to the tent of meeting.

According to one rabbinic tradition, the tent of meeting was two thousand cubits outside the camp.[7] Fun fact? That is the distance the Israelites kept between themselves and the ark of the covenant. That is also the allowable walking distance on the Sabbath. It was close enough to see, so it wasn't out of sight, out of mind. But it was far enough to be out of earshot—free of interruption, free of distraction, free of white noise. This is how Moses got off the grid.

Where do you meet with God?

When do you meet with God?

If you can't answer those questions, it's time to make an appointment. And you won't *find time;* you have to *make time.* We need rhythms and routines. We need systems and structures. That said, we also need to leave room for some spontaneity!

During the wilderness wanderings, Moses has a near nervous breakdown. All right, he has more than one. He's at the end of his rope when God tells him to gather seventy elders. This, of course, would have included Nahshon. "I will take some of the Spirit that is on you," God said to Moses, "and put it on them."[8] Why? It takes teamwork to make the dream work! The elders outside the camp started prophesying their praise, but there is a bit of a twist.

Two elders, Eldad and Medad, remained in the camp. There are differing opinions as to why they stayed back. According to one rabbinic tradition, "Eldad and Medad said to themselves: 'We are not worthy of such distinction.'"[9] Regardless, even though they were socially distanced and sheltered in place, they started prophesying *in the camp!*

Wait—let me get this straight. God told the elders to gather at the tent of meeting outside the camp, but He still blessed the elders inside the camp? In other words, God set up a structure, set up a system. Then God moved outside the system, outside the structure He Himself had set up? Again, we need structure! But we dare not box God in by boxing God out! The Holy Spirit can show up anytime, anywhere. And He can do it in some strange and mysterious ways.

This is good news when it comes to making and breaking habits.

I waited until day 30 to share this simple truth: The Holy Spirit is the prompt. The Holy Spirit is the pattern. The Holy Spirit is the prize. I have a theory of everything, and it's this: *the answer to every prayer is more of the Holy Spirit.*

I know what you're thinking: *I need love.* Yes, you do! You also need joy, peace, patience, kindness, goodness, faithfulness, gentleness, and self-control.[10] Guess what? Those are fruit of the Spirit, so what you really need is more of the Spirit who produces that fruit. The same goes for the gifts of the Spirit.

I have no idea what habit you're trying to make or break, but I do know this: it's going to take the Holy Spirit's help. The Holy Spirit is the *x* factor, the *it* factor. Without the Holy Spirit, I'm below average. With the help of the Holy Spirit, all things are possible.

The only ceiling on your intimacy with God and impact on the world is daily spiritual disciplines! And that's what it takes—daily discipline. You've got to put these habits into practice, deliberate practice. The good news? The Holy Spirit is the difference between the best you can do and the best God can do!

How do I make it a habit?

Choose your own adventure.

As a father, Edward Packard loved telling bedtime stories to his daughters. His stories revolved around an imaginary character named Pete and his many adventures. Occasionally Packard would run out of ideas, so he'd have his daughters play the protagonist in the story and share their suggestions for story lines. He couldn't help but notice how enthused they became when they were able to choose their own adventure![11]

Packard was also an author, and those bedtime stories inspired the Choose Your Own Adventure book series. His idea was rejected by nine publishers before someone saw the vision for it.

In a sense, making or breaking a habit is a choose-your-own-adventure story. You can't control the outcome, but you can control the inputs. You play the part of protagonist. How? By identifying the prompt, interrupting the pattern, and imagining the prize.

Remember the challenge on day 26? Make it a game! This is a form of that. It's adding an element of fun. It's adding an element of surprise. It's gaming the system 2.0. The good news is that God is setting us up! He has already prepared good works in advance.[12] All we have to do is step into our destiny. How? Daily habits!

We've arrived at the end of this thirty-day challenge, and it feels like we just began. Can I offer a simple reminder? There may be milestones, but *there is no finish line!* Some of you need to read this book all over again right now. Pick a habit, any habit. Make it measurable, meaningful, and maintainable. Then wade into the water once again, right up to your nostrils if need be.

As far as Nahshon knew, it was the last day of his life. It seemed like a no-win situation—death by Egyptian army or death by drowning. Like the rest of the characters in this book—everyone from Diana Nyad to Deborah, from Chris Nikic to Caleb, from General McAuliffe to Jonathan—Nahshon chose his own adventure. And it made all the difference in the world.

Remember Marcus Bullock? He applied for forty-one jobs!

Remember Chris Norton? It took him seven years to walk seven yards!

Remember Rebecca Lee Crumpler? She had to break two glass ceilings!

Almost anyone can accomplish almost anything if they work at it long enough, hard enough, and smart enough. How? Do it for a day! Destiny is not a mystery. Destiny is daily habits. Show me your habits, and I'll show you your future.

It's too soon to quit.

It's too late to stop.

Choose your own adventure!

Notes

Introduction: Domino Habits

1. Matthew 7:2.
2. Motivational speaker Jim Rohn is famous for saying that we'll become the average of the five people we spend the most time with. The science of social networks seems to suggest that the number is much higher. I chose the number twelve because that is the number of disciples Jesus chose and, when it comes to this idea, they are exhibit A.
3. David T. Neal, Wendy Wood, and Jeffrey M. Quinn, "Habits—a Repeat Performance," *Current Directions in Psychological Science* 15, no. 4 (August 2006): 198–202, https://dornsife .usc.edu/assets/sites/208/docs/Neal.Wood.Quinn.2006.pdf.
4. William James, "The Laws of Habit," in *Talks to Teachers on Psychology and to Students on Some of Life's Ideals* (Mineola, NY: Dover, 1962), 33.
5. Wikipedia, s.v. "Operant Conditioning," last modified April 19, 2021, 07:28, https://en.wikipedia.org/wiki/Operant _conditioning.
6. "The Habit Loop," Habitica Wiki, https://habitica.fandom .com/wiki/The_Habit_Loop.
7. Matthew 5:21–22, 27–28, 33–34, 38–39, 43–44.
8. See Matthew 5:39.
9. Matthew 5:40–41, 44.
10. Matthew 25:23.
11. Matthew 6:4, NLT.
12. "Domino Toppling World Records," Rekord-Klub SAXONIA, www.recordholders.org/en/records/domino-toppling.html.

13. Colin Schultz, "Just Twenty-Nine Dominoes Could Knock Down the Empire State Building," *Smithsonian Magazine*, January 17, 2013, www.smithsonianmag.com/smart-news/just-twenty-nine-dominoes-could-knock-down-the-empire-state-building-2232941.
14. Genesis 11:6, NLT.
15. Teresa Amabile and Steven Kramer, *The Progress Principle: Using Small Wins to Ignite Joy, Engagement, and Creativity at Work* (Boston: Harvard Business Review, 2011), 3.
16. Jearl Walker, "The Amateur Scientist: Deep Think on Dominoes Falling in a Row and Leaning Out from the Edge of a Table," *Scientific American* 251, no. 2 (August 1984): 122–29, www.jstor.org/stable/24969441.
17. Peter H. Diamandis, "The Difference Between Linear and Exponential Thinking," Big Think, May 22, 2013, https://bigthink.com/in-their-own-words/the-difference-between-linear-and-exponential-thinking.
18. R. B. Matthews and Doug McCutcheon, "Compound Interest May Not Be Einstein's Eighth Wonder, but It Is a Powerful Tool for Investors," *Globe and Mail*, November 12, 2019, www.theglobeandmail.com/investing/investment-ideas/article-compound-interest-may-not-be-einsteins-eighth-wonder-but-it-is-a.

Day 1: Wade into the Water

The epigraph is taken from Glenn David Bauscher, *The Comparative Original Aramaic New Testament in Plain English* (New South Wales, Australia: Lulu, 2013), 596.
1. Hayim Nahman Bialik and Yehoshua Hana Ravnitzky, eds., *The Book of Legends—Sefer Ha-Aggadah: Legends from the Talmud and Midrash*, trans. William G. Braude (New York: Schocken, 1992), 72.
2. Exodus 14:15, ESV.
3. Psalm 114:3, from *The Comparative 1st Century Aramaic Bible in Plain English*.
4. 2 Corinthians 12:9.
5. Joshua 3:8, NLT.
6. Ariston Anderson, "Tim Ferriss: On the Creative Process

and Getting Your Work Noticed," 99U, November 20, 2012, https://99u.adobe.com/articles/7252/tim-ferriss-on-the -creative-process-and-getting-your-work-noticed.

Day 2: Take the Stairs

1. Everett M. Rogers, *Diffusion of Innovations, 4th ed.* (New York: Free Press, 1995), 262.
2. Carol S. Dweck, *Mindset: The New Psychology of Success,* rev. ed. (New York: Ballantine, 2016).
3. Benjamin Bloom, quoted in Carol S. Dweck, *Mindset: The New Psychology of Success,* rev. ed. (New York: Ballantine, 2016), 65.
4. Oswald Chambers, "June 13: Getting There," My Utmost for His Highest, https://utmost.org/classic/getting-there-3 -classic.
5. Elisa B. Jones, "The Fun Theory," Penn State's SC200 Course Blog, September 16, 2015, https://sites.psu.edu/siowfa15/ 2015/09/16/the-fun-theory.
6. Kelsey Ramos, "Volkswagen Brings the Fun: Giant Piano Stairs and Other 'Fun Theory' Marketing," *Los Angeles Times* (blog), October 15, 2009, https://latimesblogs.latimes .com/money_co/2009/10/volkswagen-brings-the-fun -giant-piano-stairs-and-other-fun-theory-marketing.html.
7. Edwin H. Friedman, *A Failure of Nerve: Leadership in the Age of the Quick Fix,* ed. Margaret M. Treadwell and Edward W. Beal (New York: Seabury, 2007), 201.
8. Matthew 5:41.

Day 3: Get Off the Grid

1. A version of this can be found at "Sample Wisecracks from Yakov Smirnoff," July 4, 1986, www.latimes.com/archives/ la-xpm-1986-07-04-ca-688-story.html.
2. John Heywood, *The Proverbs and Epigrams of John Hey-wood (A.D. 1562)* (n.p.: Spenser Society, 1867), 21, 26, 30, 167.
3. Mark Hilliard, "Games, Flat-Pack Furniture and Cakes: How Behavioural Economics Could Help," *Irish Times,* Novem-

ber 24, 2014, www.irishtimes.com/business/games-flat-pack
-furniture-and-cakes-how-behavioural-economics-could
-help-1.2010605.

4. This formula combines ideas acquired from a variety of
books including these: David Epstein, *Range: Why General-
ists Triumph in a Specialized World* (New York: Riverhead
Books, 2019); Anders Ericsson and Robert Pool, *Peak:
Secrets from the New Science of Expertise* (New York: Mari-
ner Books, 2017); and James Clear, *Atomic Habits: An Easy
& Proven Way to Build Good Habits & Break Bad Ones*
(New York: Avery, 2018).

5. Robert A. Bjork, "Institutional Impediments to Effective
Training," epilogue to *Learning, Remembering, Believing:
Enhanced Human Performance,* ed. Daniel Druckman and
Robert A. Bjork (Washington, DC: National Academy
Press, 1994), 299.

6. Peter Economy, "Use the 40 Percent Rule to Break Through
Every Obstacle and Achieve the Impossible," *Inc.,* April 23,
2019, www.inc.com/peter-economy/use-40-percent-rule-to
-achieve-impossible.html.

7. Lewis Carroll, *Through the Looking-Glass,* in *Alice's Adventures in Wonderland & Through the Looking-Glass* (Ware,
UK: Wordsworth Classics, 1993), 161.

8. Kōsuke Koyama, *Three Mile an Hour God* (London: SCM,
2015).

9. Mark Woods, "Corrie ten Boom: 10 Quotes from the Author of *The Hiding Place*," Christian Today, April 15, 2016,
www.christiantoday.com/article/corrie.ten.boom.10
.quotes.from.the.author.of.the.hiding.place/84034.htm.

Day 4: Lick the Honey

1. "Why You Never Go on Spontaneous Adventures," Medium,
April 12, 2016, https://medium.com/the-livday-tapestry/
why-spontaneity-is-rare-5e2b92c92fe4.

2. "Why You Never Go."

3. Barry Newman, "Dutch Managers Will Descend on U.S.'s
Best-Known Airport," *Wall Street Journal,* May 13, 1997,
www.wsj.com/articles/SB863472646131512500.

4. Richard H. Thaler and Cass R. Sunstein, *Nudge: Improving Decisions About Health, Wealth, and Happiness*, rev. ed. (New York: Penguin, 2009), 37–39.

5. OECD, *Tools and Ethics for Applied Behavioural Insights: The BASIC Toolkit* (Paris: OECD, 2019), 98.

6. David Golinkin, "Torah Is as Sweet as Honey," *The Jerusalem Post*, May 22, 2007, www.jpost.com/jewish-world/judaism/torah-is-as-sweet-as-honey.

7. Psalm 34:8.

8. Andrew Lasane, "10 Foods That Never (or Almost Never) Expire," Mental Floss, April 7, 2016, www.mentalfloss.com/article/67560/10-foods-never-or-almost-never-expire.

9. Randy Pausch, *The Last Lecture* (New York: Hyperion, 2008), 158.

10. William Glasser, *Positive Addiction* (New York: Harper Colophon, 1985), 1.

11. Glasser, *Positive Addiction*, 42–43, 50.

12. 2 Corinthians 10:5.

13. Deuteronomy 17:18–19.

Day 5: Circle the Mountain

1. Wikipedia, s.v. "*Kaihōgyō*," last modified February 15, 2021, 08:45, https://en.wikipedia.org/wiki/Kaih%C5%8Dgy%C5%8D.

2. Johann Wolfgang von Goethe, quoted in Mark Hall, "At the Moment of Commitment," *The Alchemist's Journey* (blog), July 1, 2019, https://thealchemistsjourney.com/2019/07/01/at-the-moment-of-commitment.

3. Acts 21:26. NLT.

4. "Herschel Walker," Academy of Achievement, last revised February 17, 2021, https://achievement.org/achiever/herschel-walker.

5. Herschel Walker, quoted in Jade Scipioni, "Why NFL Great Herschel Walker Still Does 2,000 Sit-Ups a Day," FOX Business, April 19, 2018, www.foxbusiness.com/features/why-nfl-great-herschel-walker-still-does-2000-sit-ups-a-day.

6. Matthew 17:20.

7. Ephesians 3:20.

8. Anders Ericsson and Robert Pool, *Peak: Secrets from the New Science of Expertise* (Boston: Houghton Mifflin Harcourt, 2016), 40.
9. "Target Heart Rate and Estimated Maximum Heart Rate," Centers for Disease Control and Prevention, last reviewed October 14, 2020, www.cdc.gov/physicalactivity/basics/measuring/heartrate.htm.
10. Benjamin Franklin, *The Autobiography of Benjamin Franklin* (Boston: Houghton, Mifflin, 1888), 102–3.
11. Franklin, *Autobiography*, 110.
12. Jack Hollis, quoted in Kaiser Permanente, "Kaiser Permanente Study Finds Keeping a Food Diary Doubles Diet Weight Loss," EurekAlert!, July 8, 2008, www.eurekalert.org/pub_releases/2008-07/kpdo-kps062308.php.
13. "Step Four," Alcoholics Anonymous, www.aa.org/assets/en_us/en_step4.pdf.

Day 6: Stack the Habit

1. Charles Duhigg, *The Power of Habit: Why We Do What We Do in Life and Business* (New York: Random House, 2014), 34.
2. "Why Popcorn Smells So Good," *Tampa Bay Times*, October 7, 2005, www.tampabay.com/archive/1994/07/28/why-popcorn-smells-so-good.
3. Exodus 30:7–8.
4. Numbers 15:38–40.
5. "C. G. Jung," Goodreads, www.goodreads.com/quotes/44379-until-you-make-the-unconscious-conscious-it-will-direct-your.
6. Bruce Goldman, "New Imaging Method Developed at Stanford Reveals Stunning Details of Brain Connections," Stanford Medicine News Center, November 17, 2010, https://med.stanford.edu/news/all-news/2010/11/new-imaging-method-developed-at-stanford-reveals-stunning-details-of-brain-connections.html; Maggie Masetti, "How Many Stars in the Milky Way?," *Blueshift* (blog), NASA, July 22, 2015, https://asd.gsfc.nasa.gov/blueshift/index.php/2015/07/22/how-many-stars-in-the-milky-way.

7. Read Montague, quoted in Jonah Lehrer, *How We Decide* (Boston: Houghton Mifflin Harcourt, 2009), 41.
8. Romans 7:15.
9. Psalm 37:4, NASB.
10. "The Water in You: Water and the Human Body," USGS: Science for a Changing World, www.usgs.gov/special-topic/water-science-school/science/water-you-water-and-human-body?qt-science_center_objects=0#qt-science_center_objects.

Day 7: Take the Shot

1. *Jump Shot: The Kenny Sailors Story,* directed by Jacob Hamilton (Nashville, TN: Aspiration Entertainment, 2019), www.jumpshotmovie.com.
2. Matthew 5:3–10.
3. Ayun Halliday, "The Power of Conformity: 1962 Episode of *Candid Camera* Reveals the Strange Psychology of Riding Elevators," Open Culture, November 7, 2016, www.openculture.com/2016/11/the-power-of-conformity-1962-episode-of-candid-camera-reveals-the-psychology-of-riding-elevators.html.
4. Romans 12:2, NASB.
5. Saul McLeod, "Solomon Asch—Conformity Experiment," Simply Psychology, December 28, 2018, www.simplypsychology.org/asch-conformity.html.
6. R. A. Torrey, *The Person and Work of the Holy Spirit,* rev. ed. (Grand Rapids, MI: Zondervan, 1974), 10.
7. Gordon MacKenzie, *Orbiting the Giant Hairball: A Corporate Fool's Guide to Surviving with Grace* (New York: Viking, 1998), 19–20, 23–24.
8. Matthew 18:3.
9. Lim Wy Wen, "Ho, Ho, Ha, Ha, Ha," The Star, May 10, 2009, www.thestar.com.my/lifestyle/health/2009/05/10/ho-ho-ha-ha-ha.
10. "Stress Relief from Laughter? It's No Joke," Mayo Clinic, April 5, 2019, www.mayoclinic.org/healthy-lifestyle/stress-management/in-depth/stress-relief/art-20044456.

11. Rolf Smith, *The 7 Levels of Change: Create, Innovate and Motivate with the Secrets of the World's Largest Corporations* (Arlington, TX: Summit, 1997), 49.
12. John Putzier, *Get Weird! 101 Innovative Ways to Make Your Company a Great Place to Work* (New York: AMACOM, 2001), 7–8.
13. Albert Bandura, Joan E. Grusec, and Frances L. Menlove, "Vicarious Extinction of Avoidance Behavior," *Journal of Personality and Social Psychology* 5, no. 1 (1967): 16–23, https://doi.org/10.1037/h0024182.

Day 8: Remember the Future

1. James Stockdale, quoted in Jim Collins, *Good to Great: Why Some Companies Make the Leap . . . and Others Don't* (New York: HarperBusiness, 2001), 85.
2. Revelation 11:15.
3. Oswald Chambers, "August 3: The Big Compelling of God," *My Utmost for His Highest*, https://utmost.org/classic/the -big-compelling-of-god-classic.
4. "Winston Churchill," Goodreads, www.goodreads.com/ quotes/535242-the-farther-back-you-can-look-the-farther -forward-you.
5. Revelation 7:9.
6. Stockdale, quoted in Collins, *Good to Great*, 85.
7. Stockdale, quoted in Collins, *Good to Great*, 85.
8. John 16:33.
9. Hebrews 11:1.
10. Charles Duhigg, *The Power of Habit: Why We Do What We Do in Life and Business* (New York: Random House, 2014), 115.
11. Philippians 4:7.
12. Simon Ponsonby, *More: How You Can Have More of the Spirit When You Already Have Everything in Christ* (Colorado Springs, CO: David C Cook, 2009), 52.
13. Dan Sullivan, foreword to *Unhackable*, by Kary Oberbrunner (Powell, OH: Ethos Collective, 2020), xviii.
14. Sullivan, foreword to *Unhackable*, xviii.

Habit 1—Flip the Script

1. Haley Goldberg-Shine, "The One Question I Ask to Stop Negative Thoughts from Ruining My Day: No Meditation Needed," Fast Company, July 28, 2017, www.fastcompany.com/40444942/the-one-question-i-ask-myself-to-stop-negative-thoughts-from-ruining-my-day.
2. Proverbs 23:7, KJV.
3. *Amistad*, "Anthony Hopkins: John Quincy Adams," IMDB, www.imdb.com/title/tt0118607/characters/nm0000164.
4. Eric Barker, *Barking up the Wrong Tree: The Surprising Science Behind Why Everything You Know About Success Is (Mostly) Wrong* (New York: HarperOne, 2017), 75.

Day 9: Change Your Story

1. "Bob Beamon," Black History in America, www.myblackhistory.net/Bob_Beamon.htm.
2. Ralph Boston, quoted in Andy Andrews, *The Bottom of the Pool: Thinking Beyond Your Boundaries to Achieve Extraordinary Results* (Nashville, TN: W Publishing, 2019), 13.
3. Walt Kelly, "36. 'We Have Met the Enemy and He Is Us,'" Billy Ireland Cartoon Library & Museum, Ohio State University, April 22, 1971, https://library.osu.edu/site/40stories/2020/01/05/we-have-met-the-enemy.
4. Romans 8:31, NKJV.
5. 1 John 4:4, NKJV.
6. Romans 8:28, NKJV.
7. Philippians 4:13, NKJV.
8. This quote is attributed to a few people. I'm drawing from Jay Shetty, *Think like a Monk: Train Your Mind for Peace and Purpose Every Day* (New York: Simon & Schuster, 2020), ix.
9. "Berakhot 8a," in *The William Davidson Talmud*, Sefaria, www.sefaria.org/Berakhot.8a.17?lang=bi&with=all&lang2=en.
10. Levi Cooper, "World of the Sages: The Four Cubits of Halacha," *The Jerusalem Post*, August 16, 2006, www.jpost.com/jewish-world/judaism/world-of-the-sages-the-four-cubits-of-halacha.

11. Gordon Hempton, "Silence and the Presence of Everything," *On Being with Krista Tippett*, podcast, May 10, 2012, https://onbeing.org/programs/gordon-hempton-silence-and-the-presence-of-everything.
12. Clyde Haberman, "Raising Her Voice in Pursuit of a Quieter City," *New York Times*, October 6, 2013, www.nytimes.com/2013/10/07/nyregion/arline-bronzaft-seeks-a-less-noisy-new-york.html.
13. Psalm 46:10.
14. Henri J. M. Nouwen, *Life of the Beloved: Spiritual Living in a Secular World* (New York: Crossroad, 2002), 37.
15. Mark Batterson, "Whisper: How to Hear the Voice of God," YouVersion, www.bible.com/reading-plans/8721-whisper-how-hear-the-voice-of-god-mark-batterson.

Day 10: Fix Your Focus

1. Anthony McAuliffe, quoted in Pat Williams, *The Magic of Teamwork: Proven Principles for Building a Winning Team* (Nashville, TN: Thomas Nelson, 1997), chap. 2, Kindle.
2. Mark Batterson, *Double Blessing: Don't Settle for Less Than You're Called to Bless* (Colorado Springs, CO: Multnomah, 2020), 70.
3. Genesis 50:20.
4. Martin E. P. Seligman, *Learned Optimism: How to Change Your Mind and Your Life* (New York: Vintage Books, 2006), 15.
5. Daniel Kahneman et al., "Would You Be Happier If You Were Richer? A Focusing Illusion," *Science* 312, no. 5782 (June 30, 2006): 1908–10, www.jstor.org/stable/3846429?seq=1.
6. David G. Myers, *The Pursuit of Happiness: Discovering the Pathway to Fulfillment, Well-Being, and Enduring Personal Joy* (New York: William Morrow, 1993), 66–67.
7. Philippians 4:8, NLT.
8. Richard Restak, *Mozart's Brain and the Fighter Pilot: Unleashing Your Brain's Potential* (New York: Three Rivers, 2001), 92.

9. Restak, *Mozart's Brain*, 92.
10. Numbers 13:31.
11. Numbers 13:33.
12. Charles Horton Cooley, quoted in Jay Shetty, *Think like a Monk: Train Your Mind for Peace and Purpose Every Day* (New York: Simon & Schuster, 2020), 3.
13. Charles Horton Cooley, *Human Nature and the Social Order* (New York: Charles Scribner's Sons, 1902), 152.
14. James 1:23–24.
15. Psalm 17:8; Ephesians 2:10, ESV; Romans 8:37.
16. A. W. Tozer, *The Knowledge of the Holy* (New York: Harper-One, 1961), vii.
17. Victoria H. Medvec, Scott F. Madey, and Thomas Gilovich, "When Less Is More: Counterfactual Thinking and Satisfaction Among Olympic Medalists," *Journal of Personality and Social Psychology* 69, no. 4 (1995): 603–10, https://doi.org/10.1037/0022-3514.69.4.603.

Day 11: Know Your Name

1. Diana Nyad, quoted in Greg Myre, "On Fifth Try, Diana Nyad Completes Cuba-Florida Swim," NPR, September 2, 2013, www.npr.org/sections/thetwo-way/2013/09/02/218207861/diana-nyad-in-homestretch-of-cuba-florida-swim.
2. Diana Nyad, *Find a Way: The Inspiring Story of One Woman's Pursuit of a Lifelong Dream* (New York: Vintage Books, 2016), 27–28 (quote modified to remove phonetic spelling of Greek accent).
3. Mark Batterson, *Double Blessing: Don't Settle for Less Than You're Called to Bless* (Colorado Springs, CO: Multnomah, 2020), 57–58.
4. Genesis 1:27; Psalm 17:8; Ephesians 2:10, ESV.
5. Ephesians 1:3–14.
6. Genesis 1:27.
7. Philip Swann, "The Human Heart Is a Perpetual Idol Factory," *Evangelical Magazine* (March/April 2021), 16, www.evangelicalmagazine.com/article/the-human-heart-is-a-perpetual-idol-factory.

8. Numbers 6:24–26.
9. Numbers 6:27, NKJV.
10. Judges 6:34, AMPC.
11. Genesis 22:14; Exodus 17:15; Ezekiel 48:35; Isaiah 9:6.
12. Jeremiah 1:6–7.
13. "Johann Wolfgang von Goethe," Goodreads, www.goodreads .com/quotes/33242-if-you-treat-an-individual-as-he-is-he -will.
14. Dan Jackson, "11 Crazy Things Actors Have Done to Prepare for Roles," Thrillist, February 28, 2018, www.google .com/amp/s/www.thrillist.com/amphtml/entertainment/ nation/method-acting-stories.
15. Matthew 5:29–30.
16. Matthew 6:21.

Habit 2—Kiss the Wave

1. Ludwig Spohr, quoted in Arthur C. Brooks, "Opinion: This Holiday Season, We Can All Learn a Lesson from Beethoven," *Washington Post,* December 13, 2019, www .washingtonpost.com/opinions/this-holiday-season-we -can-all-learn-a-lesson-from-beethoven/2019/12/13/ 71f21aba-1d0e-11ea-b4c1-fd0d91b60d9e_story.html.
2. "The 20 Greatest Symphonies of All Time," *BBC Music Magazine,* September 25, 2018, www.classical-music.com/ features/works/20-greatest-symphonies-all-time.
3. Brooks, "Opinion: This Holiday Season."
4. "6 Quotes Spurgeon Didn't Say," Spurgeon Center, August 8, 2017, www.spurgeon.org/resource-library/blog-entries/ 6-quotes-spurgeon-didnt-say. (But were often attributed to Spurgeon.)
5. Dan Witters and Jim Harter, "Worry and Stress Fuel Record Drop in U.S. Life Satisfaction," Gallup, May 8, 2020, https:// news.gallup.com/poll/310250/worry-stress-fuel-record -drop-life-satisfaction.aspx.
6. Mark 4:39, KJV.
7. George Foreman, *God in My Corner* (Nashville, TN: Thomas Nelson, 2007), 132–33.

Day 12: Do It Scared

1. Douglas Murray, *The Madness of Crowds: Gender, Race and Identity* (London: Bloomsbury Continuum, 2021), 107.
2. James Thurber, "The Day the Dam Broke," Library of America: Story of the Week, https://storyoftheweek.loa.org/2019/12/the-day-dam-broke.html.
3. Robert A. Johnson, *Owning Your Own Shadow: Understanding the Dark Side of the Psyche* (New York: HarperCollins, 1993), 92.
4. *Ford v Ferrari*, directed by James Mangold (Los Angeles: 20th Century Fox, 2019), "Quotes," IMDb, www.imdb.com/title/tt1950186/characters/nm0000354.
5. Exodus 14:13, ESV.
6. Nadia Kounang, "What Is the Science Behind Fear?," CNN Health, October 29, 2015, www.cnn.com/2015/10/29/health/science-of-fear/index.html.
7. 1 John 4:18, ESV.
8. Exodus 14:4, NLT.
9. Ashley Lateef, "10 Inspiring Quotes from Corrie ten Boom," *Guideposts*, www.guideposts.org/better-living/life-advice/finding-life-purpose/10-inspiring-quotes-from-corrie-ten-boom.
10. Daniel Kahneman, *Thinking, Fast and Slow* (New York: Farrar, Straus and Giroux, 2011), 123–24.
11. Acts 27:29.
12. Mihai Andrei, "How Big Is the Universe?," ZME Science, April 6, 2021, www.zmescience.com/other/feature-post/how-big-is-the-universe.
13. Tryon Edwards, *A Dictionary of Thoughts: Being a Cyclopedia of Laconic Quotations from the Best Authors of the World, Both Ancient and Modern* (Detroit: F. B. Dickerson, 1908), 324.

Day 13: Walk the Wire

1. "A High-Wire Prayer over Niagara Falls," CBN, www1.cbn.com/700club/high-wire-prayer-over-niagara-falls.
2. I heard Andy say this at a Catalyst conference.

3. Job 11:6.
4. John 9:2–3.
5. Robert A. Johnson, *Owning Your Own Shadow: Understanding the Dark Side of the Psyche* (New York: Harper-Collins, 1993), 92.
6. Ephesians 4:1–2.
7. Dale Carnegie, *How to Win Friends and Influence People* (New York: Pocket Books, 1964), 37.
8. Proverbs 15:1.

Day 14: Connect the Dots

1. Peter Wohlleben, *The Hidden Life of Trees: What They Feel, How They Communicate*, trans. Jane Billinghurst (Vancouver: Greystone Books, 2015), 131–32.
2. Daniel 2:23.
3. Daniel 2:14.
4. Jenny Nguyen, "The Surprising Things a Master Sommelier Can Teach You About Wine," *Forbes*, November 17, 2014, www.forbes.com/sites/jennguyen/2014/11/17/the-surprising-things-a-master-sommelier-can-teach-you-about-wine/?sh=6bab709d48ca.
5. Steve Jobs, "2005 Stanford Commencement Address" (speech, Stanford University, Stanford, CA, June 12, 2005), https://news.stanford.edu/2005/06/14/jobs-061505.
6. Abraham Heschel, quoted in David W. Blight, "After the Flood Recedes," *Atlantic*, April 26, 2020, www.theatlantic.com/ideas/archive/2020/04/after-flood-recedes/610693.
7. "Walter Brueggemann: The Prophetic Imagination," *On Being with Krista Tippett*, last updated December 20, 2018, https://onbeing.org/programs/walter-brueggemann-the-prophetic-imagination-dec2018.
8. 1 Samuel 17:37, ESV.
9. David Brier, "What Is Innovation?," *Fast Company: Leadership Now*, November 1, 2013, www.fastcompany.com/3020950/what-is-innovation.
10. "Catherine Cox Miles," Human Intelligence, www.intelltheory.com/cox.shtml.

Habit 3—Eat the Frog

1. "Eat a Live Frog Every Morning, and Nothing Worse Will Happen to You the Rest of the Day," Quote Investigator, April 3, 2013, https://quoteinvestigator.com/2013/04/03/eat-frog.
2. Patrick Kiger, "The French Ambassador Was Teddy Roosevelt's Hiking Buddy," *Boundary Stones* (blog), September 20, 2014, https://boundarystones.weta.org/2014/09/20/french-ambassador-was-teddy-roosevelts-hiking-buddy.

Day 15: Do It Difficult

1. Christopher Klein, "When Teddy Roosevelt Was Shot in 1912, a Speech May Have Saved His Life," History, updated July 21, 2019, www.history.com/news/shot-in-the-chest-100-years-ago-teddy-roosevelt-kept-on-talking.
2. Wikipedia, s.v. "Dan Tyler Moore," last modified March 11, 2021, https://en.wikipedia.org/wiki/Dan_Tyler_Moore.
3. Theodore Roosevelt, "The Strenuous Life" (speech, Hamilton Club, Chicago, IL, April 10, 1899), https://voicesofdemocracy.umd.edu/roosevelt-strenuous-life-1899-speech-text.
4. 2 Corinthians 11:23–27.
5. "Margaret Thatcher," Goodreads, www.goodreads.com/quotes/66737-look-at-a-day-when-you-are-supremely-satisfied-at.
6. Dr. Paul Brand and Philip Yancey, *The Gift of Pain: Why We Hurt and What We Can Do About It* (Grand Rapids, MI: Zondervan, 1997), 55.
7. Hebrews 12:2.
8. Luke 22:42.
9. David Brooks, *The Road to Character* (New York: Random House, 2015), 52, 60.
10. Dwight D. Eisenhower, quoted in Brooks, *The Road to Character*, 61.
11. Luke 9:23; 2 Corinthians 10:5.

Day 16: Make Decisions Against Yourself

1. Walter Mischel, Ebbe B. Ebbesen, and Antonette Raskoff Zeiss, "Cognitive and Attentional Mechanisms in Delay of Gratification," *Journal of Personality and Social Psychology* 21, no. 2 (1972): 204–18, https://doi.org/10.1037/h0032198.

2. Mischel, Ebbesen, and Zeiss, "Cognitive and Attentional Mechanisms," 206, https://higher-order-thinking.com/wp-content/uploads/2018/09/cognitive_and_attentional_mechanisms_in_delay_of_gratification.pdf.

3. Mischel, Ebbesen, and Zeiss, "Cognitive and Attentional Mechanisms," 207, https://higher-order-thinking.com/wp-content/uploads/2018/09/cognitive_and_attentional_mechanisms_in_delay_of_gratification.pdf.

4. Daniel Goleman, *Emotional Intelligence: Why It Can Matter More Than IQ* (New York: Bantam, 2006), 80–82.

5. Steven Salzberg, "Can Intermittent Fasting Reset Your Immune System?," *Forbes,* January 6, 2020, www.forbes.com/sites/stevensalzberg/2020/01/06/can-intermittent-fasting-reset-your-immune-system/?sh=4a095c427ac2.

6. "What Is the Strongest Muscle in the Human Body?," Everyday Mysteries: Fun Science Facts from the Library of Congress, November 19, 2019, www.loc.gov/everyday-mysteries/biology-and-human-anatomy/item/what-is-the-strongest-muscle-in-the-human-body.

7. Matthew 4:4.

8. 1 Corinthians 10:23, BSB.

9. Brett McKay and Kate McKay, "Lessons in Manliness: The Childhood of Theodore Roosevelt," The Art of Manliness, February 4, 2008, www.artofmanliness.com/articles/lessons-in-manliness-the-childhood-of-theodore-roosevelt.

10. "Why People Become Overweight," Harvard Health Publishing, June 24, 2019, www.health.harvard.edu/staying-healthy/why-people-become-overweight.

Day 17: Live Not by Lies

1. Aleksandr Solzhenitsyn, "Live Not by Lies," trans. Yermolai Solzhenitsyn, February 12, 1974, The Aleksandr Solzhenitsyn Center, www.solzhenitsyncenter.org/live-not-by-lies.
2. Matthew 10:16.
3. Genesis 3:1, NLT.
4. Nathan Azrin, quoted in Charles Duhigg, *The Power of Habit: Why We Do What We Do in Life and Business* (New York: Random House, 2014), 76.
5. 2 Corinthians 2:11.
6. John 5:1–9.
7. "Chapter 53: On the Reception of Guests," in *The Rule of Saint Benedict,* trans. Leonard J. Doyle, The Order of Saint Benedict, http://archive.osb.org/rb/text/rbeaad1.html.
8. "The World According to Mister Rogers," Today, October 10, 2003, www.today.com/popculture/world-according -mister-rogers-1C9014197.
9. Emily Dickinson, "I Dwell in Possibility," in Helen Vendler, *Dickinson: Selected Poems and Commentaries* (Cambridge, MA: Belknap, 2010), 222.
10. Thanks to A. W. Tozer for this idea! "Tozer Devotional: The Secret of Life Is Theological," The Alliance, December 12, 2020, www.cmalliance.org/devotions/tozer?id=554.

Habit 4—Fly the Kite

1. M. Robinson, "The Kite That Bridged a River," Kitehistory .com, 2005, www.kitehistory.com/Miscellaneous/Homan _Walsh.htm.
2. Zechariah 4:10, NLT.
3. Winston Churchill, quoted in Fred Glueckstein, "Churchill as Bricklayer," *Finest Hour* 157 (Winter 2012–13): 34, https://winstonchurchill.org/publications/finest-hour/ finest-hour-157/churchill-as-bricklayer.
4. Glueckstein, "Churchill as Bricklayer."
5. Kobe Bryant, *The Mamba Mentality: How I Play* (New York: MCD), 25.
6. Bryant, *Mamba Mentality,* 28.

Day 18: Do It Small

1. "Americans Check Their Phones 96 Times a Day," Asurion, November 21, 2019, www.asurion.com/about/press-releases/americans-check-their-phones-96-times-a-day.
2. Rochi Zalani, "Screen Time Statistics 2021: Your Smartphone Is Hurting You," Elite Content Marketer, June 2, 2021, https://elitecontentmarketer.com/screen-time-statistics.
3. Exodus 23:30.
4. John Wooden, quoted in John C. Maxwell, *Today Matters: 12 Daily Practices to Guarantee Tomorrow's Success* (New York: Warner Faith, 2004), 34.
5. Anders Ericsson and Robert Pool, *Peak: Secrets from the New Science of Expertise* (Boston: Mariner Books, 2017), 14.
6. London Philharmonic Orchestra and David Parry, *The 50 Greatest Pieces of Classical Music*, X5 Music Group, 2009.
7. Emil Zátopek, quoted in Richard Askwith, *Today We Die a Little! The Inimitable Emil Zátopek, the Greatest Olympic Runner of All Time* (New York: Nation Books, 2016), 199.

Day 19: Exercise Your Authority

1. Blake Stilwell, "Here's What NASA Says Is the Perfect Length for a Power Nap," Business Insider, March 26, 2019, www.businessinsider.in/thelife/heres-what-nasa-says-is-the-perfect-length-for-a-power-nap/articleshow/6857035.cms.
2. Mark 4:38.
3. Matthew 21:18–19; John 2:1–10; 11:38–44.
4. Romans 8:37.
5. Martin Luther King Jr., "I Have a Dream" (speech, March on Washington, Washington, DC, August 28, 1963), www.npr.org/2010/01/18/122701268/i-have-a-dream-speech-in-its-entirety.
6. Martin Luther King Jr., "Facing the Challenge of a New Age (1957)," in *A Testament of Hope: The Essential Writings and Speeches of Martin Luther King, Jr.*, ed. James Melvin Washington (New York: HarperCollins, 1991), 140.

7. Martin Luther King Jr., "Nonviolence: The Only Road to Freedom (1966)," in *Testament of Hope*, 58.
8. Martin Luther King Jr., "Letter from Birmingham Jail," April 16, 1963, The Martin Luther King, Jr. Research and Education Institute, Stanford University, https://kinginstitute .stanford.edu/sites/mlk/files/letterfrombirmingham_wwcw _0.pdf.
9. Matthew 5:39–41; Luke 6:27–28.

Day 20: Enough Is Enough

1. Chris Nikic, quoted in Christopher Brito, "Florida Man Becomes First Person with Down Syndrome to Finish Ironman Triathlon," CBS News, November 10, 2020, www .cbsnews.com/news/chris-nikic-ironman-triathalon-down -syndrome.
2. Zechariah 4:6.
3. Zechariah 4:7.
4. Exodus 14:21–22; Joshua 10:12–13; 2 Kings 6:5–7; John 2:1–10.
5. Psalm 23:6, ESV.
6. Philippians 1:6.
7. Romans 8:28, NKJV.
8. Romans 8:31, NKJV.
9. Joshua 14:10–11.
10. Mark Batterson, *Win the Day: 7 Habits to Help You Stress Less & Accomplish More* (Colorado Springs, CO: Multnomah, 2020), 164.
11. Attributed to Henry Ford; see "Whether You Believe You Can Do a Thing or Not, You Are Right," Quote Investigator, February 3, 2015, https://quoteinvestigator.com/2015/02/ 03/you-can.
12. Romans 12:2.
13. Sean Alfano, "Because the Doctor Isn't Always Right," CBS News, May 7, 2006, www.cbsnews.com/news/because-the -doctor-isnt-always-right.

Habit 5—Cut the Rope

1. Spencer Klaw, "'All Safe, Gentleman, All Safe!,'" *American Heritage* 29, no. 5 (August/September 1978), www.american heritage.com/all-safe-gentlemen-all-safe.
2. "Escalators & Moving Walks," Otis, www.otis.com/en/us/products-services/products/escalators-and-moving-walks.
3. Reed Hastings and Erin Meyer, *No Rules: Netflix and the Culture of Reinvention* (New York: Penguin, 2020), xi.
4. "Internet/Broadband Fact Sheet," Pew Research Center, April 7, 2021, www.pewresearch.org/internet/fact-sheet/internet-broadband.
5. Stefan Campbell, "Netflix Net Worth 2021," *The Small Business Blog,* https://thesmallbusinessblog.net/netflix-net-worth.
6. Thomas Gilovich and Victoria Medvec, "The Temporal Pattern to the Experience of Regret," *Journal of Personality and Social Psychology* 67, no. 3 (October 1994): 357–65, www.researchgate.net/publication/15232839_The_Temporal_Pattern_to_the_Experience_of_Regret.

Day 21: Change the Routine

1. David Gordon and Maribeth Meyers-Anderson, *Phoenix: Therapeutic Patterns of Milton H. Erickson* (Cupertino, CA: Meta Publications, 1981), 111–12.
2. Malcolm Gladwell, *David and Goliath: Underdogs, Misfits, and the Art of Battling Giants* (New York: Little, Brown, 2013), 11.
3. G. K. Chesterton, *Orthodoxy* (CreateSpace Independent Publishing Platform, 2015), 9.
4. 1 Samuel 17:45.
5. Luke 6:28.
6. Romans 2:4.
7. 2 Kings 6:23.
8. Joshua 2:1–21.
9. Matthew 1:5–6.
10. Ben Johnson, "The Great Horse Manure Crisis of 1894," Historic UK, www.historic-uk.com/HistoryUK/Historyof Britain/Great-Horse-Manure-Crisis-of-1894.

Day 22: Pick a Fight

1. Susan B. Anthony, quoted in Lynn Sherr, *Failure Is Impossible: Susan B. Anthony in Her Own Words* (New York: Crown, 1996), 117.
2. Anthony, quoted in Sherr, *Failure Is Impossible*, 324.
3. Judges 5:7.
4. Malcolm Gladwell, *The Tipping Point: How Little Things Can Make a Big Difference* (Boston: Bay Back, 2002), back cover.
5. Judges 5:7, NLT.
6. Michael J. Gelb, *How to Think Like Leonardo Da Vinci* (New York: Delacorte, 1998), 38.
7. Hayim Nahman Bialik and Yehoshua Hana Ravnitzky, eds., *The Book of Legends—Sefer Ha-Aggadah: Legends from the Talmud and Midrash*, trans. William G. Braude (New York: Schocken Books, 1992), 109:23.
8. Judges 5:31, NLT.
9. *Rocky III*, directed by Sylvester Stallone (Beverly Hills, CA: MGM, 1982).
10. C. G. Jung, "Commentary on *The Secret of the Golden Flower*," in *Jung on Active Imagination*, ed. Joan Chodorow (Princeton, NJ: Princeton University Press, 1997), 73–74.
11. "James Corbett," Goodreads, www.goodreads.com/quotes/540142-fight-one-more-round-when-your-feet-are-so-tired.
12. 1 Corinthians 9:26–27.
13. 2 Timothy 4:7.
14. Ephesians 6:13.

Day 23: Do It Now

1. Ed Catmull, *Creativity, Inc.: Overcoming the Unseen Forces That Stand in the Way of True Inspiration* (New York: Random House, 2014), 176.
2. Catmull, *Creativity, Inc.*, 176.
3. Mike Fleming, Jr., "Candice Bergen to Tell Story of Her Legendary Ventriloquist Father Edgar Bergen for Big Screen," Deadline, April 30, 2013, https://deadline.com/2013/04/

candice-bergen-to-tell-story-of-her-legendary-ventriloquist
-father-edgar-bergen-for-big-screen-486808.
4. 1 Samuel 14:2.
5. 1 Samuel 14:6.
6. Martin Luther King Jr., "Beyond Vietnam—A Time to Break Silence" (speech, Riverside Church, New York, NY, April 4, 1967), www.americanrhetoric.com/speeches/mlk atimetobreaksilence.htm.
7. John 4:35.
8. "Parkinson's Law," The Economist, www.economist.com/news/1955/11/19/parkinsons-law.

Habit 6—Wind the Clock

1. Tony Campolo, "If I Should Wake Before I Die," Preaching Today.com, www.preachingtoday.com/sermons/sermons/2005/august/124.html.
2. Nagin Cox, "What Time Is It on Mars?," TEDxBeaconStreet, November 2016, TED video, 13:48, https://tedxbeaconstreet.com/videos/living-on-two-planets-mars-time.
3. Jonathan Larson, "Seasons of Love," in Rent, 1996.
4. Psalm 90:12.

Day 24: Tip the Cap

1. Akin Oyedele and Taylor Borden, "Hilton Was Just Named the Best Company to Work for in the US. Here's How the Iconic Hilton Family Built Their Wealth," Business Insider, February 20, 2020, www.businessinsider.com/how-the -hilton-family-got-so-rich-2014-10#throughout-the-1920s -hilton-continued-to-buy-and-build-hotels-in-texas-he -finally-expanded-beyond-the-state-in-1942-3. Also see Brandon Hilgemann, "Hilton Hotels Were Built on Prayer," Pro Preacher, April 20, 2016, www.propreacher.com/hilton -hotels-built-prayer.
2. John Heywood, The Proverbs and Epigrams of John Heywood (A.D. 1562) (n.p.: Spenser Society, 1867), 30.
3. Heywood, Proverbs, 133.

4. "Physiology," Britannica, www.britannica.com/science/information-theory/Physiology.
5. Anne Trafton, "In the Blink of an Eye: MIT Neuroscientists Find the Brain Can Identify Images Seen for as Little as 13 Milliseconds," MIT News, January 16, 2014, https://news.mit.edu/2014/in-the-blink-of-an-eye-0116.
6. Aaron Abrams, "Data Storage: How Many Words Is a Picture Really Worth?," Nortridge Software Company, September 11, 2014, www.nortridge.com/blog/data-storage-how-many-words-is-a-picture-really-worth.
7. Daniel Terdiman, "Elon Musk at SXSW: 'I'd Like to Die on Mars, Just Not on Impact," CNET, March 9, 2013, www.cnet.com/news/elon-musk-at-sxsw-id-like-to-die-on-mars-just-not-on-impact.
8. Wikipedia, s.v. "Jim Carrey Filmography," last modified June 22, 2021, 19:31, https://en.wikipedia.org/wiki/Jim_Carrey_filmography.
9. "Jim Carrey Net Worth: How Much Is Jim Carrey Worth?," Celebrity Net Worth, www.celebritynetworth.com/richest-celebrities/actors/jim-carrey-net-worth.
10. Matthew 16:26, BSB.
11. Aristotle, *On the Soul,* in On the Soul *and Other Psychological Works,* trans. and ed. Fred D. Miller Jr. (Oxford: Oxford University Press, 2018), 59.
12. R. A. Torrey, quoted in George Sweeting and Donald Sweeting, *Lessons from the Life of Moody* (Chicago: Moody, 1989), 129.
13. Luke 23:34, ESV.
14. Deuteronomy 6:4.

Day 25: Do the Math

1. Korczak Ziolkowski, quoted in Alan Leftridge, *The Best of the Black Hills* (Helena, MT: Farcountry, 2017), 21.
2. Kyle Butt, "Noah's Ark—A Flawless Floater," Apologetics Press, www.apologeticspress.org/APContent.aspx?category=22&article=562.
3. "Facts on Noah's Ark," Christian Information Ministries, www.ldolphin.org/cisflood.html.

4. Hayim Nahman Bialik and Yehoshua Hana Ravnitzky, eds., *The Book of Legends—Sefer Ha-Aggadah: Legends from the Talmud and Midrash,* trans. William G. Braude (New York: Schocken Books, 1992), 27:120.

5. H. Tankovska, "Daily Social Media Usage Worldwide 2012–2020," Statista, February 8, 2021, www.statista.com/statistics/433871/daily-social-media-usage-worldwide.

6. Charles Dickens, *David Copperfield,* ed. Jeremy Tambling, rev. ed. (London: Penguin, 2004), 179.

7. "Send Photos Delivered as Postcards to Any Person in Any Prison Instantly," Flikshop, www.flikshop.com.

8. Gemma Curtis, "Your Life in Numbers: How Long Do You Spend Sleeping? Watching TV? Working? We Take a Look at a Whole Life and Examine How Precious Time Is," Sleep Matters Club, www.dreams.co.uk/sleep-matters-club/your -life-in-numbers-infographic.

9. Matt Plummer, "Interruptions Steal a Ton of Your Time. Here Are 3 Ways to Get Those Hours Back: The Cost of Interruptions in the Workplace Is Clear. So Are the Solutions," Inc., January 30, 2019, www.inc.com/matt-plummer/interruptions-steal-a-ton-of-your-time-here-are-3-ways -to-get-those-hours-back.html.

10. Psalm 90:12.

Day 26: Play the Long Game

1. "Archive Fact Sheet: The History of Guinness," Guinness Storehouse, www.guinness-storehouse.com/content/pdf/archive-factsheets/general-history/company-history.pdf.

2. Julie Baldwin, "Theology on Tap," The Imaginative Conservative, February 17, 2012, https://theimaginativeconservative .org/2012/02/theology-on-tap.html.

3. "Visingsö Oak Forest," Atlas Obscura, www.atlasobscura .com/places/visingso-oak-forest, and Stewart Brand, *The Clock of the Long Now: Time and Responsibility* (New York: Basic Books, 1999), 162.

4. 2 Peter 3:8.

5. Acts 2:1–4.

6. Stephen R. Covey, *The 7 Habits of Highly Effective People:*

Powerful Lessons in Personal Change, rev. ed. (New York: Simon & Schuster, 2020), 109.

7. John 8:58, NKJV.
8. Joshua 10:12–13; 2 Kings 20:8–11, NLT.
9. Joshua 6:2.
10. Ephesians 2:10, ESV.
11. Eric Barker, *Barking up the Wrong Tree: The Surprising Science Behind Why Everything You Know About Success Is (Mostly) Wrong* (New York: HarperOne, 2017), 83.
12. Barker, *Barking Up,* 84.
13. Mark Batterson, *Win the Day: 7 Habits to Help You Stress Less & Accomplish More* (Colorado Springs, CO: Multnomah, 2020), 202.

Habit 7–Seed the Clouds

1. Quoted in Ginger Strand, *The Brothers Vonnegut: Science and Fiction in the House of Magic* (New York: Farrar, Straus and Giroux, 2015), 58.
2. 1 Kings 18:42–45.
3. Joshua 6:8–20; 2 Kings 5:10–14.
4. Hayim Nahman Bialik and Yehoshua Hana Ravnitzky, eds., *The Book of Legends—Sefer Ha-Aggadah: Legends from the Talmud and Midrash,* trans. William G. Braude (New York: Schocken Books, 1992), 202.
5. Psalm 126:1, NASB.
6. Bialik and Ravnitzky, eds., *Book of Legends,* 203.
7. *New World Encyclopedia,* s.v. "Arnold J. Toynbee," www.newworldencyclopedia.org/entry/Arnold_J._Toynbee.
8. *New World Encyclopedia,* s.v. "Arnold J. Toynbee."
9. R. T. Kendall, *The Anointing: Yesterday, Today, Tomorrow* (Lake Mary, FL: Charisma House, 2003), 133.

Day 27: It Takes a Team

1. Proverbs 27:17.
2. Giorgio Vasari, *The Lives of the Most Excellent Painters, Sculptors, and Architects,* ed. Philip Jacks, trans. Gaston du C. de Vere (New York: Modern Library, 2006), 200.

3. Lin-Manuel Miranda, "The World Was Wide Enough," in *Hamilton,* 2015.

4. Diana Nyad, quoted in Greg Myre, "On Fifth Try, Diana Nyad Completes Cuba-Florida Swim," NPR, September 2, 2013, www.npr.org/sections/thetwo-way/2013/09/02/218207861/diana-nyad-in-homestretch-of-cuba-florida-swim.

5. Chauncey Mabe, "Storyteller Alex Haley Dies at 70," South Florida Sun Sentinel, February 11, 1992, www.sun-sentinel.com/news/fl-xpm-1992-02-11-9201080096-story.html.

6. Acts 4:13.

7. Nicholas A. Christakis and James H. Fowler, "The Spread of Obesity in a Large Social Network over 32 Years," *The New England Journal of Medicine,* July 26, 2007, www.nejm.org/doi/full/10.1056/NEJMsa066082.

8. "The Class the Stars Fell On," West Point in the Making of America, National Museum of American History, https://americanhistory.si.edu/westpoint/history_6b.html.

9. Hebrews 10:24.

10. Nathan Brannen, "Only 1,497 Humans Have Ever Broken the 4-Minute Mile—and I'm One of the Them," CBC, June 27, 2018, www.cbc.ca/playersvoice/entry/only-1497-humans-have-ever-broken-the-4-minute-mile-and-im-one-of-them.

11. "Junto Club," Benjamin Franklin Historical Society, www.benjamin-franklin-history.org/junto-club.

12. Harry Clarke Noyes, "The Goose Story," *Arcs News* 7, No. 1, January 1992, https://socialwork.buffalo.edu/content/dam/socialwork/home/self-care-kit/the-goose-story-noyes.pdf.

Day 28: Prophesy Your Praise

1. David Sharrock, "Cellist of Sarajevo, Vedran Smailovic, Is Wounded by Words," *The Times,* June 7, 2008, www.thetimes.co.uk/article/cellist-of-sarajevo-vedran-smailovic-is-wounded-by-words-9mlbns72qv5.

2. Ephesians 6:12, NKJV.

3. 2 Corinthians 10:4.

4. Ephesians 3:20.

5. 2 Corinthians 12:9.

6. 2 Chronicles 20:12, BSB.
7. 2 Chronicles 20:15, BSB.
8. 2 Chronicles 20:21, NLT.
9. 2 Chronicles 20:22, NLT.
10. Timothy Keller and John Inazu, *Uncommon Ground: Living Faithfully in a World of Difference* (Nashville, TN: Thomas Nelson, 2020), 87.
11. Acts 13:2.
12. All Sons & Daughters, "Great Are You, Lord," by Jason Ingram, Leslie Jordan, and David Leonard, *Live*, Integrity Music, 2013.
13. Darrell Evans, "Trading My Sorrows (Yes, Lord)," *Freedom*, Integrity Music, 1998.
14. Mark Batterson, *Win the Day: 7 Daily Habits to Help You Stress Less & Accomplish More* (Colorado Springs, CO: Multnomah, 2020), 11–25.
15. Martin Luther King Jr., "Letter from Birmingham Jail," April 16, 1963, The Martin Luther King, Jr. Research and Education Institute, Stanford University, https://kinginstitute.stanford.edu/sites/mlk/files/letterfrombirmingham_wwcw_0.pdf.
16. "Praying with My Legs," Repair the World, https://werepair.org/wp-content/uploads/2017/12/Praying-with-My-Legs.pdf.
17. Abraham Herschel, *The Prophets* (New York: HarperPerennial, 2001), 12.
18. Herschel, *The Prophets*, 4.

Day 29: Swim Upstream

1. Jaclyn Long, "Rebecca Lee Crumpler: Physician, Author, Pioneer," *Picture a Scientist* (blog), Harvard University, December 24, 2020, https://sitn.hms.harvard.edu/flash/2020/rebecca-lee-crumpler-physician-author-pioneer.
2. "Dr. Rebecca Lee Crumpler," National Park Service, https://nps.gov/people/dr-rebecca-lee-crumpler.htm.
3. Joshua 3:16.
4. Dan Heath, *Upstream: The Quest to Solve Problems Before They Happen* (New York: Avid Reader, 2020), 2.

5. David Brooks, *The Road to Character* (New York: Random House, 2015), xi.
6. Rebecca Trounson, "John Goddard Dies at 88; Adventurer Fulfilled Most of Childhood Goals," *Los Angeles Times*, May 21, 2013, www.latimes.com/local/obituaries/la-me-john -goddard-20130521-story.html.
7. You can find the link to this document here: "Win the Day," Mark Batterson, www.markbatterson.com/books/wintheday.
8. Hebrews 11:1, NIRV.

Day 30: Choose Your Own Adventure

1. Lee Stetson, *The Wild Muir: Twenty-Two of John Muir's Greatest Adventures* (Berkeley, CA: Heyday, 1994), 21.
2. John Murdock, "John Muir's God of Nature," First Things, July 25, 2013, www.firstthings.com/web-exclusives/2013/07/ john-muirs-god-of-nature.
3. Stetson, *The Wild Muir*, 109–10.
4. Genesis 15:5.
5. Leviticus 6:1–5.
6. Luke 19:8.
7. Hayim Nahman Bialik and Yehoshua Hana Ravnitzky, eds., *The Book of Legends—Sefer Ha-Aggadah: Legends from the Talmud and Midrash*, trans. William G. Braude (New York: Schocken Books, 1992), 432:295.
8. Numbers 11:17, ESV.
9. Bialik and Ravnitzky, eds., *Book of Legends*, 100:132.
10. Galatians 5:22–23.
11. Wikipedia, s.v. "*Choose Your Own Adventure*," last modified June 24, 2021, 11:45, https://en.wikipedia.org/wiki/ Choose_Your_Own_Adventure.
12. Ephesians 2:10.

MARK BATTERSON is the lead pastor of National Community Church (National.CC) in Washington, DC. One church with multiple campuses, NCC also owns and operates Ebenezers Coffeehouse, the Miracle Theatre, and the DC Dream Center. NCC is currently developing a city block into the Capital Turnaround. This 100,000-square-foot space will include an event venue, child development center, mixed-use marketplace, and coworking space.

Mark holds a doctor of ministry degree from Regent University and is the *New York Times* bestselling author of twenty-one books, including *The Circle Maker, In a Pit with a Lion on a Snowy Day, Play the Man, Chase the Lion, Whisper, Double Blessing,* and, most recently, *Win the Day.* He and his wife, Lora, have three children and live on Capitol Hill.

You can follow Mark @markbatterson on Twitter, Instagram, and Facebook.

You can find Mark online at www.markbatterson.com.

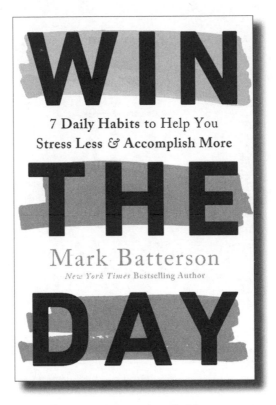

**Free resources available at
markbatterson.com/wintheday**

- Sermon Series Video, Graphics, and Downloads
- Small Group Discussion Guide
- Steps to Setting Life Goals
- Life Goal List
- And More!

MULTNOMAH

waterbrookmultnomah.com

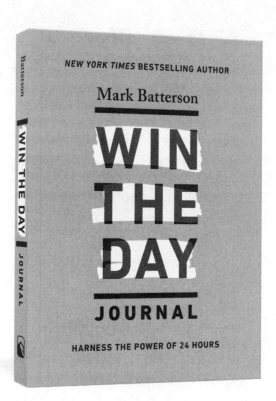

NEW YORK TIMES BESTSELLING AUTHOR

Mark Batterson

WIN THE DAY

JOURNAL

HARNESS THE POWER OF 24 HOURS

(spine) Batterson · WIN THE DAY | JOURNAL

Unlock the power of twenty-four hours and tackle your God-sized goals with this step-by-step journal that guides readers through the seven life-changing habits at the core of *Win the Day.*

MULTNOMAH

waterbrookmultnomah.com

Don't miss any of Mark Batterson
and Summer Batterson Dailey's
children's books.

Bring the whimsical storytelling
to the children in your life!